The Leader's Bookshelf

The Leader's Bookshelf

25 Great Books and Their Readers

Martin Cohen

ROWMAN & LITTLEFIELD
Lanham • Boulder • New York • London

Published by Rowman & Littlefield
An imprint of The Rowman & Littlefield Publishing Group, Inc.
4501 Forbes Boulevard, Suite 200, Lanham, Maryland 20706
www.rowman.com

86-90 Paul Street, London EC2A 4NE

Distributed by NATIONAL BOOK NETWORK

British Library Cataloguing in Publication Information Available

Library of Congress Cataloging-in-Publication Data Is Available

ISBN: 978-1-5381-3576-1 (cloth)
ISBN: 978-1-5381-6737-3 (paper : alk. paper)
ISBN: 978-1-5381-3577-8 (electronic)

∞™ The paper used in this publication meets the minimum requirements of American National Standard for Information Sciences—Permanence of Paper for Printed Library Materials, ANSI/NISO Z39.48-1992.

Contents

✛

Acknowledgments

One of the themes of this book is that 'no book is an island', in the sense that books often connect to earlier books (which in turn usually connect to others, and so on.) But in another sense too, books are not really the product of just one solitary individual, "the author", but rather depend on a more subtle network of contributors and enthusiasts. And so here, I would like to explicitly thank some of those who helped this book to grow from hazy idea to a final—reasonably well-defined!—text.

First of all, I should like to thank my researcher, Paula, who is also my sister and twin! We have many things NOT in common, but here in this project we were able to work together with a very precious empathy and shared values, identifying interesting characters for the chapters, discussing the detail of the narratives. When the book reached the stage of searching for a publisher, and indeed through all the projection processes, I have been very lucky to have a wonderful and tireless literary agent in New York's Mark Gottlieb. One of the pleasures of this book was that it took me to that city and I was able to meet and have a coffee with Mark high up in one of those iconic skyscrapers.

Once the book was really underway though, my thanks are to my editors at Rowman and Littlefield, particularly Suzanne Staszak-Silva and Natalie Mandziuk, who saw in the original, rather different manuscript, an elegant statue trapped in a block of marble, as it were, while my production editor, Elaine McGarraugh, helped us navigate several rather alarming crises in the vexed year of 2020.

I would like to rethank my illustrator, Judith Zolumio, for her pictures and indeed her personal enthusiasm for the project, and also a special shout out must go to Milo Cohen for his picture—and support—for the project too.

Of course, there are lots of other people involved who have helped as well, and if a tight production schedule prevents me from naming them here, I hope they will accept my genuine, if generalised, appreciation for all that they have done too.

Martin Cohen
Lewes, UK

✛
Introduction

This is a book about books. In the process it explores the lives of some remarkable people—inventors, scientists, business gurus, and political leaders—but it's not just a book about people and their life stories. Rather it is a book about ideas—and inspirations. Because it turns out that the paths of many famous people start out with a particular book that inspired them when they were young. And so exploring these shared ideas, dreams, and inspirations is the heart of this book. Inspiration, in fact, is the thread that ties together individuals with characters and backgrounds as diverse as Jimmy Carter and Henry Ford, Jane Goodall and Barack Obama, Malcolm X and Judge Clarence Thomas.

Each chapter typically consists of two such famous people, each with their own extraordinary tale. The first person introduced is more historical, usually revealing the character and motivations of someone most of us have heard of without really ever knowing much about—like Thomas Edison or Malcolm X. Biographies like these reveal that life is truly stranger than fiction. Paired with each such figure is a more recent soulmate, someone different in many respects yet nonetheless linked across the years by a shared philosophy—and a love of books. And I think their inspirations can become our inspirations too.

Of course, there's never been any shortage of sources of advice on the ingredients of success. Today, there are a veritable plethora of advisors and experts offering advice on how to get rich, be successful, and impress people. More than that, there are expensive business school and university courses promising pretty much the same, and last but not least, there are the books.

1

"When their advice is good, then the advisors, the professors, the entrepreneurs and the authors deserve to be celebrated, paid highly, and feted with garlands. When it is not so good, though, they deserve to be unceremoniously pickled, sawn in half, boiled, minced, and torn apart by chariots." That's the advice offered by the great Chinese strategist Sun Tzu in his classic work, *The Art of War*, written no less than 1,500 years ago! I've refreshed the translation slightly; and although the last line is pretty literal and maybe dates it a bit, the message itself is timeless: the search for wise advice goes back as long as there have been human societies, and this certainly played a key role in the working of the ancient Chinese imperial court.

Indeed, since the time of the ancient Chinese sages, the advice industry has ballooned. And as the penalties for giving dodgy tips in a book or offering up duff strategies to politicians have evidently been reduced, inevitably a lot of the stuff around now *is* rather useless. Nonetheless, it is worth noting that even as Sun Tzu warned people about bad advice, he joined the very same "books for self-improvement" industry by writing it down, if not exactly as a book at least as a bundle of bamboo strips. (In 1972, a set of such strips dating from the Han Dynasty was found in a tomb in Yinque Mountain in eastern China.) All of which just goes to show (you can't get away from it) that books are the indispensable tools for success. And, however success may be defined, since surely most of us have hopes of achieving some aspect of it in life, the problem is a practical and strategic one: how to get from A to B. Books—whether reference tomes or fantasy fiction—are the indispensable tool for doing just that.

Take Warren Buffett, the business magnate, who I look at alongside John Rockefeller in chapter 8. The CEO of Berkshire Hathaway and investor nicknamed "the Oracle" for his uncanny knack for spotting money-spinning opportunities seems to read books like athletes practice for tournaments. When asked what he thought was the key to his own achievements, he is supposed to have pointed to a nearby pile of waiting hardbacks and said, "Read 500 pages like this every day. That's how knowledge works. It builds up, like compound interest."

After all that reading, Buffett only has 20 percent of his day left for things like eating, driving to the bookstore, and maybe talking to journalists. We might think that a better life balance is perhaps struck by Bill Gates, founder of the huge computer company Microsoft, who is almost as rich and yet claims to read merely one book a week. A lot of them are business texts, although his personal blog, GatesNotes, features over 150 book recommendations for everything from scientific histories to novels and biographies to in-depth studies of social issues. The blog even offers short lists of beach reading, but even this is pretty serious stuff—books like *The Magic of Reality* by Richard Dawkins and *What If* by Randall Munroe. The subtitle of that last book is *Serious Scientific Answers to Absurd Hypothetical Questions*.

But back to *The Art of War*. Both Larry Ellison and Marc Benioff, respectively the hugely successful CEOs of software giants Oracle and Salesforce, credit Sun Tzu's work as the text that's been most instrumental to their own careers. Ellison is considered one of the tech industry's most combative figures, and, he says, he learned the art of mastering that anger from Sun Tzu and even advised his friend Benioff, "You're angry? Ignore the anger." As for Benioff, he liked the book so much that he even wrote a foreword for a 2008 reprint of the ancient classic. In this he reveals, "Since I first read *The Art of War* more than a dozen years ago, I have applied its concepts to many areas of my life. The tenets of the book provided me the concept to enter an industry dominated by much bigger players—and gave us the strategies to render them powerless. Ultimately, it is how Salesforce.com took on the entire software industry."

Well, there's someone who evidently never misses the chance to promote his business. Nonetheless, even if he had not been content just plugging his own company, there really is a lot that can be learned from the book. *The Art of War* is considered *the* classic work on strategy—life strategies, business strategies, military strategies. Hundreds of books examining its insights have been published in many different languages, and its ideas have been applied to fiefs as diverse as business management and sports training.

You see, *The Art of War* is only superficially about military tactics; at its heart, it is about human values. And so too, ultimately, are all great books.

Or take Mark Cuban, also in the book-a-week club. He's another investor, for a slightly different emphasis, who says that he reads for three hours every day, especially books about big ideas in politics and psychology. Cuban explains why in his own book, called *How to Win at the Sport of Business*. "I would continually search for new ideas. I read every book and magazine I could. Heck, three bucks for a magazine, twenty bucks for a book," he wrote. "One good idea would lead to a customer or a solution, and those magazines and books paid for themselves many times over." But he soon realized that while the information he was getting was publicly available, most people had simply never sought it out.

The notion of big ideas brings me to the reading habits of Elon Musk. Musk is a slightly different case again: a South African engineer who now makes rockets but originally made billions from the Internet payment service PayPal. He too is an avid reader, inspired as a child by epic fiction like *Lord of the Rings* and slightly less epic stuff too, like Asimov's Foundation series, which centers on the fall of the Galactic Empire, and even the subversive and dryly witty *Hitchhiker's Guide to the Galaxy*. These are books read as escapism, as entertainment. Yet, for Musk, each and every one of them provided inspirational role models—heroes with ambitious strategies to save the world—just as more conventional biographies of great historical figures like Benjamin Franklin (also on his reading list) did.

It's another take on the observation offered by Tom Corley, author of *Rich Habits: The Daily Success Habits of Wealthy Individuals*, that rich people (who Corley defines as those with an annual income of $160,000 or more and a liquid net worth of $3.2 million-plus) tend to choose educational books and publications over novels, tabloids, and magazines. Corley thinks successful people obsess over biographies and autobiographies of other successful people in order to glean guidance and inspiration. But hold on a minute. Back to that question of what it means to be "successful": What do I mean—what does anyone mean—by that anyway?

I'm using the word "success" rather carefully in this book because there's a well-established link between being successful and being rich and famous, but there's also a less appreciated one between the belief that fame and wealth bring happiness and low self-esteem and depression. In fact, people who pursue life goals more effectively are not motivated by the pursuit of wealth and fame but by other life goals. These are people who, for example, want to explore the secrets of atoms, rather than people who think there is money to be made from physics. It's a small difference, in a sense, but a vital one. Harry Kroto, who I look at in detail in chapter 7, a Nobel Prize winner and discoverer of the carbon atom shaped like a Buckminster Fuller geodesic dome, illustrates just this. One of Kroto's favorite books is *Lord of the Rings*, a work of pure imagination, and one of his favorite quotes from it is "All who wander are not lost." After winning the prize and becoming quite a celebrity, Kroto spent his time not talking to business conferences for hefty fees but instead talking to young people in schools to try to communicate his vision of science as a voyage of discovery to be undertaken for its own sake.

Similarly, psychologists have found that people with a strong drive to become famous, or merely an all-consuming interest in those who are already famous, are likely to have deficiencies in their own language, learning, and thinking skills. Not here the ingredients of success! Celebrity worshippers tend to be moody, emotional, and neurotic, at least according to the British writer Paul Martin in a book called *Making Happy People*. Martin goes on to make an interesting connection between celebrity worship and what he calls "a more fundamental desire to emulate successful individuals." According to this theory, which, like the best theories, on its face appears to be only common sense, we are evolutionarily disposed to take note of the successful individuals in our group, partly to learn from their behavior and partly to share their success. However, as Martin also says, the "malignant shadow of social comparison" is dissatisfaction with our own opportunities, activities, and indeed physical selves.

The bottom line is that success is about intrinsic motivation and rewards, not about extrinsic goals. It's about finding something that you enjoy doing for its own sake, that you think is worth doing in itself, and not about strategies based on sacrifices now for rewards down the line. Reading for success, for example, should not be undertaken only as a means to an end but instead should be valued because the right sort of reading is itself stimulating and empowering. Contrast the vast pile of books that Buffett is contentedly munching through with the 80 percent or so of UK workers who equally cheerfully reported to researchers that they had undertaken no work-related learning at all in the recent past. The reason that they didn't read? They enjoyed other things more. But the point such respondents miss is this: discovering new things and obtaining new insights can be both exhilarating and stimulating. Successful people are often those who found this out early on in life.

In exploring the life stories of such people, I've found that behind many great tales of achievement lies much more than a collection of smart tactics. Beliefs and values guide grand strategies too. But it's not always the same plan or strategy, which, if you think about it, shouldn't come as a surprise. If there really were just one recipe for success, well, everyone would be using it already. No, the thing that unifies these disparate approaches is that they all provided for their owners a kind of conceptual grid onto which a wide range of day-to-day creative, scientific, or business practices are able to develop and grow. For Sergey Brin and Larry Page, the founders of Google, for example, the grid was Charles Darwin's notions of natural mutation and iteration. With Henry Ford, the man who pioneered the assembly line, the grid was an obscure, ethereal theory of life as a sequence of reincarnations. And for both Oprah Winfrey and Steve Jobs, the grid was existentialist ideas about the pursuit of authenticity. In all these cases, a grand, indeed often philosophical, theory meshed perfectly with a practical business strategy. I explore the life stories of all these remarkable people in this book.

This flexible interplay between the theoretical and the practical aspects of ideas is illustrated by two dramatically different cases: those of Jane Goodall and Walt Disney. Goodall is the inspirational anthropologist whose work living with and closely observing chimpanzees and other primates in Africa revolutionized our understanding of both these rare and endangered animals and ourselves. Goodall, who I look at in detail in my first chapter, admits that the germ of her future research lay in two children's books about animals: *Doctor Dolittle* and *The Jungle Book*.

As for Walt Disney (who I do not look at in further detail), the mention of *The Jungle Book* immediately creates a link to the magic worlds brought to life in his animated films. But there the similarities end, as Disney was a committed social conservative and self-proclaimed God-fearing American patriot who openly admired fascist philosophers and even created his own totalitarian micro-republic originally called the Experimental Prototype Community of Tomorrow (EPCOT). This later became a very different kind of escapist utopia called Disneyland, but even so, under the glittering surface, Big Brother was omnipresent, exerting an iron control. In Disneyland, homes belonged to the state. Long fingernails and long hair for male employees were punishable, and even the emotions that must be worn on their faces at all times were stipulated! And yet, the same philosophy also helped Disney to inspire his staff, to see the power of branding and marketing, and to grow from a struggling artist to a great filmmaker and entertainment visionary.

But let's get back to the present. Rest assured the aim is not to send you off to the library to dig out books on twentieth-century fascist philosophers—or indeed to push any particular kind of books on you. Rather, I want to do something different and more direct by focusing on the big ideas that lie behind some of the world's great personal stories. Skills will—the philosophical ideas often—still be part of it, and amazing insights too, but the vital ingredient of guiding strategies and framework beliefs will be given the attention I think they richly deserve but rarely get.

So this book has two big goals: first, to restate the power of books in an era when words are cheap, and second, to provide examples of people who've found in books the inspiration to achieve great things. Because after all my research, the one habit I've found successful people have in common is a very simple one, and it's easily copied. They read *a lot*.

Here, in a nutshell, is the key to the relationship between innovators and books. Many people read books, but only a few search them for ideas—and then use them. It might be called the difference between active and passive reading. Active reading, reading for ideas, is an approach that amazingly few people use (or at least use properly), yet it is one that's proven its worth time and again.

Remember all those examples of successful people dropping out of school or forgoing a formal education? (Check out how many people in this book fit in that category!) Less often noted is that many of these taught themselves, primarily from books. But forget any idea of simply reading the same books that made other people great—far less checking Facebook groups or immersing yourself in the Sunday papers. No, the tricky aspect is that it is not just any old reading that will do; we must read books that speak directly to our aims and aspirations, our dreams and illusions.

And don't even try to count on your daily reading of social media posts. Real reading is different. A good book may well be the product of tens of thousands of hours of thinking and research—quite different from the hasty cut-and-paste encouraged by the relentless churn of the Internet and news cycle.

In the chapters that follow, I'll be taking a close look at some iconic examples of people who have been inspired by books that they read, often when they were young. I'll pick out the key sections or ideas in the texts that they themselves mention, and sometimes I'll suggest those that they just seem to embody. Each chapter will identify two great readers—one typically very well-known, even iconic, figure from recent history and the other a more contemporary figure but definitely someone we might wish to learn from. I'll also sum up the books themselves, partly in the main text but also through book boxes—like the one below for Sun Tzu's *The Art of War*. In the process, I hope you'll discover—or rediscover—some of the reasons why books are an open and waiting doorway that can take you anywhere you wish to go.

THE ART OF WAR
AUTHOR: SUN TZU
PUBLISHED: CIRCA 700–800 CE

Historians aren't sure when the book was written or even who wrote it, although traditionally it is credited to a Chinese military leader known as Sun Tzu. However, like many other Chinese classics, it is more than likely that the book is really a compilation of generations of Chinese theories and teachings on military strategy—but it's not just that. The lessons of *The Art of War* apply across all areas of life, from businesses seeking strategic advantage to individuals looking for wise advice on the conduct of their daily lives. And it does so because the advice in it is very wise and still resonates with readers today.

It is said that, for more than a thousand years, rulers across Asia consulted the text as they plotted their military conquests. However, it did not reach the Western world until the end of the eighteenth century, when a Jesuit missionary called Jean Joseph Marie Amiot translated the book into French. (Some historians believe that the French emperor Napoleon then became the first Western leader to follow its teachings.) It was finally translated into English in 1905 under the title *The Book of War*. Ever since then, it's sold pretty well too, but it is claimed that things really took off in 2001, when the television mobster Tony Soprano told his therapist that he'd been reading the book. After that, the book was in such demand that Oxford University Press had to print twenty-five thousand extra copies.

The Art of War offers specific battle strategies—for example, one tells commanders how to move armies through inhospitable terrain, while another explains how to use and respond to different types of weapons—but they also give more general advice about conflicts and their resolution. Rules like "He will win who knows when to fight and when not to fight" and "Victory usually goes to the army who has better trained officers and men" can be applied to all kinds of disagreements and challenges.

The book also offers practical strategies for success, such as, "War is a game of deception. Therefore feign incapability when in fact capable; feign inactivity when ready to strike; appear to be far way when actually nearby . . . When the enemy is greedy for gains, put out a bait to lure him; when he is in disorder, attack and overcome him; when he boasts substantial strength, be doubly prepared against him; and when he is formidable, evade him. If he is given to anger, provoke him. If he is timid and careful, encourage his arrogance. If his forces are rested, wear them down. If he is united as one, divide him. Attack when he is least prepared."

However, perhaps one of *The Art of War*'s most important and counter-intuitive messages (although very much in keeping with Taoist principles of yielding) is that warfare is considered something essentially undesirable and to be avoided. Sun Tzu writes, "Those who are not fully aware of the harm in waging war are equally unable to understand fully the method of conducting war advantageously." Instead, "he who is skilled in war subdues the enemy without fighting. He captures the enemy's cities without assaulting them. He overthrows the enemy's kingdom without prolonged operations in the field . . . This is the method of attacking by stratagem."

Above all, the text emphasizes the importance of not only *morale* but morals too. It advises rulers very firmly to "find out which sovereign possesses more moral influence, which general is more capable, which side has the advantages of heaven and earth, which army is better disciplined, whose troops are better armed and trained, which command is more impartial in meting out rewards and punishments, and I will be able to forecast which side will be victorious."

1

✛

Meet the Wild Things

Barack Obama and Jane Goodall

For both Barack Obama and Jane Goodall, success in life seems to have come about through combining practical work with their most idealistic beliefs. For Obama, America's forty-fourth president, it was the appeal of taming wild things; for the anthropologist, Goodall, it was Doctor Dolittle talking to the animals. In both cases, the idealism seems to have been planted in childhood by two very different children's books. Ridiculous? Maybe not; psychologists often say it is at the most tender ages that ideas are planted and future paths are determined. So let's consider first the deceptively simple case of Obama and *Where the Wild Things Are*.

Politicians seem to need to read books without actually having the spare time to do so. Studying the reading habits of presidents of the United States is therefore an activity that requires particular skepticism, especially as politicians' words always seem to be carefully crafted for an ever-skeptical public audience. After all, is it really plausible that so many presidents from Abraham Lincoln down only loved the classics and rejected mere popular fiction, or is it more likely that they *thought* they should privilege the classics? Books are a more individual taste than that. I can well believe that Herbert Hoover, the engineer whose presidency started off with the Wall Street crash, kept himself stimulated and up to date with books on metallurgy. Yet, there too, I suppose that Hoover was projecting an image of himself as a political engineer.

Skepticism aside though, some presidents simply were book lovers, from Theodore Roosevelt, who consumed books at a rate of one a day, to Barack Obama, who not only reads voraciously but writes best sellers too.

Obama's reading list offers plenty of texts that a president *should* be reading, like the writings of Abraham Lincoln, the Reverend Martin Luther King Jr., Mahatma Gandhi, and Nelson Mandela. Obama says that he found such books were "particularly helpful" when he needed a sense of solidarity, adding that "during very difficult moments, this job can be very isolating . . . So sometimes you have to sort of hop across history to find folks who have been similarly feeling isolated, and that's been useful."

Obama is a curious figure, though, and his claimed *favorite* books reflect that ambiguous side. Here we find two books of fiction feature prominently: Ernest Hemingway's *For Whom the Bell Tolls*, a ripping yarn that also deals with subtle issues of personal belief and political duties, and in very different vein, an illustrated children's book, *Where the Wild Things Are* by Maurice Sendak.

As president of the United States, Obama needs only a little introduction—but he does need one nonetheless, not least because here is a man who started off, like so many remarkable figures, with little apparently in his favor. He was born on August 4, 1961, in Honolulu, Hawaii, to Barack Obama Sr. and Stanley Ann Dunham. She hailed from Kansas, and I don't know why she was given a man's name, but in any case she was always called Ann. His parents divorced, and Barack spent most of his childhood years in Honolulu being looked after by his grandparents while his mother attended the University of Hawaii at Manoa. Just before his fourth birthday, his mother married Lolo Soetoro, who was originally from Indonesia, and two years later she took the young Obama with her to that country. Later, Obama returned to Honolulu to attend Punahou High School, graduating in 1979, and it was at this point that he finally arrived in the mainland United States, to study at Occidental College, Columbia University, and finally Harvard Law School. In the process he worked at various times as a community organizer, lawyer, and college lecturer.

Of all these roles, publicly at least, Obama has made his organizing days central to his political identity. When he announced his candidacy for president, he said the "best education" he ever had was not at colleges or universities but rather the time he spent discovering the science of communities in Chicago. Indeed, Obama's inspirational chant, "Yes, we can," goes back to these days when he wished to inspire Chicago's citizens and groups to realize their dreams.

The flip side of listening to others to help implement their life strategies is that you don't develop one yourself. And indeed, in his superb 1995 autobiography, *Dreams from My Father: A Story of Race and Inheritance,* no particular philosophy is offered. Instead, Obama says he sought as a youth to reject the values he had been fed from "TV sitcoms and philosophy books." It is a strange combination and a worrying aside.

Morality is also absent from his book *The Audacity of Hope,* with one exception—Obama refers to his work ethic not once but seven times! Apart from this, Obama presents himself simply as a technician, an organizer. He doesn't seem interested in ethics or solving other grand questions. In fact, when asked for an opinion about the origins of life, he short-circuited the debate, saying that it was "above his pay grade"—a characteristic response that would be funnier if it hadn't come from someone whose real life would include ruling on the ramifications of such matters.

Indeed, the Obama administration's record seems to reveal a tin ear for ethics, by which I mean a preference to see issues in purely instrumental terms, with precedents set in terms of data privacy, citizenship, and, most brutal of all, the use of drones to target—even at great cost to innocent civilians—the United States' enemies. (This is a point Malala Yousafzai would make years later to Obama—see chapter 10.)

It is all a far cry from the heady optimism of *The Audacity of Hope,* where Obama says, "What troubled me was the process—or lack of process—by which the White House and its Congressional allies disposed of opposing views; the sense that the rules of governing no longer applied, and that there were no fixed meanings or standards to which we could appeal."

He even says that it was as if those in power had decided that constitutional limits "were niceties that only got in the way, that they complicated what was obvious (the need to stop terrorists) or impeded what was right . . . and could therefore be disregarded, or bent to strong wills."

But back to the books he read. In a July 2008 interview that Obama gave *Rolling Stone* cofounder Jann Wenner shortly after his nomination as the Democratic candidate for the US presidency, Obama discusses both his plans and his influences in some detail. Asked to list three books that inspired him, he offers Toni Morrison's *Song of Solomon,* the tragedies of William Shakespeare, and "probably" Hemingway's *For Whom the Bell Tolls.*

For Whom the Bell Tolls is a war story based on the author's observations (as a journalist) of the bitter civil war in Spain in the 1930s. It is full of gritty passages with a life-or-death flavor that appeal to the spirit of the Spanish Republicans in their ultimately futile bid to stave off the better-equipped fascist forces.

The title, by the way, comes from a much older poem by John Donne. It has become a popular aphorism, usually given as "Ask not for whom the bell tolls: it tolls for thee," but when taken out of its original context like that, it loses a lot of the sense, which is about the shared values of humanity.

> No man is an Island, entire in itself;
> every man is a piece of the continent,
> a part of the main.
> If a clod be washed away by the sea,
> Europe is the less, as well as if a promontory were,
> as well as if a manor of your friends or of your own were.
> Any man's death diminishes me, because I am involved in mankind;
> and therefore never send to know for whom the bell tolls; it tolls for thee.

Perhaps Obama, ever the cautious speaker, thought it a dangerous choice. Yet later, in 2018, at the memorial service for Obama's former presidential rival and frequent political adversary Senator John McCain—a memorial that dwelled at length on the Vietnam veteran's patriotism and personality—Obama directly quoted the book, which was also said to be one of McCain's favorites: "Today is only one day in all the days that will ever be. But what will happen in all the other days that ever come can depend on what you do today."

That's a great line for a politician, as is "There is nothing else than now," which Hemingway has Robert Jordan, the hero in his book, say at one point, before continuing, "There is neither yesterday, certainly, nor is there any tomorrow. How old must you be before you know that? There is only now, and if now is only two days, then two days is your life and every-thing in it will be in proportion. This is how you live a life in two days. And if you stop complaining and asking for what you never will get, you will have a good life. A good life is not measured by any biblical span."

However, Hemingway has more dramatic things than mere votes in mind, of course. As he explains a little later,

> Dying was nothing and he had no picture of it nor fear of it in his mind. But living was a field of grain blowing in the wind on the side of a hill. Living was a hawk in the sky. Living was an earthen jar of water in the dust of the threshing with the grain flailed out and the chaff blowing. Living was a horse between your legs and a carbine under one leg and a hill and a valley and a stream with trees along it and the far side of the valley and the hills beyond.

"If the function of a writer is to reveal reality," the literary editor Max-well Perkins wrote to Hemingway shortly after reading the manuscript, "no one ever so completely performed it." The publisher also described it as greater in power, broader in scope, and "more intensely emotional" than any of the author's previous works and "as one of the best war novels of all time."

Personally, though, I didn't like it. I found it two-dimensional and unreflective, both in its tale of the antifascist guerilla unit in the mountains of Spain and the subsidiary tale of his love for the beautiful Maria. I can well imagine a soldier like McCain having found it a powerful read, but as an inspiration for Obama it has always seemed to me to strike a slightly duff note.

Instead, for me, *Where the Wild Things Are* speaks with more authenticity. And indeed, Obama makes much greater reference to this—on the face of it—less important text. *Wild Things* even features prominently in an interview Obama gave to the *New York Times*' chief book critic Michiko Kakutani in the week before finally stepping down from the presidency, when he talks about the role that books had played during his presidency and throughout his life. Here, in a relaxed and unpretentious account, Obama describes how books guided him out of his turbulent and disconnected teenage years and helped him to figure out who he was, what he thought, and what was important. They also helped him at an earlier stage of what he calls a "peripatetic and sometimes lonely" boyhood when these "worlds that were portable" provided "companionship." (Peripatetic? I had to look that up too. It means traveling from place to place. And although Obama insists he doesn't do philosophy, the word originates as a description of Aristotle's followers.)

Wild Things is a book that talks to a young boy, at odds with his mother, lost in the threatening jungle of life. Indeed, there is a video clip of Barack Obama and his wife, Michelle, reading the storybook to their children on the White House lawn, complete with growls and claws, as part of the annual Easter Egg Roll. Obama can be found saying, "I love that book, and my wife still thinks that I'm Max: that I'm getting into mischief all the time."

Pen drawing of an imaginary "wild thing" by Milo (who is, at the time, the same age as Max in the book).

The story, which consists of only 338 words, concerns a young boy called Max who, after dressing in a wolf costume, wreaks such havoc at home that he is sent to bed without his supper. However, Max's bedroom then mysteriously changes into a jungle, and the boy winds up sailing to an island inhabited by vicious beasts. Far from being scared, though, Max faces down the creatures and ends up hailed as "King of the Wild Things" as well as enjoying a playful romp with his new subjects. Is there a revealing insight here into Barack Obama's stint in Washington? And if so, what tricks might President Obama have borrowed from Sendak's Max?

WHERE THE WILD THINGS ARE
AUTHOR: MAURICE SENDAK
PUBLISHED: 1963

Although just ten sentences long, *Where the Wild Things Are* is considered by many as a masterpiece of children's literature, inspiring operas, ballets, songs, and film adaptations. It is, however, quite an odd, even disquieting, book.

As the book opens, we find the hero, a young boy called Max, armed with a very large hammer. He is wearing a wolf suit and generally making mischief, such as chasing his dog about with a fork. His mother, who appears in the story only as a disembodied voice, shouts at Max that he is a "WILD THING!" to which Max responds by shouting back, "I'LL EAT YOU UP!"

Because of this, he is sent to bed without dinner. There, in his bedroom, his rage continues to burn, and soon trees begin to grow from the floor and his room becomes a forest. Max enters the forest before coming upon a boat that he takes across the ocean to "where the wild things are."

Right on cue, these appear from the jungle, with sharp, pointed teeth and menacing claws, but Max confronts them and soon so thoroughly dominates that he becomes their king!

It all becomes a rather wild, frenzied romp, but after a while, Max begins to feel lonely and wish that he were "where someone loved him best of all." He journeys home, leaving the wild things behind, and arrives back "into the night of his very own room, where he found his supper waiting for him." And what's more, the book finishes, it was still hot.

In a 2009 article reflecting on the eve of *Wild Things'* cinematic interpretation, the contemporary American psychologist Richard Gottlieb analyzed Maurice Sendak's book for *The Psychologist*. Gottlieb has no doubt that its central message of the book is that destructive rage allows children to survive disappointments and loss. *Where the Wild Things Are* vividly captures this dark truth.

Gottlieb also recalls the writer Francis Spufford's description of *Where the Wild Things Are* as "one of the very few picture books to make an entirely deliberate, and beautiful, use of the psychoanalytic story of anger." According to Spufford, Sendak's writing is a study of intense emotions—including disappointment, fury, and even cannibalistic rage—and their transformation through creative activity. Could similar ingredients be said to exist in an inner-city community like Chicago—or, more generally, in the voting public—that all politicians must attempt to transform into positive energy?

In a pair of interviews with Leonard Marcus spaced five years apart (in 1988 and 1993), Sendak explains that the book begins with a child in a fit of bad temper triggered in part by destructive fantasies. This rage then results in an altered state of consciousness similar to that which occurs in a dream or even in an act of artistic creation. This altered state in turn then allows the child to confront the initial rage and achieve mastery over it.

Having conquered his anger, Max is drawn by the smell of food—representing maternal warmth and security—and returns home to find his mother's love evidenced by the dinner she left in his room.

For Spufford, Sendak's tale addresses our deepest, frequently repressed, concerns about ourselves. He says it meets children in a place of "anguished inner struggle" made up of such previously unspoken things as being consumed by sudden anger with their mother and fighting to control their own feelings.

What's the author's own personal story? It seems that Sendak's own childhood was a miserable one. Born in Brooklyn in 1928, he was the youngest of three children. His parents, Phillip and Sadie, had emigrated from Poland before World War I. The families they left behind, although never known firsthand by young Maurice, had a great influence on the emotional tone of his childhood. "My father's entire family was destroyed in the Holocaust. I grew up in a house that was in a constant state of mourning," he said in an interview with Leonard Marcus in 2002. He has described his mother as disturbed and depressed and has alluded frequently to her lack of emotional availability, her preoccupation, and her chronic sadness. Death was a constant presence, if not as a fact then as a fantasy, worry, or deep concern. Maurice himself was a sickly child, suffering from scarlet fever, and his parents worried constantly about his health.

On top of all this, the year Maurice was born, his father lost every cent he had in a financial disaster. The morning of Maurice's bar mitzvah, his father received news that his family had been wiped out by the Nazis. As for his remaining relatives, Sendak says they gave him the creeps. He has revealed that his models for drawing the *Wild Things* characters were his Jewish relatives who used to visit his family weekly when he was a child. They terrified him, and he dreaded their visits, because it always seemed to him that they might eat everything the family had. They also threatened him directly, he recalled, when they would pinch his cheek and tell him they would eat him up.

From around 1952 (when he was twenty-four years old), Sendak created what he called variously "fantasy sketches," "stream-of-consciousness doodles," and "dream pictures" while listening to classical music. His aim was not unlike that of a patient in psychoanalytic treatment, consisting of "letting whatever came into my mind come out on the paper, and my only conscious intention was to complete a whole 'story' on one page . . . beginning and ending, if possible, with the music itself." He said that some of these were "purely fantastic meanderings that seem to roam carelessly through the unconscious." Cannibalistic fantasies feature prominently, with themes of devouring and regurgitation. This last is quite a theme in psychiatry, the most common "eating disorder" in infancy.

What children need to survive, Sendak seems to suggest, are disappointments, losses, and, most important, destructive rages! In Sendak's book, survival results from going to where the wild things are, albeit in the altered states of dream and daydream. Once there, as Richard Gottlieb has put it, the child can conquer them, and then they can return. Obama, it seems, adopted a very similar approach when he channeled not just the hopes and aspirations but also the rage and disappointment of voters by offering them not merely a political program but the right to dream. Obama is often considered a very cool, unemotional leader, almost a "technocrat" —but behind that surface is a much more complex and psychologically aware figure, one who evidently still enjoys the coded messages and Freudian interpretations of this deceptively simple children's book.

Nonetheless, with *Wild Things*, it's as well to realize that we're really talking about psychology and metaphors, because otherwise this kind of story hardly augers well for the furry creatures and wild beasts of the real world. Unfortunately that distinction may be difficult to explain to very young children. So it's perhaps fortunate for animals everywhere that Jane Goodall's favorite children's book offers a very different message.

Today, Jane Goodall is the inspirational anthropologist whose work living with and closely observing chimpanzees and other primates in Africa revolutionized our understanding both of these rare and endangered animals and of ourselves. However, Goodall admits that the germ of her future research lay in three children's books: two about animals—Hugh Lofting's *Doctor Dolittle* and Robert Louis Stevenson's *Jungle Book*—and a series of short stores by Edgar Rice Burroughs about a community of apes who raise a young boy called Tarzan. We usually think of Tarzan via the whimsical portrayals in television and films, but the apes in the Tarzan novels are made of more serious stuff. They have both a rudimentary society and a rudimentary morality. They negotiate and have discussions as a group involving concepts as abstract as ethical rights.

Indeed, Burroughs says that apes live in societies with unwritten laws. A more scientific account of animal life called *The Miracle of Life* (that Goodall's grandmother got for her free by saving up coupons from cereal packets) contains considerable discussion of biology and behavior. Goodall told the website Radicalreads that she spent hours poring over the small print of those magical pages. "It was not a book written for children, but I was absolutely absorbed as I learned about the diversity of life on earth, the age of the dinosaurs, evolution and Charles Darwin, the early explorers and naturalists—and the amazing variety and adaptations of the animals around the world."

Nonetheless, it is the fictional accounts that seem to have really lit Goodall's original fire. In a 2016 World Books Day interview published by the Jane Goodall Institute, she recalls that

> the first book that really made an impression was *The Story of Dr. Dolittle* by Hugh Lofting. An English country doctor who lived in Puddleby-on-the-Marsh who was taught how to speak to animals by his parrot, Polynesia . . . Mum got it for me from the library—we could not afford new books. I read it at least twice before it had to go back. In fact I loved it so much that Danny (my grandmother, with whom Mum, my sister Judy and I went to live after war broke out and my father joined up in the army) gave it to me as a great treat for Christmas, 1944. It was one of the most exciting presents I remember—my very own book!

In an earlier interview, in 2010, after Kathryn Reed asked the "iconic friend of the chimpanzees" to talk both about her past practical work in the field and what she thought were the greatest similarities she had observed between humans and the anthropoid monkeys, Goodall replied, "The non-verbal communication, kissing, embracing, holding hands, patting on the back, swaggering, throwing rocks, using tools, making tools, nurturing infants; showing real altruism by rescuing infants, adopting them, caring for them. And then on the reverse side you get this brutal behavior and a kind of primitive inclination to war as well."

In chapter 2 of *The Story of Doctor Dolittle*, there is this message too, delivered by the parrot to the good doctor: "But animals don't always speak with their mouths. They talk with their ears, with their feet, with their tails, with everything. Sometimes they don't want to make a noise." And the parrot points at the dog, called Jip, wrinkling his nose. "What's that mean?" asks the doctor. "That means 'Can't you see that it has stopped raining?,'" Polynesia answered. "He is asking you a question. Dogs nearly always use their noses to ask questions."

THE STORY OF DR. DOLITTLE
AUTHOR: HUGH LOFTING
PUBLISHED: 1920

The plot is admirably simple. Doctor John Dolittle loves animals. He has rabbits in his pantry, white mice in his piano, and a hedgehog living in his cellar. He has a horse, a cow, and several birds, including Dab-dab the duck, Polynesia the parrot, and Too-too the owl. In fact, we're told, his office overflows with animal friends, and when he walks down the street the dogs run out to follow him and the crows start caw-cawing their approval. Of course, many people teach their parrots to speak a little English, but the big breakthrough for Dolittle comes one day when Polynesia the parrot teaches him the language of the animals. After this, Doctor Dolittle travels the world, as far away as Africa, to help his new friends.

The book was an instant hit. But when it was written, its author's concerns were less with animals as such and more with encouraging children to respect the different peoples of the world, using animals as a kind of metaphor. In his afterword for the book, Lofting straightforwardly says, "If we make children see that all races, given equal mental and physical chances for development have about the same batting averages of good and bad, we shall have laid another very substantial foundation stone in the edifice of peace and internationalism."

If that seems a strange thing, bear in mind that Dr. Dolittle made his very first appearance not in the book but in letters that Lofting wrote to his children while serving as a soldier in World War I.

Valerie Jane Morris-Goodall's first contact with apes came as a very young child when her father, a London businessman called Mortimer Morris-Goodall, gave her a stuffed chimpanzee named Jubilee. Jane's mother was worried that the chimpanzee might give Jane nightmares, but Jane loved it. (I hasten to explain we are talking about fluffy toys stuffed with foam rubber, nothing worse!) At the time of writing, Jubilee still sits on Goodall's dresser in London.

Amazingly, for someone who later became an iconic figure in the study of primate behavior, Goodall had no formal training in zoology or biology. In fact, she had no university degree at all when she followed her passion for animals to the farm of a friend in the Kenya highlands in 1957. At first, the only role she had was that of a secretary, until one day, acting on a friend's advice, she telephoned the famous Kenyan archaeologist and paleontologist Louis Leakey with no other thought than to make an appointment to discuss animals. It just so happened that Leakey, believing that the study of existing great apes could provide indications of the behavior of early hominids, invited Goodall to Olduvai Gorge in Tanganyika (present-day Tanzania), where he laid out his plans.

To start, Leakey sent Goodall to London to study primate behavior and to learn about their anatomy. As part of her research, she also returned to Gombe Stream National Park in Tanganyika, this time accompanied by her mother, whose presence was necessary to satisfy the safety requirements of their chief warden, David Anstey. With Leakey's assistance and funding, Goodall (who, remember, had no degree) arrived at Newnham College, Cambridge, and obtained a PhD in ethology, the scientific study of animal behavior. She was only the eighth person to be allowed to study for a PhD there without first having obtained an undergraduate degree!

Her thesis drew on her first five years of study at the Gombe Reserve and detailed the behavior of free-living chimpanzees. Goodall observed things that researchers more conventionally trained, or perhaps just with more conventional mindsets, had overlooked. For a start, instead of numbering the chimpanzees she observed, she gave them names such as Fifi and David Greybeard and noted their unique and individual personalities, an unconventional idea at the time. (Numbering was a nearly universal practice and thought to be important so that researchers would not become attached to the subjects they were studying. But, of course, this naming of animals is a major part of the appeal and charm of Doctor Dolittle.)

As Goodall puts it in a 1996 PBS documentary called *Jane Goodall's Wild Chimpanzees*, she found that "it isn't only human beings who have personality, who are capable of rational thought [and] emotions like joy and sorrow." She also observed behaviors such as hugs, kisses, pats on the back, and even tickling, all the kinds of actions that we normally consider unique to human interaction. She built up a theory that such gestures were evidence of "the close, supportive, affectionate bonds that develop between family members and other individuals within a community" and that such things suggest that similarities between humans and chimpanzees go far beyond mere genetics and can be seen in emotion, intelligence, and family and social relationships.

THE SOCIAL LIFE OF CHIMPANZEES

Among those whom Goodall named during her years in Gombe were

- David Greybeard, a gray-chinned male and the first chimp to accept Goodall as a friend;
- Goliath, a friend of David Greybeard, originally the alpha male of the troop;
- Mike, who through his cunning and improvisation displaced Goliath as the alpha male;
- Humphrey, a big, strong, bullying male;
- Gigi, a large, sterile female who delighted in being the "aunt" of any young chimps or humans;
- Mr. McGregor, another belligerent older male;
- Flo, a motherly, high-ranking female, and her children, Figan, Faben, Freud, Fifi, and Flint; and
- Frodo, Fifi's second-oldest child, an aggressive male who would frequently attack Jane and ultimately force her to leave the troop.

Goodall's research is renowned in the scientific community for challenging two long-standing beliefs of the day: that only humans could construct and use tools and that chimpanzees were vegetarians. As to the first, Goodall recounts observing chimpanzees *fishing* for termites. In her book *Reason for Hope: A Spiritual Journey*, she describes watching one feeding at a termite mound by repeatedly placing stalks of grass into termite holes and removing them covered with clinging, tasty termites. She also describes how the chimps would take twigs from trees and strip off the leaves to make the twig more effective, a form of object modification that is the rudimentary beginnings of tool making. Humans had long distinguished ourselves from the rest of the animal kingdom as "man the toolmaker." In response to Goodall's revolutionary findings, Louis Leakey wrote, "We must now redefine man, redefine tool, or accept chimpanzees as human."

It is a perspective Dr. Dolittle shares as well, as when he announces,

> I do not understand the human race
> Has so little love for creatures with a different face.
> Treating animals like people is no madness or disgrace.
> I do not understand the human race.

However, in some ways, life at Gombe Stream was very different from the imaginary paradise of animal cooperation conjured up in *Doctor Dolittle*. Goodall found and reported a hitherto unrecorded aggressive side to chimpanzee behavior. For one thing, she found that the chimps systematically hunted and ate their smaller, weaker near relatives—such as colobus monkeys. Goodall records watching one hunting group isolate a colobus monkey high in a tree, block all possible exits, and then capture and kill it.

The chimpanzees then each took parts of the carcass, sharing with other members of the troop in response to begging behaviors. Incredibly, given that this aspect of chimp behavior had not been noted before, it turned out the chimps at Gombe killed and ate as much as one-third of the colobus population in the park each year. In such ways, Goodall's work challenged and revolutionized the study of chimpanzees and the other primates.

In *Reason for Hope*, Goodall says of her discovery, "During the first ten years of the study I had believed . . . that the Gombe chimpanzees were, for the most part, rather nicer than human beings. . . . Then suddenly we found that chimpanzees could be brutal—that they, like us, had a darker side to their nature."

Nonetheless, she managed to develop a close bond with the chimpanzees and to become the only human, to this day, ever accepted into chimpanzee society, as the lowest-ranking member of a troop for twenty-two months!

Throughout her life, Goodall has worked (and at the time of writing continues to work) tirelessly—and fearlessly—on behalf of Africa's wild chimpanzees, even in her eighties contributing to a shift in the scientific understanding of how similar these animals really are to ourselves, both in their complex social behaviors and in their abilities to understand and communicate. Just as important as changing the expert view has been her influence on popular opinion. A prolific writer (like Obama), perhaps her best-known book is *In the Shadow of Man*, published in 1971 and since translated into forty-eight languages. We even had a copy in my home—but it was read less often than *Doctor Dolittle*!

2

✛

Roll the Dice

Larry Page, Sergey Brin, and Richard Branson

"Try everything and see what works" has long been the philosophy behind both Larry Page and Sergey Brin's "hopeful monsters" strategy at Google and Richard Branson's business experiments at Virgin. All three entrepreneurs illustrate a philosophy that could be called Darwinism, but, if so, that's only one strand of it.

Take Google. As an Internet search company, it works at a fundamentally different pace from other industries. Web software changes continuously. You don't plan it rigidly; you let it evolve day by day in response to customer behavior. The faster and more flexibly things evolve, the more successful your products will be. That's the "hopeful" part.

The flip side with this approach, though, is that no one really knows where Google is going—or what its ultimate effects will be. Will Google destroy libraries, films, or books? That's the "monster" part of random evolution. Add to which, there is indubitably another side of Google: a taste for killing things. Fortunately, so far, it's mainly been the company's own products! Even so, killing a product is usually considered a shameful thing for a business. It disappoints customers, and it looks like an admission of failure. So most companies downplay any change of plan as merely a change of emphasis or a readjustment. Google, however, does the exact opposite. It trumpets to the world that it's terminating products. Turning off Google Reader or Google Desktop is an accomplishment to be proud of!

Michael Mace, author of the business strategies book *Map the Future* and former director of worldwide customer and competitive analysis at Apple, says that Google doesn't seem to respond to the rules and logic used by the rest of the business world. It passes up what look like obvious opportunities, invests heavily in things that look like black holes, and proudly announces product cancelations that the rest of us would view as an embarrassment.

Yet, if Google is seen as a kind of ongoing autonomous experiment, the cancelations are just as exciting, and certainly as informative, as the successes. The downside with such try-outs, as Doctor Frankenstein found, is that they have a nasty habit of ending up in chaos, even dangerously out of control. We must hope that Page and Brin's creation retains some memory of its mysteriously dismantled founding credo: don't be evil.

Any talk of corporations conducting autonomous experiments brings to mind the highly successful entrepreneur Richard Branson. On the surface, he has little in common with the Google founders. Branson is from an earlier, groovier generation and started out in the music biz. Today, however, his companies, under the brand name Virgin, range from insurance to space flight. And for decades he has enthusiastically applied to his businesses the same spirit of "try everything and see what works" that permeates Silicon Valley start-ups.

Richard Branson is now a billionaire who lives on a tropical island, but I remember him starting out as a British hippy with a couple of grubby record shops, including one in my hometown of Brighton, busy making his name promoting trendy punk bands and selling vinyl records.

Where the Google founders are academic high-fliers who seem to relax by designing 3-D printers in Lego (no, really! Page did this), Branson is refreshingly populist. Not for him sweeping scientific theories like Darwinism. Instead, Branson claims to have been directly influenced by a cult 1971 classic called *Dice Man* by Luke Rhinehart—actually a pseudonym for George Powers Cockcroft, a reclusive figure who says that he admires Zen philosophies. Selling more than two million copies, the book offers a refreshingly subversive way to deal with the complexity of modern life: "let the dice decide."

DICE MAN
AUTHOR: LUKE RHINEHART (AKA GEORGE POWERS COCKROFT)
PUBLISHED: 1971

Dice Man tells the story of a psychiatrist who, feeling bored and unfulfilled, begins making life decisions based on the casting of dice. He creates lists of six possible actions for himself and then "lets the roll of the dice decide." The outcomes he gambles with are not sophisticated stuff, and along the way he breaks lots of taboos, including committing murder, breaking psychiatric patients out of hospitals, and causing all kinds of chaos. The novel became a cult classic for its subversive approach to life in general and antipsychiatry sentiments in particular. At the same time, due to its central message as well as its treatment of crime and sexuality, it was considered controversial. On its initial publication, the cover bore the confident strapline, "Few novels can change your life. This one will."

The key point of the text—and it must be remembered it is only a fictional story and not really an alternative life strategy being presented—is that while some of the actions he lets the dice decide are merely whimsical and eccentric, others go against his own sense of morality, not to mention the law. At the end of the tale, Rhinehart is finally forced to choose between his promise to obey the dice and the rules of both society and his own conscience.

Many people have called the book out as dreadful, and mainstream reviewers shunned it. And yet, especially with outright criminality removed, the idea *is* intriguing. Indeed, the germ of the book came from a course Crockcroft led while teaching psychology at a US college. One class focused on freedom and the ideas of the philosophers Nietzsche and Sartre, and he challenged the students to consider whether the ultimate freedom was to get away from actions dictated by force of habit or simple causality and instead make all their decisions by casting dice. He was so struck by the response that he decided to write the book.

Older and wiser now, Cockcroft stresses the value of considering the range of possibilities that exist before each act (the roll of the dice requires you to think of only six possible outcomes), and he links his youthful folly to wider debates in business science where an element of chance is introduced to enhance creativity.

Tip: If you are tempted to try this, make sure none of the outcomes you consider are too rash or really outside the bounds of acceptability. Shouting out a snatch of song on the hour, as Branson already did, may already be on the very edge of tolerable!

The crux of the dice strategy is deciding how much power you give them. In the novel, Cockcroft actually allows the technique to decide such things as who to marry! As the book puts it, "Once you hand over your life to the dice, anything can happen." In real life too, Branson has admitted openly that the book influenced his decision making, particularly in the early days of his Virgin Records label.

In an interview with the main British TV magazine, nostalgically called *The Radio Times*, Branson has said, "I was very much under the influence of the *Dice Man* books . . . It's where you compile lists of actions and, after throwing the dice, have to adhere to whatever number you've placed by that particular instruction."

By way of an example, Branson recalls what happened when he used the technique while on a trip from the UK to Finland to see a pop group called Wigwam just prior to the release of their LP. "I had made this list of things to do and threw the dice, which told me that for all that day I had to scream loudly on the hour every hour for twelve hours." Yes, you read it right. Branson created some pretty weird options for himself.

"So there I am at the Wigwam gig and the band are playing not the loudest song in their set. I can see the hour coming up, thinking, you know, oh, please finish the song so my shriek can be lost in the applause." According to a Press Association report, when Branson was asked if the crowd managed to drown out his screams, he admitted, "Not a hope. I had to just bellow it out. Dreadful for everyone, really. . . . I had to do it again during their encore."

If this just sounds like a media personality trying to be a bit wacky, the reality of Branson's life really has been to let randomness decide events. For example, he only came up with the name for his chart hits music series "Now That's What I Call Music!" because he spotted a sign with those words in a bric-a-brac shop. What's more, he was in the shop not to buy bric-a-brac (which would have been logical) but to woo the girl who worked there. She later became his wife. It seems that another lucky roll of the dice, metaphorical if not actual, came in 1992 when Branson's business empire was creaking under the strain of maintaining his airline, Virgin Atlantic. He decided to sell off his profitable music industry operation, Virgin Records, to EMI to provide a cash lifeline, gambling his core asset on what looked like a risky new venture.

Branson goes further into the nature of this kind of gamble at length in his autobiography, *The Virgin Way: Everything I Know about Leadership*. He starts by stating that luck is one of the most misunderstood and underappreciated factors in life. He insists that luck is really about taking risks. "Those people and businesses that are generally considered fortunate or luckier than others are usually also the ones that are prepared to take the greatest risks and, by association, are also prepared to fall flat on their faces every so often."

Today, Branson, as the founder of the Virgin Group, has an estimated net worth of $5 billion. But he surely took a risk when he dropped out of school (plus, it was a pretty posh school) at the age of fifteen to produce a magazine to campaign against the Vietnam War instead. No money in that, but it did lead to his first moneymaking scheme: *Student* magazine. He managed to get some big-name interviews but wasn't focused on turning a profit.

After that, Branson pivoted into very different territory—music. He rolled the dice (metaphorically) and launched a mail-order record business. It started as a way to make the magazine pay, but it soon grew into the profitable music and entertainment business called Virgin Records. Hole in one!

Branson offers the example of a golfer doing this, saying that he once watched a golfer chip out of a deep greenside bunker in the final round of the British Open golf championship. The shot was too high, but the ball just clipped the top of the flagpole and dropped right into the hole. The TV commentator exclaimed, "Oh my goodness, what a lucky shot!"

According to Branson, the golfer was not so much lucky as he was reaping the rewards of thousands of hours spent practicing how to get a golf ball out of a bunker and onto the green. The shot illustrated the old saying "The harder I practice, the luckier I get."

Certainly, over the years (like that golfer) Branson has often been accused of being lucky in business, but he insists that he's entitled to some credit because "a lot of very hard work has played a major part in any luck that has come my way." It does seem that sometimes he *has* just been fortunate, the early success of Virgin Records being the classic example. The company turned an almost immediate profit in the UK, but in the music business you need a presence in the United States to really succeed. Branson kept encountering closed doors there though. One time, he had a meeting with the legendary head of Atlantic Records, Ahmet Ertegun, during which he hoped to persuade him to take on Virgin's first-ever album release, Mike Oldfield's *Tubular Bells*. The record had already become a huge hit in the UK, but no one seemed very interested in the United States. Indeed, Ertegun insisted that an all-instrumental album like *Tubular Bells* would not sell in North America.

There was certainly nothing charmed about that meeting, but while Ertegun just happened to be playing the album in his office (and still trying to figure out what all the fuss in Britain was about) in walked movie director William Friedkin in search of some backing music for his new movie.

Even as Ertegun moved to turn the music off, Friedkin heard a snatch of *Tubular Bells* and instantly loved it. The result was that Branson got a US deal with Atlantic that included the use of his band's music in one of the 1970s' biggest blockbuster movies: *The Exorcist*. Thus *Tubular Bells* was introduced to a generation of young people and a global audience.

Now Branson says that you could call the success of *Tubular Bells* luck if you want, but he had worked hard at trying to win over Ertegun. Branson's efforts were vital to getting the record into Ertegun's office in the first place.

Or consider another time that Branson rolled the metaphorical dice that came when his flight from some Caribbean island to Puerto Rico was canceled. It seemed that he was going to miss an important meeting. Not willing to miss a rendezvous with a new female acquaintance, Branson simply found a chartered jet and put up a sign: "$29 per ticket." He quickly sold out the plane's other seats, made it to Puerto Rico, and discovered a taste for running an airline.

What do you do if you discover such a thing? (My ten-year-old has such a taste too.) Well, what Branson did was to ring up Boeing the next day and ask to borrow a plane with the option to return it if in a year things hadn't worked out. It sounds like a pretty hopeful, not to say hopeless, approach, but here's where it seems that luck once again came in. Although Branson didn't know it, Boeing, in fact, had their own agenda in the UK, and it suited them to have a low-cost rival challenging British Airways' then monopoly.

"I got lucky," Branson writes. "Right place. Right time."

Indeed, plans that work can seem like lucky guesses—like rolling the luck dice or spinning the roulette wheel—but Branson says that he has often covered so many options that he is bound to get lucky sometimes. No wonder he says his company slogan is "Screw it, just do it." Branson runs hundreds of different businesses under the Virgin brand, and, of course, his approach has also brought its own share of wrong turns and miscalculations. Here are a few examples of failures where his luck seemed to desert him:

- *Soft drinks.* Remember Virgin Cola? The drink was too similar to "the real thing" to make any impact—Branson let it go to the wall.
- *Motor sales.* Hello and goodbye to Virgin Cars, intended to change the way cars were bought. It too sunk without a trace.
- *Online music.* Ditto for Virgin Digital, Branson's attempt to rival Apple's iTunes. It struggled and consumed a lot of cash before disappearing in 2007.

Actually, during the initial test flight of Virgin's first and then only plane, Branson's dice seemed unlucky as a flock of birds flew into the engine of the rented Boeing 747, causing extensive damage. The cost of repairs to jumbo jets is enormous; the company couldn't borrow money for repairs without being certified, and the airline couldn't get certified to start carrying passengers without a working plane!

Branson had to gamble the resources of his other companies to get the repairs done. But his airline got the certification it needed, and Virgin's inaugural flight from Gatwick to Newark was a success. Mind you, when Branson, as the wealthy owner of Virgin Atlantic Airways, was asked how to become a millionaire, he had a quick answer: "There's really nothing to it. Start as a billionaire and then buy an airline."

A curious tale Branson told James Altucher during a podcast takes on the nature of chance. When Branson's children were eighteen and twenty-one, he took them to a casino and gave them $200 each to play with. The point was not to give them a taste for gambling but rather to teach them, on the contrary, that gambling was a mug's game and that the only way to make money in a casino is to be the owner. Sure enough, after half an hour they had lost all their money and went to have a reflective drink together. However, as they were doing this, a cheer went up from one of the gambling tables and someone came over and told them that one of their chips had actually just come up as a huge winner! Branson insisted his children didn't misread the lesson though: he redistributed all the winning tokens to the other players and left the casino.

THE STRANGER
AUTHOR: ALBERT CAMUS
PUBLISHED: 1942

The French writer Albert Camus wrote a celebrated first novel called *The Stranger* (or sometimes *The Outsider*), which parallels Luke Rhinehart's book in several ways. In his book, Camus too tries to reveal the absurd, random character of the universe by creating a character, Meursault, who (like Branson) has rather abruptly discontinued his education and is now working as a clerk with a shipping company. Meursault follows none of the normal assumptions about life and is without social ambition let alone belief in any religious or rational meaning in the universe. In Camus's tale, a series of chance events leads Meursault to eventually commit murder and be condemned to death.

In real life, by contrast, Branson's interest in randomness and challenging social conventions seems to have served him well. Or perhaps we might just say, the real-life Branson, like the Google founders, seems to have been fortunate in certain key rolls of the dice.

Mathematicians know that the outcomes of dice only appear to be random; over time they can be precisely computed. This was at the heart of Google founders Larry Page and Sergey Brin's scientific approach to trying everything.

Take their core idea of making a new kind of Internet search engine based on the number of links Web pages have. This wasn't originally arrived at as part of a business strategy but rather arose in a more happenstance, random way that both Darwin and Rhinehart would have liked. While a doctoral student at Stanford University in California, Page came up with multiple competing projects across various areas and then asked his supervisor, Terry Winograd, to help select a winner. More or less on the spur of the moment, Winograd said that the one described as something to do with the link structure of the Web "seems like a really good idea."

From this small exchange, Page, along with his friend Brin, developed a search algorithm approach called PageRank. It was Brin who had the idea that information on the Web could be ordered in a hierarchy by link popularity. At its simplest, this means that a Web page is ranked higher the more links there are to it. Page and Brin were always aware, though, of the quality issue implied by the endless generation of new pages on the Web, usually effortlessly created without any editorial control or standards, or as Page put it in an early account, "The reason that PageRank is interesting is that there are many cases where simple citation counting does not correspond to our commonsense notion of importance."

An academic paper (coauthored by Rajeev Motwani and Terry Winograd) described PageRank and also sketched out an initial prototype of the Google search engine. Shortly after, Google Inc., the company behind the search engine, was founded.

PAGERANK

An early step in the Google project was a paper entitled "The PageRank Citation Ranking: Bringing Order to the Web." Published by Brin and Page in 1998, its solution to the problem of dodgy links and measuring quality on the Web is set out, dautingly, like this: "Let A be a square matrix with the rows and columns corresponding to web pages. Let $A_{u,v}$ =1/Nu if there is an edge from u to v and $A_{u,v}$=0 if not. If we treat R as a vector over web pages, then we have R=cAR. So R is an eigenvector of A with eigen value c. In fact, we want the dominant eigenvector of A. It may be computed by repeatedly applying A to any non-degenerate start vector."

What is an eigenvector? Glad you asked. "In linear algebra, an eigenvector or characteristic vector of a linear transformation is a non-zero vector that only changes by a scalar factor when that linear transformation is applied to it." Here's the point: Google's success derives in large part from a fiendishly clever mathematical algorithm that ranks the importance of Web pages.

But before you begin to feel that all this is just too complicated and mathsy for ordinary folks like us, note that in practice Google often answers queries by directing users to the Wikipedia page containing the search term in its title. That's not got anything to do with links, let alone eigenvectors, but is simply a quick solution to getting reasonably well-structured answers to simple queries. In other words, it's a practical fix that implies the complicated math-driven method fails. It's not particularly clever, let alone elegant—but it works.

The big idea, then, behind Google emerged by chance from a swirl of scholarly (not business) debate. Even the name Google itself emerged from events with a random, not to say Darwinian, flavor. When I say "Darwinian," I mean an approach that is free and open at the outset but then systematically reduces itself to a sole possibility. Before natural selection can act to favor a feature, you need to have a range of traits to select from, a range provided by the ways in which individual animals (whether humans, giraffes, or finches, as shown on the next page) are different from each other. Likewise, sometimes unexpectedly interesting results can be obtained by adding a random word to a search query. Try it sometime! More generally, working off-topic words and themes into your thinking is one way to prompt new insights and discovery.

Darwin's big idea, then, the one that changed the way we see the world, was that evolution is a two-step process: random mutation is the raw material creating a range of possibilities, and natural selection is the guiding force that cuts them all down to just one. In a similar way, randomness and order combine in Google's algorithms.

The website Conservapedia has long noted that Google is a big promoter of Darwin and atheistic science even to the point of giving special recognition to the anniversary of his birthday, which the search engine calls Darwin Day. Now, Conservapedia is an American encyclopedia project written with a narrow political agenda, but on this they are right: if you want to understand the driving philosophy of Google, you can do a lot worse than returning to the ideas of Charles Darwin—in particular, the conviction that life on earth is a kind of vast, random experiment in which only the fastest, strongest, fittest life-forms survive. Nor, in fact, do you have to look too hard to see that the views and ideas of this great English theorist seem to predominate in this twenty-first-century Californian enterprise. The nineteenth-century naturalist whose insights would rapidly spread from botany and biology to influence fields as diverse as politics, sociology, and even art is truly the ghost in the Google machine.

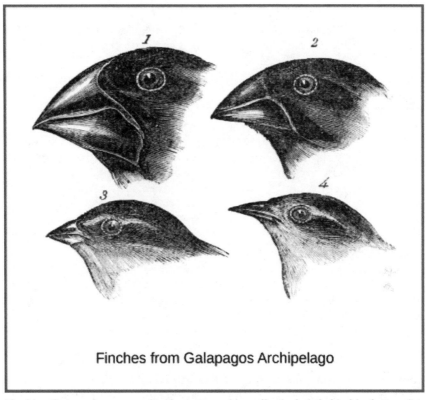

Finches from Galapagos Archipelago

The idea that randomness and order can combine effectively is behind both Darwin's theory and in Google's algorithms. This famous image is supposed to illustrate how natural selection led to very different beaks for the finches of the Galapagos. (Darwin, *Journal of Researches into the Natural History and Geology of the Countries Visited during the Voyage of the H.M.S. Beagle Round the World*, 2nd ed. London: John Murray, 1845. https://www.biodiversitylibrary .org/page/2010582#page/7/mode/1up.)

That said, whatever the Google philosophy really is, it seems to take second place to practical requirements. Illustrative of this is the fact that, originally, Page and Brin called their search engine BackRub, which has nothing to do with rubbing backs but instead, in their minds, something to do with back links. Would you use a search engine called BackRub? Me neither, especially if I were seeking objective information from an array of similar products. Fortunately, one day in September 1997, Page invited several other graduate students, including Sean Anderson, Tamara Munzner, and Lucas Pereira, to brainstorm better names for the new search technology.

Anderson suggested the word "googolplex," and Page responded verbally with the shortened form, "googol." Ten squared (or ten raised to the power of two) is a hundred, and ten cubed (or ten raised to the power of three) is a thousand, but a googol is 10^{100}, ten raised to the power of a hundred. In decimal notation, it is written as the digit 1 followed by one hundred zeroes: 10,000,000,000,000,000,000,000,000,000,000,000, 000,000,000,000,000,000,000,000,000,000,000,000,000,000,000,000, 000,000.

The computer nerds all liked the idea so much they immediately checked whether it was available as a domain name on the Internet. However, by mistake (chance!), Anderson entered the name as "google.com," and it was this that was found to be available. Page still liked the name, and within hours he took the step of registering it. The domain name record is dated September 15, 1997: Google's birthday.

The search engine's evocative name thus came about by chance. The other elements of Google were much more calculated but at the same time play less of a role in explaining the company's success. After all, in the mid-1990s, just as Google was coming into existence, other equally smart people were developing search engines. Even the key Google concept of PageRank is influenced by other studies of how academic citations reflect the relative value of papers (notably the research by Eugene Garfield in the 1950s at the University of Pennsylvania) and by the creation of HyperSearch, at the time a revolutionary new kind of search engine, by Massimo Marchiori at the University of Padua.

Nonetheless, the reality that Google is a creature that has always competed in the Internet jungle and had to survive by being bigger and better than everyone else—rather than being actually new and different—is underlined by the fact that today, although the name PageRank is a trademark of Google, and the PageRank process has been patented, the patent is actually assigned to Stanford University, not to Google. However, Google has exclusive license rights on the patent for which, in return, the university received 1.8 million shares. The shares were sold in 2005 for $336 million. Peanuts! All of which goes to emphasize that Page and Brin's genius does not lie in "invention" but rather in being able to commercialize the technology first—put another way, *in being the fastest to adapt.*

And so we turn to the book that seems to have had a remarkable influence on the Google founders—even if they've never referenced it publicly. *On the Origin of Species by Means of Natural Selection, or the Preservation of Favored Races in the Struggle for Life* was originally published way back in 1859 and has never been out of print.

Although Darwin's book was remarkable for its scientific details, that is not why it had such political impact. Rather, there's another aspect to Darwin's theory, which is the conviction that life on earth is perpetually engaged in a zero-sum struggle for existence. And this other, character-

ON THE ORIGIN OF SPECIES
AUTHOR: CHARLES DARWIN
PUBLISHED: 1859

Rarely has a scholarly work so deeply influenced modern society and thought. The book itself has a curious history. It started as a much longer compendious account of all Darwin's research into the riddle of life on this planet. Darwin's idea was originally to organize and record the key points of some 2,500 diary pages and notes made while traveling the world on the ship HMS *Beagle*. This famous voyage from 1831 to 1836 had taken in the Cape Verde Islands; coastal regions of Brazil, Uruguay, and Argentina; and the Galapagos Islands, to name only the most famous destinations. Darwin, we might say, had been busy following the "try everything, no preconceptions" approach. But then chance changed his plans significantly.

By June 18, 1858, Darwin had finished a quarter of a million words and even had a working title for what he envisaged as a three-volume account: *Natural Selection*. But that day he received a letter from Alfred Russel Wallace, an English socialist who had been collecting botanical specimens in the Malay Archipelago. In his letter, Wallace sketched out a theory very like Darwin's own!

Fearing that his own work would be overtaken by Wallace's, Darwin immediately resolved to write a much briefer abstract of his ideas, and it is *this* shorter and much more readable account that became the book that would change the world.

istically Darwinian, element that has helped transform Google from a start-up launched in a garage to a colossus with ambitions to become the world's first media company with revenues of a trillion dollars ($1,000 billion) is less playful. Everyone's heard tales about Google's quirky, fun side, including mouthwatering stock options, perks such as free meals and massages, and a daunting and sometimes just plain weird recruitment process. But running through the company's DNA is also a darker strand: a ruthless killer instinct.

This instinct (along with extraordinary chutzpah) has led Brin and Page to take on the world's biggest corporate animals. This is the dark side of the "try everything, no preconceptions" mindset. Sometimes it seems as if Google has never come across an industry it doesn't want to disrupt. The behemoth has spread its tentacles into an ever-growing array of businesses, including advertising, telecoms, and digital-navigation software. It's started using drones to deliver medical supplies and even takeaway food to Googlers' doors. The company's habit of selling services cheaply or giving them away for free has endeared it to consumers—and outflanked regulators. But the same tactics have enraged competitors, who complain their new rival is out to destroy the economics of entire industries.

One of the biggest potential competitors was Microsoft, sometimes nicknamed the Beast of Redmond (or was the company in reality already less of a dangerous beast and more of a clumping great dinosaur?). In 2003, Brin told the *New York Times* that he wouldn't knowingly challenge Microsoft: "We are not putting ourselves in the bull's-eye as Netscape did," he said, referencing Netscape's disastrous battle against Microsoft Explorer to be the world's choice of Web browser.

And yet only a year later (in the company's 2004 initial public stock offering), Microsoft was precisely listed as one of three strategic competitors, and in 2006, when Google's then chairman, Eric Schmidt, was asked who the company's main rivals were, he listed just two: Yahoo, because, like Google, they had "a targeted advertising network," and Microsoft, because it had plans to enter the search market. It's not entirely clear how Yahoo's cofounders, Jerry Yang and David Filo, felt about being seen as a strategic enemy considering they'd originally lent the Google founders a generous hand to get started. But then, it's a jungle out there!

Not that that's how Brin explained the company policy at an executive Q&A for a Google press day: "We just certainly see the history with that particular company, Microsoft, behaving anti-competitively, being a convicted monopoly and not necessarily playing fair in other situations—like Netscape and whatnot," he said, before adding sanctimoniously, "so I think we want to focus early on and make sure that we at least are looking at the areas where perhaps power can be abused."

What this meant was that within the company spirit of "trying everything," Google had soon thrown down the gauntlet on virtually every path that Microsoft was following. As Janet Lowe describes in her book *Google Speaks: Secrets of the World's Greatest Billionaire Entrepreneurs*, they opened a recruiting office not far from Microsoft's office in Redmond, Washington, and made raids on Microsoft's talent pool. They developed and offered free Google Apps, an online productivity software similar to Microsoft Office. Then came Gmail, also free, and in 2008, Google launched Chrome, the free browser that challenged one of Microsoft's most lucrative products, Internet Explorer.

"The benefit of free is that you get 100 percent of the market," Eric Schmidt, Google's chief executive, explained to Ken Auletta, an American writer, journalist, and media critic for *The New Yorker*, in an interview. "Free is the right answer." For Google, perhaps, but for both its competitors and other more humble life-forms, like regional newspapers and authors, free was often unsustainable. For many, as Auletta puts it, "'free' became a death certificate."

WOLVES

If, occasionally, Google helps young start-ups, it can more usually be found clawing to pieces elderly prey. Because, above all, in Darwin's theory, nature is red in tooth and claw. Animals and organisms compete to survive and prosper. At one point in *Origin of Species*, Darwin offers, "In order to make it clear how, as I believe, natural selection acts, I must beg permission to give one or two imaginary illustrations. Let us take the case of a wolf which preys on various animals, securing some by craft, some by strength, some by fleetness; and let us suppose that the fleetest prey, a deer for instance, had from any change in the country increased in numbers, or that other prey had decreased in numbers, during the season of the year when the wolf is hardest pressed for food."

Darwin's answer is emphatic: "I can under such circumstances see no reason to doubt that the swiftest and slimmest wolves would have the best chance of surviving, and so be preserved or selected."

Of course, business executives know it's a rough, tough world. However, Microsoft's chairperson, Steve Bulmer, wasn't keen for his company to become someone else's dinner, let alone just another fossil. He declared in public, unambiguously, "I'm going to f***ing kill Google."

Yet at the Googleplex, on the surface at least, there was no such passion. Instead, there was only a steady if rather dull fine-tuning of methodologies. There is a revealing conversation with Sergey Brin, back in 2009, explaining how he and Larry Page created a multibillion-dollar business in just a few years. "We've been very successful with advertising," he said. You could say that again! Indeed, Google makes its money by selling advertisements, typically for a handful of cents. The clever bit is it sells vast numbers of them.

Curiously, when they were at Stanford, Page and Brin criticized search engines that had become too "advertising oriented." And when, for many years, Google listed ten ingredients for corporate success prominently on its website, item one was that placement or ranking in search results is "never sold to anyone." "These guys were opposed to advertising," Auletta quotes Ram Shriram, one of Google's first investors, in his book *Googled: The End of the World as We Know It* (Penguin, 2009). "They had a purist view of the world." Presumably the "no preconceptions, try everything" strategy eventually won out over their ideals.

In reality, a "roll the dice and see what works" Darwinian (Bransonian?) approach was always ideally suited to Google's core business of search

advertising. The Internet is so big that you have to use some sort of algo-
rithmic process to organize it, and it takes a vast series of logical experiments to fine-tune search results and the delivery of advertising around
them. Within Google's ecosystem, products like AdSense, which is currently the key driver of the company's profitability, force businesses to
compete for key words and only reward them if they choose the right ones.

Right from the start, Google refused to run with the herd, eschewed
taking banner ads, and kept quietly building its own system linked to
things people might be looking for. Brin has explained that ads related to
searches were originally considered junk content not worth much, while
affiliate fees barely paid for the pizza, and so Internet companies had
tended to compete for the more lucrative banner ads that sit at the top of
pages. Instead, Google ruthlessly upended the whole multibillion-dollar
world of advertising. "It required a lot of evolution and a lot of work,
but it happened," Brin said to journalists at the 2009 Google I/O annual
conference for developers, adding, "If you give it time to *evolve* and give
people a chance to *experiment*, much as it took us in search a long time to
find the magic answer . . . *several generations later*, we have what you think
of now as AdWords, which works very well" (emphasis added).

Here, indisputably, are the key ingredients of the Google mindset: experimentation, evolution, and testing—this last guided not only by their
engineering training but also by the laws of nature themselves. Indeed,
the engineering mindset, the Lego-modeler's mindset, is very different
from that of traditional business thinking. You test theories through controlled experiments, and you make decisions based on experimental data.
It's a Darwinian marketplace of ideas in which only the fittest creations
survive. Yet there's always a randomness, an element of chance there.

Darwin himself once said, "I love fools' experiments. I am always
making them," in which light, he would surely have welcomed Google's
seemingly random investments in businesses like Shweeb, an eco-
friendly monorail transport system powered by passengers kicking their
legs as if on a bicycle. Daft? Maybe. Google gave the company $1 million.
Then there's Clearwire, a wireless communications network. At the time,
Google said Clearwire would "provide wireless consumers with real
choices for the software applications, content and handsets that they desire." Google liked the concept so much it chipped in $500 million. Brave?
Yes. Unfortunately, the company shut down in 2015.

And then there is 23andMe, a trendy start-up founded by Anne
Wojcicki, health care analyst and wife of Sergey Brin. Indeed, this initiative was supported by a personal loan of $2.9 million from the man him-
self. 23andMe offers to decode your DNA if you provide a saliva sample
and a fistful of money. Google put a shade under $4 million into the
project, but the thinking in this case may have been rather less driven by

a taste for risky investments and more by a taste for keeping Brin's cash safe, as one of the first things the company did with its new investment was to promptly pay back his original stake!

That reminds me that, actually, Google is not as indifferent to spending as its enormous wealth might lead you to imagine. According to a *Forbes* piece on penny-pinching billionaires, David Cheriton, the Stanford professor who introduced Page and Brin to the venture capitalists at Kleiner Perkins and who subsequently became a billionaire, is a man who reuses tea bags. Reuses tea bags! It's bad enough to use bagged tea in the first place.

To sum up, Darwin's little book seems to have contributed to Google's willingness to experiment now and see what works later. However, there's that other aspect of the company's philosophy, the one that is Darwinian in a more ruthless sense. This is the conviction that in order for a few to succeed, many must perish. And as we'll see again and again in this book, it's also a reminder that it is not only people that are influenced by books; books themselves are too.

Darwin is supposed to have arrived at his insight as a result of observing animals on the Galapagos Islands during the voyage of the *Beagle*, but the real root seems to have been a famous book, written in 1798, by the English economist Thomas Malthus called *An Essay on the Principle of Population*. It is here that Malthus, obsessed with the dangers of overpopulation, warns that humanity is locked in a "struggle for existence" in which only the fittest survive and that "it follows that any being, if it vary ever so slightly in a manner profitable to itself . . . will have a better chance of survival, and thus be naturally selected."

It is known that Darwin read Malthus's essay, was much impressed by this notion, and merely expanded this theory of struggle among humans to the wider sphere of the plants and animals.

Recall that for many years, Google's motto was "Don't be evil" (it changed to "Do the right thing" in 2015), yet, as Michael Mace has noted, time and again, Google has identified a competing technology or idea, targeted it, and then gobbled it up whole. Mace adds that the behavior is a natural outcome of the way the company works. "Page says he's all about cooperation and I think he means it, but his product teams relentlessly stalk the latest hot start-up. The result is a company that talks like a charitable foundation but acts like a pack of wolves."

One of Page's key strategic moves for Google illustrates this approach. Anxious to strengthen the company's position in the sphere of mobile technology, Google bought Motorola Mobility for over $12 billion. The purchase was certainly disastrous for the Motorola workforce, who were slashed from 10,000 to 3,800 (AP, 2014). Despite this, Google continued to hemorrhage money, and shareholders pressured Page and Brin to call off the experiment. On January 29, 2014, Google announced the sale of

Motorola Mobility to the Chinese PC maker Lenovo for $2.91 billion. Now, I'm not a math fiend like Brin or Page, but that looks like quite a steep drop in value. Or was it asset stripping? Google did keep bits of Motorola—notably some of their intellectual property. But this is the logic of Darwin: most of Motorola was struggling so had to perish. The successful parts, though, were given a chance to evolve and multiply. As Darwin put it, "A scientific man ought to have no wishes, no affections—a mere heart of stone."

And yet, and as I say, quite unabashed, Google prides itself on being a highly principled company pursuing the good of humanity and for many years (up until 2015 when it mysteriously disappeared) it used the motto "Don't be evil" within its corporate code of conduct. Nonmathematical, nonengineering types misread this. They assume it must mean "don't do bad things," but the evolutionary approach doesn't allow for right and wrong, only for what works. For Google, and nature, "evil" is weakness, and strength and triumph are the only acceptable outcomes.

Reducing morality to self-interest and survival skills has always been controversial, but Darwin himself didn't shy away. In fact, Darwin openly extended his theory to cover the human race and therefore challenged many social, ethical, and psychological assumptions. While *Origin* is his most admired work, he wrote others, such as *The Descent of Man* (1871), which are full of political advice:

> With savages, the weak in body or mind are soon eliminated; and those that survive commonly exhibit a vigorous state of health. We civilized men, on the other hand, do our utmost to check the process of elimination. We build asylums for the imbecile, the maimed and the sick; we institute poor-laws; and our medical men exert their utmost skill to save the life of every one to the last moment. There is reason to believe that vaccination has preserved thousands, who from a weak constitution would formerly have succumbed to small-pox. Thus the weak members of civilized societies propagate their kind. No one who has attended to the breeding of domestic animals will doubt that this must be highly injurious to the race of man. It is surprising how soon a want of care, or care wrongly directed, leads to the degeneration of a domestic race; but excepting in the case of man himself, hardly anyone is so ignorant as to allow his worst animals to breed.

Coming back to Google, there's another revealing story told about the company. In 2001, when Google was only a few years old, Page and Brin decided that the structure had become flabby and unresponsive. They called everyone to a meeting and told them that they were fired. The company was organized instead into small teams that attacked particular projects. (Some were later rehired.) This was, for them, the logical way to ensure that the wolves of Google were the fastest and fleetest.

What about the people's feelings? As to that, an interview in *The New Yorker* with Barry Diller, onetime movie mogul, offers a clue. Diller, it seems, was rather put out by what he felt to be the arrogance of the Google founders. He described visiting Page and Brin in the early days of the company and being disconcerted that Page, even as they talked, stared fixedly at the screen of his personal digital assistant (PDA). "It's one thing if you're in a room with 20 people and someone is using his P.D.A.," Diller recalled.

I said to Larry, "Is this boring?"
  "No. I'm interested. I always do this," Page said.
  "Well, you can't do this," Diller said. "Choose."
  "I'll do this," Page said matter-of-factly, not lifting his eyes from his hand-held device.

Page, it seems, lives in a parallel universe of machines and not emotions. Likewise, his company, even though it hunts in a technological world where things change very fast and even though the Darwinian philosophy it is built on stresses the danger of failing to adapt fast enough, takes a detached and long-term view. Page himself likes to talk about a fifty-year planning horizon, which sounds mad to most business strategists. Most companies have a planning cycle that doesn't run to even one year but rather is worked out in pursuit of quarterly goals. Google does just the opposite.

And all the time, the very software that runs Google searches embodies the principles of Darwinian thought. Algorithms compete to satisfy the Internet searchers. Those whose findings meet expectations will flourish, and those that fail must shrink in importance and eventually perish.

How did Darwin's theory come to have such a hold not only over Google's scientists but on the way we all think? Part of it, as I say, must be because it is a powerful general theory with social and political dimensions. *Origin of Species* has had profound implications not only for understandings of biology and nature but also for our views of human societies and morality. Nazism and Marxism both were, in the minds of their founders, Darwin's theory applied to politics.

And Darwinism explains how simple rules can lead to complex outcomes. How, for example, in living organisms, complexity emerges as the result of simple chemical reactions following certain laws. It is these more complex molecules that build up to become cells and these cells that in turn interact to become specialized organs. Organs interact to form organisms, which interact, communicate, and reproduce on ever higher scales to form, eventually, the universe.

Within Google's search engine too there are virtual molecules, again guided by rules, which together create a new kind of artificial intelligence that increasingly guides our own thinking and behavior. But what if the search engine itself were really alive in the sense of possessing some kind of consciousness, what then might it be thinking? Surely it would be something like this: "From my early youth I have had the strongest desire to understand or explain whatever I observed. . . . To group all facts under some general laws."

As a Google search will show you, in a fraction of a second, these are the words of Charles Darwin.

3

Save the Planet—
One Page at a Time!

Rachel Carson and Frans Lanting

Books have played a key role in widening the circle of human concern to include the natural world and the environment. But what inspired their authors? For some of them at least, it seems that it was not so much dry facts or even direct experiences as imaginary tales in which nature was just one character in a compelling human narrative. Such books can range all the way from grand literary monuments to humble children's stories.

Rachel Carson's *Silent Spring* is a true example of a book that has changed the way people see the natural world. Indeed, it is considered one of the most influential green polemics ever written. It asks hard questions about whether and why humans have the right to control nature, to decide who lives or dies, or to poison and destroy nonhuman life. And, in many ways, its author seems to have been always destined to be interested in nature and the environment. Nevertheless, it turns out that the precise direction her interests took, and her success in communicating her passion, owe a lot to *Moby Dick*, written a good century earlier by New York–born Herman Melville.

The debt that Carson's writing owes in stylistic and emotional terms to Melville is amply reflected by the fact that her first three books, *Under the Sea Wind* (1941), *The Sea around Us* (1951), and *The Edge of the Sea* (1955) were all, well, about the sea! This from someone born and brought up in inland United States, 350 miles distant from the Atlantic Ocean. Like *Moby Dick*, all these were gripping accounts of the interaction of human and marine life in the open seas. In these first books, Carson wrote about how islands were formed, how currents change and merge, how temperature affects sea life, and how erosion impacts not just shorelines but also salinity, fish populations, and tiny micro-organisms, embracing a larger environmental ethic including all of nature's interactive and interdependent systems. Carson applies a cool, scientific eye to such questions.

On the surface, though, Melville's novel is a very different kind of writing. It is supposed to be sailor Ishmael's account of the obsessive quest of Ahab, captain of the whaling ship *Pequod*, to exact revenge on Moby Dick, the giant white sperm whale that on the ship's previous voyage bit off Captain Ahab's leg at the knee. *The New Yorker* says of it, "*Moby Dick* is not a novel. It's barely a book at all. It's more an act of transference, of ideas and evocations hung around the vast and unknowable shape of the whale, an extended musing on the strange meeting of human history and natural history" (Philip Hoare, "What *Moby Dick* Means to Me," November 3, 2011).

MOBY DICK
AUTHOR: HERMAN MELVILLE
PUBLISHED: 1851
(ORIGINALLY UNDER THE TITLE *THE WHALE* AND
SOMETIMES HYPHENATED TOO)

Moby Dick is considered one of America's greatest literary works. It is the story of one man, Captain Ahab's, quest for revenge on a whale that on a previous voyage bit off his leg at the knee. Among the characters of the boat called the *Pequod* are First Mate Ishmael and his friend Queequeg, the latter of whom falls ill, prompting a coffin to be built in anticipation of his demise. Later on in the story, the coffin becomes a lifeboat for Ishmael. (An image we might, slightly irrelevantly, note that Hergé, creator of Tintin, plays with evocatively in his tale "The Cigars of the Pharaoh.")

Without spoiling the plot, it is fair to say that Moby Dick is eventually tracked down, and a great fight ensues in which the whale is victorious, the ship is destroyed, and everyone is killed—except Ishmael. (Well, maybe I have spoiled it a little.)

The enduring appeal of the book lies in two quite different elements. The first is a rich narrative style in which multiple threads are intertwined, including religion, human psychology, and ethics. But the second element is much more direct and practical: the descriptions of nature and the sea. Melville himself had firsthand experience of whaling, having spent time aboard a whaling vessel called the *Acushnet*. He also conducted detailed research for his book, reading about, among other things, the real-life drama of a whaling vessel called the *Essex* that in 1820 was attacked by a sperm whale thousands of miles off the coast of South America. The *Essex* sank, and the twenty-man crew was forced to make for shore—suffering dehydration, starvation, and exposure on the open ocean—in the ship's whaleboats. Soon after they made landfall, the survivors resorted to eating the bodies of the crewmen who had already died. When that proved insufficient, members of the crew drew lots to determine whom they would sacrifice so that the others could live!

That was an influence on the author, though not on the tale itself, which is essentially focused on the life-and-death struggle of the crew of the *Pequod* and the slow but inexorable turning of the wheels of fate.

What does a grand story about human obsession and revenge have to do with the science of pesticide use? On the face of it, nothing at all, and the link has been downplayed by Carson's biographers. Nonetheless, I am sure that one tale did lead to a world-changing other. It is in the emotional content that the debt to *Moby Dick* lies. This says a little bit about how books work and how one book can lead to another—and a whole lot more about the subtle ways in which our lives can be influenced by them.

On May 27, 1907, Rachel Louise Carson was born on a sixty-five-acre farm on a hill just up the Allegheny River from Pittsburgh. Her father was an insurance salesperson, but her mother seems to have had the greater influence on her life. A former schoolteacher (and before that a singer), she gently instilled in her daughter a passion for nature and the outdoors, aided by Anna Botsford Comstock's *Handbook of Nature Study*, the surrounding lush woods and waterways all of which combined to become her classroom. She once wrote in *The Saturday Review of Literature* that she had taught her daughter "as a tiny child joy in the out-of-doors and the lore of birds, insects, and residents of streams and ponds."

As a child, Rachel loved reading, and she began writing stories (often involving animals) at age eight. Her first foray into publishing, at the tender age of ten, was with a story printed in *Saint Nicholas* magazine, a monthly that included among its contributors authors Louisa May Alcott, Frances Hodgson Burnett, Mark Twain, Laura E. Richards, and Joel Chandler Harris.

An early favorite seam of reading was Beatrix Potter's tales of rabbit families, but these were later followed by the novels of Gene Stratton-Porter, herself an early nature campaigner, especially on behalf of birds, while in her teen years the sea was a common thread brought alive in the novels of Herman Melville, Joseph Conrad, and Robert Louis Stevenson.

At college, Carson originally opted to study English, but with the encouragement of biology professor Mary Scott Skinker (and this despite the fact that career opportunities for women in the sciences were extremely rare at that time), she soon switched to biology, eventually earning a master's degree in zoology. Despite initial concerns that, in her new field, she would have to give up writing, Carson discovered that the new focus actually gave her "something to write about" (as Linda Lear notes in her autobiography *Rachel Carson* [1997, 80], referencing correspondence by Carson. Indeed, Lear uses the phrase as the title for the fourth chapter in the autobiography).

Carson might have continued working toward a doctorate, but in 1934, at the height of the Great Depression in the United States, she was forced to abandon her studies in order to seek a full-time teaching position to help support her family. And then, in 1935, her father died suddenly, leaving the family in financial straits and Carson solely responsible for the care of her aging mother. It was thus more out of need than desire that she took what was originally supposed to be a very temporary position with the US Bureau of Fisheries, writing radio copy for a series of weekly educational broadcasts about water life entitled *Romance under the Waters*. However, it would turn out to be a very fortuitous posting.

Her supervisor, Elmer Higgins, was an enthusiastic audience and thought the first pamphlet she wrote for them was more suitable for a magazine, saying, generously, that it was "too good" for the original purpose! He advised her to offer it to *Atlantic Monthly* instead, who in due course published it as "Undersea," a vivid narrative of a journey along the ocean floor.

One of the readers of *Atlantic Monthly* was an editor at the publishing house Simon & Schuster, who promptly contacted Carson and asked if she could expand the essay into a book. This became in due course *Under the Sea Wind* (1941), which received excellent reviews even if it sold only modestly. In the meantime, Carson's article writing expanded with features in *Sun Magazine*, *Nature*, and *Collier's*.

And so, by 1948, Carson was working on material for a second book, a life history of the ocean. Chapters were serialized in various publications, including *The New Yorker*, and it was eventually published as *The Sea around Us* by Oxford University Press. Now Carson's writing really took off. The book shot on to the *New York Times* best-seller list, where it remained for eighty-six weeks. It was serialized in abridged form by *Reader's Digest*, and it won both the 1952 National Book Award for Nonfiction and the John Burroughs Medal. *The Sea's* success led to the republication of *Under the Sea Wind*, which also became a best seller.

Carson herself became a minor celebrity and was inundated with demands to give talks and answer fan mail while she worked to convert the book into a documentary. This too was very successful, but Carson was unhappy at the editing of her work to make it suitable for the screen and from then on refused to sell film rights to her work. Nonetheless, unloved or not, the documentary proceeded to win the 1953 Academy Award for Best Documentary Feature.

Thus it was with the ground laid already that Carson turned her attention toward what would in due course be her legacy issue: the mass production and government-sponsored spraying of pesticides.

The result was that by the early years of the 1960s, Carson had already become famous for a series of books announcing that the natural world was under threat. *Silent Spring* in particular (the last book published in her lifetime) is a searing indictment of the threat to the natural ecological balance through such things as the overuse of pesticides and became one of the icons of the green movement in the United States in the 1960s.

Whereas most writers, up to then, much admired the new age of science, Carson instead described "the chemical barrage" as being as crude a weapon as the caveman's club, hurled against a fabric of life that was on the one hand delicate and destructible and on the other miraculously tough, resilient, and capable of striking back in unexpected ways.

However, it was only after a *CBS Reports* TV special, "The Silent Spring of Rachel Carson," aired on April 3, 1963, that pesticide use really became a major public issue. The program included segments of Carson herself reading from *Silent Spring* interwoven with interviews with a number of other experts, mostly critics, such as Robert White-Stevens, a former biochemist and assistant director of the Agricultural Research Division of American Cyanamid, who told the public, "If man were to follow the teachings of Miss Carson, we would return to the Dark Ages, and the insects and diseases and vermin would once again inherit the earth." According to biographer Linda Lear, "In juxtaposition to the wild-eyed, loud-voiced Dr. Robert White-Stevens in white lab coat, Carson appeared anything but the hysterical alarmist that her critics contended." Reactions from the estimated audience of ten to fifteen million were overwhelmingly positive.

If a million people had already read her book, fifteen million more saw the TV show. Among them was President Kennedy, who announced that

A 1947 advertisement for DDT to control household insect pests. Well into the 1960s, when Rachel Carson's book was published, most writers much admired the new age of science. Carson instead described "the chemical barrage" as being as crude a weapon as the caveman's club. (Wikipedia Commons, "DDT Is Good for Me-e-e!," July 30, 1947. Science History Institute, Philadelphia. https://digital.sciencehistory.org /works/1831ck18w.)

the federal agencies were taking a closer look at the problem after being asked about pesticide use during a press conference. It was, all in all, a remarkable journey for a child who had grown up in a rural river town in Springdale, Pennsylvania.

In some ways, it was the careful research behind *Silent Spring* that made her words carry weight, but it was also true that the book, published by Houghton Mifflin on September 27, 1962, arrived at exactly the right time in history, just as a new idealistic generation started to see science not only as a savior but also as a threat. *Silent Spring*, in particular, marked a turning point in the understanding of the interconnections between human activities and their environmental consequences.

Carson's position in the book is that chemicals play a sinister but little-recognized role, similar to that of nuclear radiation—in changing the very nature of life. She attributed the recent decline in bird populations—in her words, the "silencing of birds"—to pesticide overuse. This is where the title comes from; it was initially just the title for the chapter on birds. The year 1959 brought the "Great Cranberry Scandal": when it was discovered that three consecutive harvests of US cranberries contained increasingly high levels of the herbicide aminotriazole. Since this was known to cause cancer in laboratory rats, the sale of all cranberry products was halted.

As it says in *Silent Spring*, "The sprays, dusts and aerosols are now applied almost universally to farms, gardens, forests and homes—non-selective chemicals that have the power to kill every insect, the good and the bad, to still the song of birds and the leaping of fish in the streams—to coat the leaves with a deadly film and to linger on in soil—all this, though the intended target may be only a few weeds or insects."

SILENT SPRING
AUTHOR: RACHEL CARSON
PUBLISHED: 1962

Silent Spring opens with a dark fable of an imaginary town in the American heartland in which a blight has fallen upon the land, turning hillsides that formerly teemed with wildlife into silent landscapes of "brown and withered vegetation, as though swept through by fire." There is only one clue as to what might have happened: "the residue of a white powder that had fallen from the sky like snow a few weeks before."

In the chapters that follow, the book weaves together carefully researched evidence on the effects of pesticides with more colorful and literary descriptions. The tale of Clear Lake, north San Francisco, for example: Once a popular fishing spot, noted for the western or "swan" grebe, whose nest floated on the lake's surface, it had been repeatedly sprayed with DDT and various other chemicals to reduce the numbers of gnats. After three applications of insecticide, the gnats were still there but the grebe were dying. Autopsies showed that fatty tissue in the birds contained levels of the insecticide many times higher than had ever been sprayed. What had happened is that the insecticide had concentrated a thousandfold as it rose up the food chain. The plankton absorbed and concentrated the initial dose, then the fish ate the plankton, and finally the birds ate the fish, with the level of the pesticide multiplying many times over at each stage.

On land too, Carson pointed out that the practice of planting large monocultures created the conditions for insect explosions and unraveled nature's own systems of checks and balances. She gave the simple example of Dutch Elm disease, which spread through the United States and Canada largely because town planners liked to line streets with a single varietal of tree. And she put the problem into a wider economic context too, saying that "pest control" was doubly misguided as the most pressing problem for agriculture in the United States at the time was that it was producing too much food, resulting in surpluses that had been created at public expense via government subsidies that also had to be dealt with at public expense. In the United States, pesticides were a solution in search of a problem.

The chemical industry responded to Carson's call for careful use of insecticides by denouncing the idea of a world without any chemicals—and sought their own emotionally charged examples in response, such as the plight of children dying from mosquito-borne illnesses in African villages. Ironically, though, the critics spread Carson's message and created interest in her book without actually persuading key figures in authority.

Carson's main argument was that pesticides have such disastrous effects on the environment that they should really be called biocides—poisons whose effects are rarely limited to the target pests. Most of *Silent Spring* is devoted to describing their deleterious effects on natural ecosystems, but later chapters also detail cases of human poisoning, cancer, and other illnesses attributed to the chemicals.

This was all in the context of a postwar world in which scientists were considered infallible, chemicals were our friends, and certainly the government's guiding light was the health and safety of its citizens. It was uncontroversial that regulation of insecticide use was the responsibility of the Department of Agriculture—a department otherwise busy encouraging and funding exactly that . Back then, the Environmental

Protection Agency did not yet exist, much less campaign groups like Greenpeace.So when Carson warned of a world in which birds had disappeared and "the spring was silent," she gave a voice to those who previously had none.

Serialization of *Silent Spring* began in *The New Yorker*, in the June 16, 1962, issue—the first nonfiction book to ever be featured in the magazine. Carson and the others involved with the publication braced for fierce criticism. It was not long in coming.

Barely had the second installment appeared than Louis McLean, the general counsel of Velsicol chemical company (exclusive manufacturer of chlordane and heptachlor) wrote to say it would sue if *The New Yorker* printed the next installment. The magazine went ahead anyway. Soon after, widening the attack to oppose publication of the book itself, McLean stated that "sinister influences" and "natural food faddists" were seeking to create the impression that "all businesses are grasping and immoral" and to reduce American agriculture to "east-curtain parity," meaning the level of the communist countries of Eastern Europe. Many conservative politicians of the period firmly believed that environmentalists were a kind of Trojan horse movement employed by the feared communist regimes of the Soviet sphere.

One of the main manufacturers of DDT (Dupont) was also among the first to react, compiling an extensive report on the book's press coverage and estimated impact on public opinion as well as joining with other companies to produce a number of brochures and articles of their own promoting and defending pesticide use.

Two chemists associated with the company American Cyanamid, Robert White-Stevens (mentioned above) and Thomas Jukes, were among the most aggressive critics, especially of Carson's analysis of DDT. They attacked Carson's scientific credentials, because her training was in marine biology rather than biochemistry, as well as her personal character. White-Stevens labeled her "a fanatic defender of the cult of the balance of nature." The snidest attack of all came from Ezra Taft Benso, a former secretary of agriculture who would later become prophet of the Mormon Church. He wondered why "a spinster with no children" should be so concerned about genetics before immediately offering his own answer: *because she was a communist.*

Yet the attacks failed. Indeed, they only made Carson more influential.

In conjunction with a new grassroots environmental movement, *Silent Spring* spurred a reversal in national policy with the creation of the US Environmental Protection Agency, tasked with identifying and evaluating the "environmental impacts" of government policies. When the EPA officially opened its doors on December 2, 1970, it had a budget of $1.4 billion and 5,800 employees, many of whom "had an enormous sense of purpose and excitement," as the first EPA administrator, Bill Ruckelshaus, put it as part of an oral history interview with Chuck Elkins. In the same interview, Ruckelshaus paid tribute to Carson's role, saying, "I would say in 1962, things changed significantly when Rachel Carson wrote her book entitled *Silent Spring*, because this introduced a new element into the public consciousness about pollution because she identified the fact that invisible pollutants—in this case, pesticides—might be having damaging and maybe even permanent effects on the environment, particularly on the survivability of species. And so this brought into the environmental movement a whole other set of people with different concerns and different demands that the government ought to be doing something."

Part of Carson's effectiveness was in fighting science with science. After all, she began the four-year project of what would become *Silent Spring* by gathering examples of environmental damage attributed to DDT. She pulled together already-existing data from many areas and synthesized the information to create the first coherent account of the effects persistent chemicals had on the environment.

But another part, and probably the more important part, was that she had a knack for taking dry facts and translating them into lyrical prose that enchanted the public. It was this aspect that enabled *Silent Spring* to launch a revolution in attitudes at all levels of society, from schoolchildren to government and industrial leaders. Carson's power lay in her scientific knowledge combined with poetic writing, which was far more effective than earlier calls to use modern technology responsibly that were made by people with only a superficial understanding of their topic.

Carson had been concerned about the use of synthetic pesticides, many of which had been developed through the military funding of science after World War II, since the mid-1940s; however, it was really the US federal government's 1957 gypsy moth eradication program that prompted her to switch her research to focus on the issue. The gypsy moth program involved aerial spraying of DDT and other pesticides—mixed with fuel oil! Since the program mandated the spraying of private land, landowners on Long Island were able to file a lawsuit opposing the practice, and although they were ultimately unsuccessful in the suit, the fact that the Supreme Court granted the petitioners the right to gain injunctions against potential environmental damage in the future created the basis for later successful environmental actions.

In *Silent Spring*, Carson recounts the story of this campaign along with nearly a dozen other real-life horror stories concerning the misuse of chemical pesticides. One chapter, for example, entitled "Indiscriminately from the Skies," details the American government's disastrous 1957 campaign of chemical warfare on fire ants. The South American invaders, unintentionally introduced in the early 1920s, were certainly a nuisance, with their painful sting and large mounds, but on its own assessment the government had previously deemed them neither a pest nor a serious threat to agriculture. However, with the advent of new methods of chemical pest control, that all changed. Suddenly the fire ants had to die!

Enormous quantities of chemical poisons were injudiciously applied to twenty million acres of farmland in an effort to eradicate what the government now insisted was a threat to livestock, despite their earlier assertions to the contrary. The losses to wildlife—and the livestock that the spraying was supposed to protect—were widespread, disastrous, and easily attributed to the spraying program, even as the government continued to deny any connection. Carson contended that the "pest eradication" program was nothing more than an ill-disguised, poorly conceived public relations campaign to sell pesticides.

As her research progressed, Carson found a sizeable community of scientists who were documenting the physiological and environmental effects of pesticides. She also took advantage of her personal connections with many government scientists, who supplied her with confidential information. From reading the scientific literature and interviewing scientists, she realized that there were two scientific camps: those who dismissed the possible dangers barring absolutely conclusive proof and those who were minded more to the "precautionary principle" and ready to consider alternatives such as biological pest control.

The result of all this, as Mark Hamilton Lytle has put it in his biography *The Gentle Subversive: Rachel Carson, Silent Spring, and the Rise of the Environmental Movement*, was that Carson "quite self-consciously decided to write a book calling into question the paradigm of scientific progress that defined post-war American culture," the overriding theme of which is the powerful—and often adverse—effect humans have on the natural world.

This is where Melville's tale of whale hunting comes back in. It has well been noted that, in Doug McLean's phrase, a "great herd of readers profess devotion to Herman Melville's classic *Moby Dick*, but novelists especially seem to love saying they love it." On The Top Ten, a website that lists authors' favorite books, *Moby Dick* is cited more often than not (and by writers as dissimilar as John Irving and Robert Coover, Bret Easton Ellis, and Joyce Carol Oates). But, as McLean notes wryly, perhaps they all love a different *Moby Dick*. Because, at various times, it's been called a whaling yarn, a theodicy, a Shakespeare-styled political tragedy, an anatomy, a queer confessional, and an environmentalist epic; and perhaps because this novel seems to hold all the world, all these readings are compatible and true. For Rachel Carson, the book seems to have inspired in two ways: first, in the insights it offers into marine life, and second, for the very different insights it offers into human motivations and psychology.

However, to understand the book's influence on Carson, a few key passages will suffice. First of all, consider one of the central characters, Flask, the third mate of the whaling ship, and his motivations. Flask, we are told, is a native of Tisbury, in Martha's Vineyard.

A short, stout, ruddy young fellow, very pugnacious concerning whales, who somehow seemed to think that the great leviathans had personally and hereditarily affronted him; and therefore it was a sort of point of honor with him, to destroy them whenever encountered. So utterly lost was he to all sense of reverence for the many marvels of their majestic bulk and mystic ways; and so dead to anything like an apprehension of any possible danger from encountering them; that in his poor opinion, the wondrous whale was but a species of magnified mouse, or at least water-rat, requiring only a little circumvention and some small application of time and trouble in order to kill and boil.

Flask is driven by a violent grudge against whales, a passion that keeps him on edge—but also prevents him from understanding how glorious and magnificent whales can be. Exactly the same attitude and folly govern human interaction with "the pests" of nature in Carson's account. At the same time, it is the poetic quality of *Moby Dick* that seems to have transmitted itself to Carson and in turn made *Silent Spring* such a powerful plea on behalf of the environment. Melville talks of "the blending cadence of waves with thoughts" and of the ocean as a deep, blue, bottomless soul, pervading mankind and nature, and of "every strange, half-seen, gliding, beautiful thing" that flickers unseen through the depths, like so many elusive thoughts.

Indeed, contemplating the ocean depths, even Ishmael feels himself to be united to all of creation in a transcendent moment—reminiscent of the sentiments of American Romanticism in the mid-nineteenth-century writings of Henry Thoreau and Ralph Waldo Emerson. (Thoreau's *Journal* was another of Carson's favorite reads.)

One of Carson's key themes is that science presents only a partial picture of nature. A passage in Melville makes a similar point:

The natural aptitude of the French for seizing the picturesqueness of things seems to be peculiarly evinced in what paintings and engravings they have of their whaling scenes. With not one tenth of England's experience in the fishery, and not the thousandth part of that of the Americans, they have nevertheless furnished both nations with the only finished sketches at all capable of conveying the real spirit of the whale hunt. For the most part, the English and American whale draughtsmen seem entirely content with presenting the mechanical outline of things, such as the vacant profile of the whale; which, so far as picturesqueness of effect is concerned, is about tantamount to sketching the profile of a pyramid.

Above all, it is the link between whales and man that Melville makes that seems to inspire Carson's own work. Because, in both the novel and the factual account, the truest picture of nature is the one that emerges through describing humanity's relationship with it. Many years later, when *CBS Reports* presented "The Silent Spring of Rachel Carson," Carson can be found saying, "We still talk in terms of conquest. We still haven't become mature enough to think of ourselves as only a tiny part of a vast and incredible universe. Man's attitude toward nature is today critically important simply because we have now acquired a fateful power to alter and destroy nature. . . . But man is a part of nature, and his war against nature is inevitably a war against himself."

At the end of *Moby Dick*, there is a scene in which the sight of the now-killed and butchered whales seems to echo *Silent Spring*'s fear of a world to come in which man's indiscriminate use of chemicals leads to a similar but land-based death of nature:

When I stand among these mighty Leviathan skeletons, skulls, tusks, jaws, ribs, and vertebrae, all characterized by partial resemblances to the existing breeds of sea-monsters; but at the same time bearing on the other hand similar affinities to the annihilated antichronical Leviathans, their incalculable seniors; I am, by a flood, borne back to that wondrous period, ere time itself can be said to have begun; for time began with man. Here Saturn's grey chaos rolls over me, and I obtain dim, shuddering glimpses into those Polar eternities; when wedged bastions of ice pressed hard upon what are now the Tropics; and in all the 25,000 miles of this world's circumference, not an inhabitable hand's breadth of land was visible. Then the whole world was the whale's; and, king of creation, he left his wake along the present lines of the Andes and the Himmalehs. Who can show a pedigree like Leviathan? Ahab's harpoon had shed older blood than the Pharaoh's. Methuselah seems a school-boy. I look round to shake hands with Shem. I am horror-struck at this antemosaic, unsourced existence of the unspeakable terrors of the whale, which, having been before all time, must needs exist after all humane ages are over.

Carson once remarked to her friends that while it was clear where her love of nature had originally come from, there was something of a mystery about where her love of writing originated. Surely *Moby Dick* fills that gap. However, for her readers, it is her ability to offer them a way to see the world from new perspectives that matters. And this is exactly the gift that another highly influential environmentalist, Frans Lanting, offers too, in his books that combine text with images.

Recall that Carson once explained that in writing *Under the Sea Wind*, in particular, she chose to tell her story from the point of view of the fish and other creatures whose world she wished to enter and explore. As biographer Mark Hamilton Lytle puts it, quoting a section of her correspondence with a friend, "their world must be portrayed as it looks and feels to them—and the narrator must not come into the story or appear to express an opinion." This was to avoid "human bias" and also to inject power and immediacy. The same aim and ambition reappears even more emphatically in the writing and photography of Lanting.

Today, Lanting is considered one of the great photographers of our time. His work appears in books, magazines, and exhibitions around the world but perhaps most notably in *National Geographic* magazine. Born in Rotterdam, the Netherlands, he earned a master's degree in economics before moving to the United States to study environmental planning. It was soon after this that he began photographing the natural world, documenting wildlife from the Amazon to Antarctica "through images that convey a passion for nature and a sense of wonder and concern about our living planet," as his website puts it. Lanting also recalls "living with albatrosses" on an island in the Atlantic Ocean and how at such times he "shrank in size and learned to see the world through other eyes."

Lanting's work has been commissioned frequently by *National Geographic*, and assignments have ranged from the bonobos of the Congo to incredible images of penguins as part of a circumnavigation by sailboat of South Georgia Island in the sub-Antarctic. In a remote part of the world, he spends weeks on platform towers to obtain rare tree-canopy views of rainbow-colored macaws, frogs in flight, and orangutans swinging on vines. He has lived for months with seabirds on isolated atolls in the Pacific Ocean, tracked lions through the African night, and camped among giant tortoises inside a volcano in the Galápagos.

Lanting is quite open about the fact that, in all of this, he was deeply influenced by a book. So, as an environmentalist, was he too, perhaps, inspired by an epic tale of the struggle between Man and nature like Melville's? Not at all; that is not how books work. Influences are much more individual and unique. In his case, he takes as his ideal the tale of a child who becomes so close to a flock of geese that he is accepted as one of them. This is Lanting's arena, poised somewhere between the worlds of man and nature, an ambassador from one to the other.

The children's classic *The Wonderful Adventures of Nils*, published in 1906 by Selma Lagerlöf, is so famous in Scandinavia that everyone knows the plot, although it's a long book and few have read it. (Of course, not being read didn't stop Lagerlöf becoming a Nobel Prize winner for her writing!) The short version, though, is that Nils, a good-for-nothing kid in late-nineteenth-century Skåne, angers the local *tomte* (a kind of elf or leprechaun), who magically transforms him into another *tomte*. Fortunately, Nils, now the size of a thumb, is adopted by a flock of geese who take him to their summer nesting grounds in Lapland. On the way, they travel all around Sweden, which for Swedish children is near enough to the whole world. In any case, as Lanting says, the geography is always firmly in the service of the narrative.

In the introduction to his book *Eye to Eye* (1997), Lanting says,

During my youth in Holland I read a children's book that made a deep impression on me . . . *The Wonderful Adventures of Nils* . . . tells the story of a boy who shrinks to the size of an elf, climbs on the back of a barnyard goose and joins a flock of wild geese migrating north. For a year Nils travels with the geese who introduce him to Eagle, Raven, Bear and other animals. He learns to see the world through their eyes. But when Nils finally returns to his family's farm and regains his former size, he loses his standing amongst the animals. The geese, suddenly afraid of their companion, take off—but not until after they plead with him to become an advocate for their needs.

And he continues,

As sentimental as it may be, this children's story has resonated with me, and even today it reflects some of my basic beliefs and aspirations as a natural-ist. I have spent much of the past two decades in the company of animals, trying to understand and interpret their ways. The conditions under which I work are often a far cry from Nils' intimacy with his wild geese. Long lenses, remotely controlled cameras, and other complicated contraptions—plus a great reserve of patience—are often prerequisites to overcoming the distance most animals like to keep from the camera.

Being tiny, of course, is an essential part of all young children's experi-ences, as are Nils's immediate worries in his new state: "Where would he get food and who would give him shelter, and who would make his bed?" It seems matters must turn even worse when he is accidentally borne away from home by the farm gander intent on following the wild geese to Lap-land. There are echoes here to other fairy tales, notably Tom Thumb, and at one point Nils even reenacts the story of the Pied Piper when he saves a town's grain stores by leading the rats away with a tiny pipe.

THE WONDERFUL ADVENTURES OF NILS
AUTHOR: SELMA LAGERLÖF
PUBLISHED: 1906

Perhaps it slightly spoils the book to discover that it was originally commis-sioned by the Swedish National Teachers' Society as a geography textbook. But maybe the dusty origin inspired the author to greater imaginative heights, because Lagerlöf's book is poetical and never allows the moralistic undercur-rent to crush Nils's naughty spirit as a child. Actually, Nils Holgersson starts the book as a *very* naughty boy: he locks his parents in the shed, trips up his mother as she is carrying milk, and is cruel to the animals on the farm. His comeuppance arrives at age fourteen on the day he traps a *tomte*, or house elf, and is shrunk as part of a lesson in what it is like to be tiny.

Reviewing the book for *The Guardian*, Philip Womack calls it "grand, beautiful, exciting and poignant," offering one of the tales within the tale as particular evidence. This is an episode in which Nils wanders the streets of Vineta, a fine city where everyone dresses well and appears fabulously wealthy. The residents even offer him the chance to enjoy similar riches—in return for a single coin. Excited, Nils rushes off in search of one, but on his return the city has vanished. A stork then explains to him that what he saw was actually a ghost city that long ago had been drowned for its greed. Spookily, it reappears for just one hour each year, during which period of grace it has the chance to return to life, but only if someone buys something for one coin. Nils, who used to be so selfish and uncaring, is now so sad for the lost city that he bursts into tears. Similarly, at the end of the book, when Nils returns to the farm and his parents plan to eat his goose companions, he remonstrates with them, saying that it would be a real sin to eat a bird that has found its way home. In the manner of the best books, his parents yield and spare the goose.

In fact, what gives the book its spice and enables it to speak directly to children, rather than talk down as so many children's books and their authors still seem to do, is the way Nils is able to transcend his parents' limited perspectives and to see things anew. Significantly, when the elf offers to return Nils to full size and humanhood the boy refuses, preferring instead to remain with his animal companions and be wild and free.

Lanting was also affected by the story within the story. It turns out, according to the introduction, that Lagerlöf's own original inspiration was a grim tale she was told by her grandmother about an incident that had occurred when the grandmother was herself a little girl. There had been a white gander on the farm, which one spring day took it into its head to fly off with a flock of wild geese who were passing by. The family was of course sure they would never see the white gander again. But many months later, the grandmother was astonished to see that the gander had returned. And he was not alone; during the summer, he had found a mate, a beautiful gray goose, and they were accompanied by half a dozen little goslings. Delighted, Selma's grandmother led the goose family to the barn, where they could eat from the trough with the other fowl. She closed the door so that they wouldn't fly off again and ran to tell her stepmother. And so to the awful ending. The stepmother said nothing. She just took out the little knife she used for slaughtering geese, and an hour later there was not one goose left alive in the barn.

For Lanting, this resonates with the moment in the book when Nils is awoken one night by a stork who says that if Nils follows him, the stork will show him something important. They fly to the seashore, where there is a strange city, quite unlike anything one would expect to find on the Swedish coast. Nils goes in through the huge gate and discovers people dressed in rich clothes from a bygone age. No one seems to notice him at first. He finds his way to the merchants' quarter. People are selling all kinds of precious goods: embroidered silks and satins, gold ornaments, glittering jewels. And now he realizes that the merchants can see him. They are holding out their wares to him, offering all these treasures. Nils tries to make them understand that he could never afford any of it; he is a poor boy. But they persist and using gestures tell him that he can have anything he wants if he can just give them one small copper coin. He searches his pockets over and over again but finds they are empty. In the end, he leaves the city, and when he turns round again it has disappeared. "It is the lost city of the sea traders," explains the stork. "They were drowned beneath the waves long ago, but once every hundred years they come back for a single night. The legend is that if they can sell a single thing to a mortal, they will be allowed to return to the world; but they never do." Nils feels his heart is going to break. He could so easily have saved all these good people and their city, but he has failed them.

It seemed to Lanting that both stories expressed the same feeling. If only people had known what was needed to save the doomed merchants and the endangered animals they could have acted in time! If only. . . .

And so Lanting's work is more than merely passive observation. He has profiled "ecological hot spots" from India to New Zealand and has created awareness of both the majesty and the plight of albatrosses, the threatened extinction of the Asiatic cheetahs of Iran, and the remarkable lives and behavior of chimpanzees in Senegal—research that meshes with Jane Goodall's by expanding our appreciation of these animals and in the process shedding new light on what it means to be human.

Also in *Eye to Eye*, Lanting recalls a story of northwestern Native Americans—a culture in which wood carvings of animals are immortalized in totem poles and masks. He explains that one summer, while touring this coastal region, a Kwakiutl elder honored him by sharing a legend that belongs to his people.

He took me to a sacred cave on his island and there, surrounded by the sweet scent of cedars, we sat down and he told me this story:

Once upon a time, he said, all creatures on the face of the earth were one. Even though they looked different on the outside, they all spoke the same language. From time to time they would come together at this cave to celebrate their unity. When they arrived at the entrance, they all took off their skins. Raven shed his feathers, Bear his fur, and Salmon her scales. Inside the cave, they danced. But one day, a human, attracted by the commotion, crawled into the cave and surprised the animals in the act of dancing.

Embarrassed by their nakedness they fled, and that was the last time they revealed themselves in this way.

There are similar stories in other traditions too; indeed there are echoes of paradise and Adam and Eve discovering the shame of nakedness here. But for Lanting, what is important here is the "mythical understanding" that underneath their separate identities all animals are one. This, he says, became the guiding principle for all his photographic work. "I aim to get past the feathers, fur and scales. I like to get under the skin. It doesn't matter whether I am focusing on a three-ton elephant or a tiny tree frog. I want to get up close and face them, eye to eye."

And thus we better understand now not only the title but the spirit of his book.

Above all, running through all Lanting's books, is a recognition of our shared animal nature. Lanting says that he seeks to offer a different perspective, to emphasize animals' own parallel worlds, to show their "full individuality" and also how animals operate as members of their own societies.

For Lanting, wildlife photography was partly an escape and partly a way to seek out animals on their own ground. "What my eyes seek in these encounters is not just the beauty traditionally revered by wildlife photographers. The perfection I seek in my photographic compositions is a means to show the strength and dignity of animals in nature." His book is his tribute to that.

Lanting's mission is to use photography to help create leverage for conservation efforts ranging from local initiatives to global campaigns, through his publications, alliances, public appearances, and active support of environmental organizations. He serves as an ambassador for the World Wildlife Fund Netherlands, on the National Council of the World Wildlife Fund USA, as well as on the Leadership Council of Conservation International.

The result is books that are stories as much as collections of images—from *Eye to Eye* (1997) to *LIFE: A Journey through Time* (2006) and onward too. "No photographer turns animals into art more completely than Frans Lanting," says *The New Yorker*, but perhaps his own words are a more accurate description of his aims and hopes. Lanting says simply that his aim is to "give voice to the natural world." Books, whether factual or fictional, textual or photographic, are our most powerful way to do that.

4

✛

Search for Life's Purpose

Steve Jobs and Evelyn Berezin

A belief in taking control of your life is at the heart of the philosophy known as existentialism. That's a long word and a rather off-putting one. But the key point about the philosophy is that it is concerned with essences and one essence in particular: the search for meaning in our own lives. We exist, yes. But to what ends, for what purpose? Sure enough, books and writing played a key role in shaping both Steve Jobs's and Evelyn Berezin's answers to that big question.

Let's start with Jobs; one of my favorite quotes of his beautifully sums up the Apple supremo's approach to life: "Your time is limited, so don't waste it living someone else's life. Don't be trapped by dogma—which is living with the results of other people's thinking. Don't let the noise of others' opinions drown out your own inner voice. And most important, have the courage to follow your heart and intuition. They somehow already know what you truly want to become. Everything else is secondary."

That's taken from his commencement speech for students at Stanford in 2005, when Jobs had already been diagnosed with cancer and was in a reflective mood, which is not to say that Jobs wasn't always pretty reflective. Indeed, a full eleven years earlier, in a PBS program entitled *One Last Thing*, the title itself being an echo of his catchphrase at the hotly awaited Apple product launches, Jobs can be found saying something similar:

> When you grow up, you tend to get told that the world is the way it is and your life is just to live your life inside the world, try to have a nice family, have fun, save a little money. That's a very limited life. Life can be much broader, once you discover one simple fact, and that is that everything around you that you call life was made up by people that were no smarter than you. And you can change it, you can influence it. That's maybe the most important thing. It's to shake off this erroneous notion that life is there and you're just going to live in it, versus embrace it, change it, improve it, make your mark upon it.

This older and wiser Jobs is here drawing on some very personal life experiences as well as one book in particular that profoundly influenced his thinking. As to the life experiences, though, way back in 1985, a young Steve Jobs in a shiny silk shirt and an oversize bow tie gave some big clues to David Sheff in a profile for *Playboy* magazine. For example, Jobs told Sheff, "When you're a carpenter making a beautiful chest of drawers, you're not going to use a piece of plywood on the back, even though it faces the wall and nobody will ever see it. You'll know it's there, so you're going to use a beautiful piece of wood on the back. For you to sleep well at night, the aesthetic, the quality, has to be carried all the way through."

Why should something people will probably never see matter? But for existentialists it's a no-brainer. The carpenter must be guided by their own values, and every aspect of the object they create has to be true to its function. For Jobs, as those working with him later found out all too well, what most people might think is "okay" is not good enough.

There's no doubt that Steve Jobs was quite an imposing figure. But before Jobs became the visionary founder of Apple, he was just a pretty ordinary, middle-class kid growing up in California, being raised by his adoptive parents, Paul and Clara Jobs. His new dad was a kind of engineer, or more precisely a machinist for a company that made lasers. According to Steve's fond account, he was "a genius with his hands" who was often tinkering in the garage. And he seems to have passed on to his adoptive son some key ideas, including ones about product design and the pursuit of perfection—ideas that would later be at the heart of the young Jobs's success with Apple. Though less often noted, it is probably true that

Clara, who was an accountant and may have contributed to Steve's skills at raising seed capital for his ideas, also contributed her parental influence.

Walter Isaacson, author of probably the most detailed biography of Jobs, recounts a lesson from Paul that was particularly influential. It seemed that the young Steve once helped his father build a fence around their family home in Mountain View. While working, Paul told the boy, "You've got to make the back of the fence, that nobody will see, just as good looking as the front of the fence. Even though nobody will see it, you will know, and that will show that you're dedicated to making something perfect."

The story illustrates that long before Jobs read any philosophy, existentialist ideas had clearly struck with the result that, years later, as the CEO of Apple, Jobs insisted that every element of the Macintosh computer be beautiful, including the bits nobody would ever see, like the circuit boards inside.

But back to school. The young Steve Jobs hated it. Lessons bored him painfully, and he reacted by engaging in acts of disobedience and defiance. He was expelled from the third grade and then, in junior high school, one day he simply refused to go back. Fortunately for him, his adoptive parents decided to try to make a fresh start in another California town. They moved to Los Altos, California, near the heart of Silicon Valley.

Steve Jobs has a curious habit of being in the right place at the right time. After the move to Silicon Valley, ideas began to flow around the young teenager—not at school, not at college, but in the neighborhood's garages. Many of his new neighbors were engineers who gathered in garage workshops after work and on weekends to talk and tinker with projects. One key player who lived just across the street was Steve Wozniak, whose father was an engineer at Hewlett Packard. "Woz" would become Jobs's inseparable "other."

Jobs explained years later that participating in these informal garage workshops gave him the realization that technology was the result of human creation, not "magical things that just appeared in one's environment." If there's ever a stage play of the Steve Jobs story, for sure one dramatic scene will be set in the interior of a garage.

So it was that when he was just twelve or thirteen, at an age when most boys would be pleased to work out how to mend a battery light for their bicycle, Jobs could be found trying to build a digital frequency counter, which is a device to measure the oscillations in an electrical circuit and extremely cutting-edge stuff—not the kind of thing you can get in a local hardware store. That being so, he ended up needing some help, at which point, Jobs thought to pick up the phone and call Bill Hewlett, the CEO of Hewlett Packard, then one of the world's most advanced technology companies. HP was a "local company," a Californian company, and sure enough Jobs found Bill's number listed in the Palo Alto phone book. As

Jobs related it to Sheff, "He answered the phone and he was real nice. He chatted with me for, like, 20 minutes. He didn't know me at all, but he ended up giving me some parts and he got me a job that summer working at Hewlett-Packard on the line, assembling frequency counters. Assembling may be too strong. I was putting in screws. It didn't matter; I was in heaven."

On his own account too, Steve's summer job at Hewlett Packard was a key experience—yet it came about in this quite extraordinary way. After all, why did Steve want a frequency counter? No one else seems to have noted it, but such things are useful for hacking phone networks. This brings us back to Woz, Steve's lifelong friend and vital collaborator. In fact, Wozniak was significantly older than Steve, at about eighteen, and he was, as Jobs put it in the *Playbox* interview, "the first person I met who knew more electronics than I did." The two became good friends; they shared not just an interest in electronics but also a sense of humor. They pulled "all kinds of pranks" together, usually rather silly ones, like making a huge flag with a rude "up yours" symbol on it to unfurl in the middle of a school graduation, and one time they made something that looked and sounded like a bomb and brought it to the school cafeteria. Ah, innocent times—boys can't play pranks like that now!

Nor indeed is it likely that the 1960 hacker generation could reproduce in today's surveillance state such key parts of the Jobs-Wozniak learning curve as their development of technology for playing the "blue-box business." This is hacker-speak for electronic devices that emitted particular beeps and whistles at particular frequencies and could allow free long-distance phone calls. Cool! One time the two called the Vatican and pretended that Wozniak was Henry Kissinger; they claimed to have actually persuaded someone there to wake the Pope up in the middle of the night.

In the Sheff profile, Jobs recalls somehow wistfully, "Woz and I are different in most ways, but there are some ways in which we're the same, and we're very close in those ways. We're sort of like two planets in their own orbits that every so often intersect. It wasn't just computers, either. Woz and I very much liked Bob Dylan's poetry, and we spent a lot of time thinking about a lot of that stuff. This was California. You could get LSD fresh made from Stanford. You could sleep on the beach at night with your girlfriend. California has a sense of experimentation and a sense of openness—openness to new possibilities."

By contrast, Jobs also explains that in most companies personal creativity and innovation is discouraged with the result that "great people leave and you end up with mediocrity. . . . I know," he tells Sheff, because "that's how Apple was built . . . Apple is built on refugees from other companies. These are the extremely bright individual contributors who were troublemakers at other companies."

Economics, being a rather conservative affair, has traditionally downplayed the role of the idiosyncratic entrepreneur in business success—and instead focused on abstract, impersonal models. Only a handful of contrarians, such as Joseph Schumpeter and Israel Kirzner, have been left to argue for the importance of the personal element in entrepreneurship. Nevertheless, recently psychologists like Martin Seligman have identified in the entrepreneur's mindset several key ingredients: autonomy, self-directedness, and creative exploration.

So far, so conventional, and few would argue against such ingredients anyway. But Jobs, unlike most computer nerds, went a step further because he always managed to stay a bit "cool." And to make sense of Jobs, more important than sensible stuff about "self-directedness" is to understand that part of the Apple difference is his interest in Eastern mysticism. This, he told Sheff, "hit the shores at about the same time." About the same time as what, you may ask? As Bob Dylan. For Jobs, in both sources, "there was a constant flow of intellectual questioning about the truth of life."

Dylan could be appreciated via open-air concerts or maybe just recordings, but serious mysticism was imbibed via books. Jobs recalls too that when he was briefly a college student at Reed College, an elite liberal arts school in Portland, Oregon, he started doing lots of LSD and reading lots of esoteric texts about spirituality. He says that it was a time when it seemed that *everyone* was reading *Be Here Now* or *Diet for a Small Planet*—two books drawn from a very short list of about ten. "You'd be hard pressed to find those books on too many college campuses today," he told Sheff. "I'm not saying it's better or worse; it's just different—very different." Referring to a standard text about business practices, he adds, "*In Search of Excellence* has taken the place of *Be Here Now*."

However, during his freshman year at Reed, it was Shunryu Suzuki's *Zen Mind, Beginner's Mind,* Chogyam Trungpa's *Cutting through Spiritual Materialism,* and Paramahansa Yogananda's *Autobiography of a Yogi* that he first devoured. The last one in particular, a guide to meditation and spirituality that Jobs had first read as a teenager, was a book he came back to and reread many times during his life.

IT was then that Jobs discovered *Be Here Now,* a guide to meditation and the wonders of psychedelic drugs by Baba Ram Dass, born Richard Alpert. This book advises things like "What we're seeing 'out there' is the projection of where we're at—the projection of the clingings of our minds" and "My life is a creative act—like a painting, or a concerto."

"It was profound," Jobs told Isaacson. "It transformed me and many of my friends." Notice that word "transformation." When Geoffrey James, an editor at the website Inc.com, compiled a list of the "12 Books Steve Jobs Wanted You to Read," what struck him most was that almost all the books were about a single individual overcoming enormous odds and obstacles in order to *transform* either the world, himself, or both.

For example, Jobs recommends *1984* by George Orwell, the dystopian novel that makes guest appearances in key Apple publicity ads. *1984* is all about one man's desperate struggle against an all-pervasive state that is committed to controlling people's thoughts and behaviors. Then there's that *Autobiography of a Yogi,* just mentioned. This is a book by one Paramahansa Yogananda, an Indian guru who offers advice drawn from his life experiences, such as, "You may control a mad elephant; You may shut the mouth of the bear and the tiger; Ride the lion and play with the cobra; By alchemy you may learn your livelihood; You may wander through the universe incognito; Make vassals of the gods; be ever youthful; You may walk in water and live in fire; But control of the mind is better and more difficult."

But, much as Jobs appreciated these books, it was *Be Here Now* that became his personal bible.

BE HERE NOW
AUTHOR: RAM DASS
PUBLISHED: 1971

Be Here Now, or in slightly longer version *Remember, Be Here Now,* is a book of new-age philosophy that was written during its author's journeys in India. The original cover featured a mandala with some esoteric images and the word "Remember" repeated four times.

The book is an account of the personal journey of Richard Alpert, PhD, into Baba Ram Dass, spiritual leader. It is a quasi-philosophical collection of metaphysical, spiritual, and religious aphorisms, accompanied by illustrations that are offered as "the core" of the book, alongside practical advice on yoga and meditation and finally a list of recommended books on spirituality and consciousness. The list is divided into "books to hang out with," "books to visit with now & then," and "books it's useful to have met."

Don Lattin's 2010 retrospective on the book titled "The Harvard Psychedelic Club" and subtitled "How Timothy Leary, Ram Dass, Huston Smith, and Andrew Weil Killed the Fifties and Ushered in a New Age for America," notes that Beatle John Lennon, no less, wrote the song "Come Together" as a campaign tune for Leary's "quixotic" race against Ronald Reagan for governor of California. The actual slogan was "Come together, join the party" and was composed as a thank-you after Leary and his wife, Rosemary, traveled to

Montreal for John and Yoko's "bed-in for peace," on June 1, 1969. This, you see, is how counterculture works, lubricated by LSD sessions and group acid trips. Don Lattin also notes rather sniffily that Alpert was a man whose spiritual side was balanced by a yearning for porn films and junk food.

Not the least extraordinary thing about the book is that it has remained in print since its initial publication and has sold over two million copies.

Steve Jobs even credited this book with getting him to try the hallucinogenic drug LSD, and no wonder as a central theme of the book is how during "a period of experimentation," Alpert/Baba Ram Dass peeled away each layer of his identity, disassociating from himself as a professor, a social cosmopolite, and lastly, as a physical being. As the book description enthuses, "Fear turned into exaltation upon the realization that at his truest, he was just his inner-self: a luminous being that he could trust indefinitely and love infinitely."

A key passage runs: "The cosmic humor is that if you desire to move mountains and you continue to purify yourself, ultimately you will arrive at the place where you are able to move mountains. But in order to arrive at this position of power, you will have had to give up being he-who-wanted-to-move-mountains so that you can be he-who-put-the-mountain-there-in-the-first-place. The humor is that finally when you have the power to move the mountain, you are the person who placed it there—so there the mountain stays."

Drugs and existentialism go together like bacon and eggs, or maybe computers and graphics. Over in France, philosophy's favorite existentialist couple, Jean-Paul Sartre and Simone de Beauvoir, who I'll say a bit more about in a moment, also famously experimented with LSD-type substances. Unfortunately for Sartre, one "bad trip" with mescaline left him with a lifelong fear of crabs, lobsters, and jellyfish, which he would see everywhere, following him in the street, sitting on his desk, even waiting for him in his bedroom. De Beauvoir only says she smoked a little marijuana in New York, and the main effect she found was that it upset her throat. But put aside practical matters: the thread running through all these experiments is a search for your real self. This is the heart of *Be Here Now*, and Ram Dass sums up the existentialist message very well when he writes, "Only when I know who I am will I know what is possible." No wonder that the book has been described as a "countercultural bible."

What qualifies someone to write such a thing? Nothing too formal. In the case of Ram Dass, while he was still plain old Richard Alpert, he had worked for a while at Harvard University conducting research on psychedelic drugs—that is, until he was rather abruptly dismissed for, ahem, "breaking university rules." Let's not go into that. Anyway, it was shortly after this that he went to India, met another American spiritual seeker called Kermit Michael Riggs (I'm not making this up), and renamed himself "Ram Dass," which means "servant of God."

> The deeper the Self-realization of a man, the more he influences the whole universe by his subtle spiritual vibrations, and the less he himself is affected by the phenomenal flux.
>   "Why be elated by material profit?" Father replied. "The one who pursues a goal of even-mindedness is neither jubilant with gain nor depressed by loss. He knows that man arrives penniless in this world, and departs without a single rupee."

The same sentiment reappears, unmistakably, in the Stanford Commencement Address, delivered by Jobs not, of course, in the capacity of an academic professor or even religious guru but instead—better!—as a fabulously successful CEO: "Your work is going to fill a large part of your life, and the only way to be truly satisfied is to do what you believe is great work. And the only way to do great work is to love what you do. If you haven't found it yet, keep looking. Don't settle. As with all matters of the heart, you'll know when you find it. And, like any great relationship, it just gets better and better as the years roll on. So keep looking until you find it. Don't settle."

Following his own early departure from academia (in fact, his "alternative reading list" is about all that Steve got out of college), Jobs decided, like many young people before and since, that he wanted to travel the world. However, the young Steve realized he had to make some money first. So, on his own account, he opened up the paper, saw a job advert that said, yes, "Have fun and make money," and called. It was Atari. "I had never had a job before other than the one when I was a kid. By some stroke of luck, they called me up the next day and hired me."

In this way, his unerring feel for the "right time, and right place" skill got Jobs his first "real job" too. Atari was just starting up then, and Jobs was employee number forty. It was a very small company that made Pong (based on tennis) and a couple of less successful games. His first project was helping a guy named Don work on a basketball game project, which was a disaster. Then there was a baseball game, and somebody else was working on a hockey game. They flopped too. But now Jobs thought that he could see why. The programmers hadn't managed to penetrate to the *essence* of what made the sports compelling in the first place. As he put it later in that revealing interview with Sheff, a special quality of the original video game, Pong, was that it "captured the principles of gravity, angular momentum and things like that, to where each game obeyed those underlying principles, and yet every game was different—sort of like life. That's the simplest example. And what computer programming can do is to capture the underlying principles, the underlying essence, and then facilitate thousands of experiences based on that perception of the underlying principles."

Anyway, while at Atari, Jobs was allowed to work at the firm in the evenings, and he used to let Woz in, largely to play the early computer games. His boss, the CEO, Nolan Bushnell, knew about this but considered it a good arrangement because "Woz was a savant, no question about it" and in this way he got "two Steves for the price of one" to build his arcade game.

One project that particularly attracted Woz was called Gran Trak. It was the first car racing game with an actual steering wheel to drive it, and Woz soon became something of a Gran Track addict. He would play it all night long while Steve was wrestling with code, but if Steve came up against a stumbling block on a project, he would get Woz to "take a break from his road rally for ten minutes" and come and help. In this informal process lay the seeds of the technical collaboration that created the Apple I computer.

So what if some Californian dudes were going to make a new kind of computer? But remember that this was a time long before computers were consumer goods, long before things like iPhones could even be dreamed of. The Apple I was just a printed circuit board. There was no case; you had to buy your own keyboard. There wasn't even a power supply, as no transformer was included.

Even so, the big step of manufacturing and selling them to make money was serious stuff. It required Jobs to sell his VW bus and Woz his Hewlett Packard calculator to finance the initial batch of Apple Is. A friend who owned one of the first computer stores provided their only retail outlet. They sold only about 150 of the very first Apple I computers—ever—but even so, as Jobs told *Playboy*, "We made about $95,000 and I started to see it as a business besides something to do."

And Jobs was now interested in the mysteries of how to build a company. The two Steves' next venture, the Apple II, was a game changer, aimed at people who didn't have to be hardware hobbyists but instead just wanted to play with a computer. The first year, 1976, they sold three or four thousand—representing about $200,000—all while the factory was literally still the garage. And a year later they had about $7 million in sales. As Jobs says, the interest and sales were "phenomenal"! In 1978, they sold $17 million worth. In 1979, $47 million. By 1980, it was $117 million, and a year later, $335 million. In 1982, it was half a billion dollars. A year later, they had a billion-dollar company.

That's the business story, and it is a wonderful tale in itself. But behind the business success lies that existential aesthetic. One of the best questions that David Sheff puts to Jobs is what does he think is "the difference between the people who have insanely great ideas and the people who pull off those insanely great ideas"? Jobs replies by comparing the Apple approach with that of IBM, saying, "How come the Mac group produced Mac and the people at IBM produced the PC*jr*? We think the Mac will sell zillions, but we didn't build Mac for anybody else. We built it for ourselves. We were the group of people who were going to judge whether it was great or not. *We weren't going to go out and do market research.* We just wanted to build the best thing we could build" (emphasis added).

Here is existentialism applied to manufacturing. Designing computers based on market research is like being a waiter taking orders in a French bar. That was not going to be Jobs's approach. Because for Jobs, every product has its own essence, its own rationale, and all other considerations are secondary. It's a daring line to follow in a competitive marketplace. But Jobs made the approach work in two world-beating companies—both at Apple and again at his film animation company, Pixar. Jobs gives a very clear account of his *commitment*, to use another key existentialist term, toward "thinking differently" when (again in the *Playboy* interview) he recalls a classic tale about Bell Telephones:

> A hundred years ago, if somebody had asked Alexander Graham Bell, "What are you going to be able to do with a telephone?" he wouldn't have been able to tell him the ways the telephone would affect the world. He didn't know that people would use the telephone to call up and find out what movies were playing that night or to order some groceries or call a relative on the other side of the globe. But remember that first the public telegraph was inaugurated, in 1844. It was an amazing breakthrough in communications. You could actually send messages from New York to San Francisco in an afternoon. People talked about putting a telegraph on every desk in America to improve productivity. But it wouldn't have worked. It required that people learn this whole sequence of strange incantations, Morse code, dots and dashes, to use the telegraph. It took about 40 hours to learn. The majority of people would never learn how to use it. So, fortunately, in the 1870s, Bell filed the patents for the telephone. It performed basically the same function as the telegraph, but people already knew how to use it. Also, the neatest thing about it was that besides allowing you to communicate with just words, *it allowed you to sing.* [Emphasis added again.]

"Allows you to sing" is a phrase that Jobs would often drop into descriptions of his computers. People often misinterpret the reference. However, in the 1985 interview, he is very clear about what he means:

> It allowed you to intone your words with meaning beyond the simple linguistics. And we're in the same situation today. Some people are saying that we ought to put an IBM PC on every desk in America to improve productivity. It won't work. The special incantations you have to learn this time are "slash

q-zs" and things like that. The manual for WordStar, the most popular word-processing program, is 400 pages thick. To write a novel, you have to read a novel—one that reads like a mystery to most people. They're not going to learn slash q-z any more than they're going to learn Morse code. That is what Macintosh is all about. It's the first "telephone" of our industry. And, besides that, the neatest thing about it, to me, is that the Macintosh lets you sing the way the telephone did. You don't simply communicate words, you have special print styles and the ability to draw and add pictures to express yourself.

For Jobs, great businesses are built up out of the bricks of intellectual playfulness, research, experimentation, analysis, and judgment. But of all of these, it's intellectual playfulness that is the most important. As one venture capitalist once put it, "Money does not get the ideas flowing. It's ideas that get the money flowing."

Jobs managed to "get the ideas flowing" because he eschewed unthinking acceptance of the views of others, what the right-wing novelist and many CEOs' favorite philosopher Ayn Rand called "second-handedness." Instead, Jobs embraced "first-handedness," or independent thinking with a Platonic orientation not toward others' opinions but toward reality, or at least "reality" as you see it. "Don't be trapped by dogma—which is living with the results of other people's thinking. Don't let the noise of others' opinions drown out your own inner voice," he advises. In true existentialist style, he continues, "To [do] something really well, you have to get it. You have to really *grok* what it's all about. It takes a passionate commitment to really thoroughly understand something, chew it up, not just quickly swallow it. Most people don't take the time to do that."

Or put short: *think different*. He then adds, "I think one of the potentials of the computer is to somehow . . . capture the fundamental, underlying principles of an experience."

In a YouTube short called "Steve Jobs Philosophy on Life," he says,

> Life can be much broader, once you discover one simple fact, and that is that everything around you that you call life was made up by people that were no smarter than you. And you can change it, you can influence it, you can build your own things that other people can use. And the minute that you understand that you can poke life and actually something will, you know if you push in, something will pop out the other side, that you can change it, you can mold it. That's maybe the most important thing. It's to shake off this erroneous notion that life is there and you're just gonna live in it, versus embrace it, change it, improve it, make your mark upon it. . . . Once you learn that, you'll never be the same again.

The quest to identify the key working principles of life and then apply them to work in your own way is a profoundly philosophical, existentialist project. So let's say a bit more about the philosophy itself.

Existentialism is a philosophy of action, an "ethic of action and self-commitment," as one of its best-known exponents, Jean-Paul Sartre, said in 1946, just after passing World War II eating boiled turnips in Paris and writing philosophy.

Actually, Sartre emphasizes what is not over what is, the latter being a rather humdrum sort of affair consisting of the kind of things that scientists, and no doubt computer programmers, examine, while the "what is not" is really much more interesting. He sums up his view (if "sums up" is ever an appropriate term in existentialist writing) thus: "The Nature of consciousness simultaneously is to be what is not and not to be what it is." And hence we come back to our own natures, our own "essences." We *exist*, yes, but how do we *define* ourselves? Or, in one of the movement's catchphrases, "existence precedes essence."

It is here that Sartre's most celebrated example, that of a waiter (or "server"), comes in:

> His movement is quick and forward, a little too precise, a little too rapid. He comes toward the patrons with a step a little too quick. He bends forward a little too eagerly; his voice, his eyes express an interest a little too solicitous for the order of the customer. Finally there he returns, trying to imitate in his walk the inflexible stiffness of some kind of automaton while carrying his tray with the recklessness of a tight-rope walker by putting it in a perpetually unstable, perpetually broken equilibrium which he perpetually re-establishes by a light movement of the hand and arm. (*Being and Nothingness*, 1943)

Sartre seems to have had a prejudice against waiters, in fact. He saw them in the same sour light that Plato saw actors, as somehow presenting a fake, false face to the world. His example belies the very function of a waiter and dismisses them with a lofty disdain that really has more to do with his privileged roots than any real philosophy. And yet, as a metaphor, it can be allowed. The waiter is performing a role that is not "authentically" theirs. When they say that the chicken fricassee is excellent today, we cannot be entirely sure whether that is really their opinion at all.

Elsewhere, Sartre's existentialism emphasizes the use of imagination, which is the purest form of freedom available to us. In a tome called *Critique of Dialectical Reason*, Sartre offers by way of example workers engaged in monotonous tasks yet having sexual fantasies, thus demonstrating the power and counterfactual freedom of the imagination. Sartre was no businessperson; indeed, he rather looked down on "all that" or adopted a radical political stance on public ownership.

Of course, most Apple employees humbly employed in the factories have no chance to use much imagination, but at Apple's Californian HQ, and even more clearly at Pixar, imagination was put center stage. No wonder Jobs once described being fired from Apple as "the best thing that could have happened because the heaviness of being successful was replaced by the lightness of being a beginner again . . . it freed me to be creative again."

It was in 1986, shortly after he was forced out of Apple Computer in a boardroom battle over management policy, that Steve Jobs bought the small computer manufacturer named Pixar from George Lucas, the director of *Star Wars*. By 1990, he was supporting the company out of his own pocket as project after project died. "We should have failed," Alvy Ray Smith, a cofounder of Pixar, says in David Price's *The Pixar Touch*. "But it seemed to me that Steve would just not suffer a defeat. He couldn't sustain it." The survival of Pixar, and its subsequent rise, is a revealing case study in Jobs's approach to innovation. Although his background was in computer hardware, he helped transform Pixar into one of the most successful studios in the history of cinema.

In November 2000, Jobs purchased an abandoned Del Monte canning factory to be Pixar's base. The original architectural plan called for three buildings: separate offices for the computer scientists, the animators, and the Pixar executives. Logical. Jobs immediately scrapped it. Instead of three buildings, there was going to be a single vast space with an airy atrium at its center. "The philosophy behind this design is that it's good to put the most important function at the heart of the building," Catmull says. "Well, what's our most important function? It's the interaction of our employees. That's why Steve put a big empty space there. He wanted to create an open area for people to always be talking to each other."

Jobs realized, however, that it wasn't enough to simply create a space; he needed to make people go there to force computer geeks and cartoonists to mix. In typical fashion, Jobs saw this as a design problem. He began with the mailboxes, which he shifted to the atrium. Then he moved the meeting rooms to the center of the building, followed by the cafeteria, the coffee bar, and the gift shop.

For years, though, Pixar's model of digitally animated movies lost money and was kept afloat primarily because Jobs believed in it and continued to fund it. Indeed, it seemed he simply couldn't stomach admitting failure. But, long after all sensible accountants would have pulled the plug, the magic worked. Following the 1995 release of *Toy Story*, every film Pixar created and released has been a commercial success, with an average international gross of more than $550 million per film.

Later on, the creativity regained at Pixar also led to a remarkable rebirth at Apple when Jobs returned to the by then ailing company. Soon, the iPhone, iTunes, and iPad all became remarkable commercial successes. And all the time Jobs followed his laid-back variety of existentialist philosophy:

Don't take it all too seriously. If you want to live your life in a creative way, as an artist, you have to not look back too much. You have to be willing to take whatever you've done and whoever you were and throw them away. What are we, anyway? Most of what we think we are is just a collection of likes and dislikes, habits, patterns.

At the core of what we are is our values, and what decisions and actions we make reflect those values.

As you are growing and changing, the more the outside world tries to reinforce an image of you that it thinks you are, the harder it is to continue to be an artist, which is why a lot of times, artists have to go, "Bye. I have to go. I'm going crazy and I'm getting out of here."

Introducing the iPad 2 in March 2011, Jobs summarized his strategy this way: "It is in Apple's DNA that technology alone is not enough—it's technology married with liberal arts, married with the humanities, that yields us the results that make our heart sing."

The existentialist refusal to be pigeonholed into being either "a scientist" or "an artist" allowed Jobs to make Apple's technology beautiful. Revealingly, Jobs's biography notes that even after he dropped out of Reed College during his freshman year, he continued to take classes in calligraphy: "I learned about serif and sans-serif typefaces, about varying the amount of space between different letter combinations, about what makes great typography great. It was beautiful, historical, artistically subtle in a way that science can't capture, and I found it fascinating. None of this had even a hope of practical application in my life. But ten years later, when we were designing the first Macintosh computer, it all came back to me."

It's said that Jobs even had the engineers' names engraved inside each one. Why? Because "real artists sign their work." Contrast all this with the West Coast Computer Fair in April 1981. There, Adam Osborne released what he described as the first truly portable personal computer. It had only a five-inch screen and hardly any memory, but it worked after a fashion. Osborne announced, "Adequacy is sufficient. All else is superfluous." Jobs was appalled at this and for days told everyone he met that Osborne was a guy who just didn't "get it." "He's not making art, *he's making shit.*"

It is revealing that even as a millionaire, Steve's house had almost no furniture in it—just a picture of Einstein, whom he admired greatly, a Tiffany lamp, a chair, and a bed. He didn't believe in having lots of things around, and he was incredibly careful in what he selected. When he returned to Apple in 1997, he took a company with 350 products and in two years reduced them to just ten. But then Jobs, talking about change and obsolescence, once said, "I think death is the most wonderful invention of life."

Speaking about life and death, which existentialists invariably come back to, there's a very revealing story about Jobs that also helps explain why he was so extraordinarily successful in turning Apple into one of the world's most iconic companies. One time he challenged an engineer called Larry Kenyon as to why the operating system took so long to boot up. (We've all stared aimlessly at blank screens wondering much the same thing.) Kenyon started a long, technical explanation that Jobs brusquely cut off. "Larry, if it could save a person's life, would you find a way to shave ten seconds off the boot time?" Kenyon conceded that he might, hardly expecting much to follow from that concession.

And now here comes the impressive bit. Jobs went over to the whiteboard in the engineer's office, grabbed a marker, and showed that since there were at least five million people who used Macintosh computers, if it took ten seconds extra to turn them on every day, then the amount of time being lost was equivalent to one hundred lifetimes—per year! A few weeks later, Larry Kenyon had found a way to save not a mere ten seconds but nearly half a minute off the boot-up time.

Of course, Steve didn't really think that computers that were slow to boot cost lives. After all, people could be rearranging their paper clips or something while the cursor was spinning. In fact, his concern was not practical at all. He wasn't interested in the current limitations of the technology or in winning a race with competing computers—far less in making a lot of money. Instead, his goal was to do something the best way imaginable.

Jobs was convinced that for an object to be truly great, it had to be completely "authentic," meaning true to its own origins and purpose. He abhorred the idea of compromises and "compatibility." It is said that he even designed the original Macintosh computers to have no cursor arrow keys—partly as a way of forcing people to use the mouse to click and point and partly to oblige software designers to use a more visual approach in the design of their programs. But user choice didn't come into it. The right approach would be forced on them whatever their inclinations.

And part of the deal was that market share was thrown away in order to produce Macs running the Mac operating system and Mac programs. Because anything else, as ZDNet's founder, Dan Farber, put it to Jobs's biographer, Isaacson, would have been like inviting the local decorator to add some brush strokes to a Picasso painting. Okay, that's an analogy, but the fact that Jobs really saw the world like this is borne out by the time he took a team from Apple to see an exhibit of Tiffany glass in San Francisco. For Jobs, the exhibition was important as it showed that something mass-produced could also be great art. Great art? *Computers*? But yes: "Here's to the crazy ones . . . because they change the world."

Most CEOs aren't crazy at all, though. They're very careful types who start with a hardheaded strategy and then at most adapt it in the light of any highfalutin, quasi-philosophical comments received. Not so Apple's visionary, Steve Jobs. He started off with a philosophy of life melded from personal experiences and a countercultural bible rooted in existentialism and then shaped his business strategy around that. Actually, to me, it still seems remarkable that something as precise and, well, technical as a computer interface could have its roots in a hippy philosophy. But maybe the weirdness of this is made more understandable when you recall the case of another great computer pioneer who was working just a decade earlier also in the United States. This is Evelyn Berezin, who found inspiration in the alternative universes of science fiction and "amazing" stories, and her own is pretty "amazing" too.

The first Apple was launched into the world in 1978. However, it was only able to do so because a decade earlier, which in computer terms is ancient history, Evelyn Berezin (pronounced "bear-a-zen") had not only set up the Redactron Corporation, a tech start-up on Long Island that was the first company exclusively engaged in manufacturing computerized typewriters, but also invented new kinds of technology able to control them.

Berezin was every bit as much of a pioneer as Jobs and Wozniak. At a time when computers were in their infancy and few women were involved in their development, her machines were bulky, slow, and noisy, but they could edit, delete, and cut and paste text. To some offices, particularly those producing standard letters with small amounts of individual content, Redactron word processors arrived "like a trunk of magic tricks" as the *New York Times* put it in its 2018 tribute to Berezin.

Redactron enthusiastically christened its computer "the Data Secretary." Early versions looked like an upright black refrigerator; input and output were both via an IBM Selectric Typewriter with a rattling golf ball printhead, and there was as yet not even a rudimentary screen for words to trickle across. And yet underneath the bland, office equipment surface was something quite revolutionary: thirteen semiconductor chips, some of which Berezin had herself designed, and a system of programmable logic patiently waiting to deliver its word-processing functions.

During the early 1970s, Redactron sold some ten thousand machines for $8,000 each. If you think that's a bit steep for a word processor, bear in mind that in today's money it is actually about $53,312—and four cents. No wonder her chief competitor, International Business Machines (IBM), didn't sell its devices but instead only rented them out. However, beyond that, IBM machines relied on electronic relays and tapes, not semiconductor chips, and so were barely in the same technological era. By 1975, Redactron had made $20 million from its word processor, or again, about seven times that at today's prices. Certainly, this was an extraordinary achievement, and doubly so, for the child of a family of barely literate refugee parents.

Of course, "Big Blue" (IBM) soon caught up technologically and later in the decade swamped the market, pursued by a herd of new brands, like Osborne, Wang, Tandy, and Kaypro. However, as the *Times* put it, for a few heady years, "Ms. Berezin was a lioness of the young tech industry, featured in magazine and news articles as an adventurous do-it-herself polymath with the logical mind of an engineer, the curiosity of an inventor and the entrepreneurial skills of a C.E.O."

Her pioneering work included designing logic boards and inventing new kinds of computer-to-computer communication, vital groundwork for the later Internet age. "Why is this woman not famous?" the British writer and entrepreneur Gwyn Headley asked in a 2010 blog post for a site called Fotolibrarian. "Without Ms. Berezin," he continued enthusiastically, "there would be no Bill Gates, no Steve Jobs, no internet, no word processors, no spreadsheets; nothing that remotely connects business with the 21st century."

Actually, that's overstating Berezin's role and significance and misunderstanding the collective nature of the advance of computers. Yet, curiously, in as much as technological breakthroughs depend on particular individuals, the same should be said of a cluster of science-fiction writers, because without their short stories in a pulp magazine called *Astounding Science-Fiction*, Evelyn Berezin would never have been tempted to become a computer scientist, there would have been no Redactron, and the arrival of the modern computer would have taken substantially longer.

I say that because even if today her name is not familiar to many, nonetheless Evelyn Berezin is truly one of a tiny group of people who made the modern world, and in her case it seems clear that she was inspired to take her then unheard of career path by reading science-fiction stories in a magazine.

In fact, many of the most famous names of the genre explored cutting-edge scientific ideas in short stories as well as later on in full-length novels, these being published in the 1930s and onward. One such was Georgiy Gamov (also known as plain George Gamow), a respected physicist who had moved from Russia to the West, where he became involved in the development of quantum theory alongside iconic figures like Niels Bohr and Ernest Rutherford. Gamov also became one of the most ardent proselytizers for the now standard but then controversial theory of the universe's origins, known as the Big Bang theory, in opposition to the then widely accepted steady-state universe theory. This had been popularized by his friend and fellow keen science-fiction writer Fred Hoyle, whose own book *The Black Cloud* (1957) is considered something of a sci-fi classic.

Actually, Gamov's stories, featuring Mr. Tompkins, such as *Mr. Tompkins in Wonderland* (1939) and *Mr. Tompkins Explores the Atom* (1944), are rather less celebrated yet still explore the wonders of science, including relativistic effects like that which would astonish the young Evelyn Berezin. The first lines of *Mr. Tompkins in Wonderland* run,

It was a bank holiday, and Mr. Tompkins, the little clerk of a big city bank, slept late and had a leisurely breakfast. Trying to plan his day, he first

First issue of *Amazing Stories*, cover art by Frank R. Paul. This copy was autographed by Gernsback, the publisher. (*Amazing Stories*, Vol. 1, No. 1. Gernsback, Hugo, "Free Download, Borrow, and Streaming." Internet Archive. Experimenter Publishing Co., April 1, 1926. https://archive.org/details/AmazingStoriesVolume01Number01 /mode/2up.)

thought about going to some afternoon movie and, opening the morning paper, turned to the entertainment page. But none of the films looked attractive to him. He detested all this Hollywood stuff, with infinite romances between popular stars. If only there were at least one film with some real adventure, something unusual and maybe even fantastic about it. But there was none. Unexpectedly, his eye fell on a little notice in the corner of the page. The local university was announcing a series of lectures on the problems of modern physics, and this afternoon's lecture was to be about Einstein's Theory of Relativity. Well, that might be something!

To which might be said, don't besiege the bookshops; there's plenty of copies to go round. Nonetheless, James Watson, one of the scientists who helped pin down the hidden workings of life via his discoveries of the famous double-helix structure of DNA, pays tribute to the great importance of Gamow's insightful contributions to many scientific debates in his autobiographical book *Genes, Girls, and Gamow: After the Double Helix* (2001)—insights perhaps like that in *The Creation of the Universe* (1952), where Gamow says, "It took less than an hour to make the atoms, a few hundred million years to make the stars and planets, but five billion years to make man!"

ASTOUNDING SCIENCE-FICTION
AUTHOR: VARIOUS
PUBLISHED: SINCE 1930

Astounding was a magazine launched in 1926 by inventor-writer Hugo Gernsback's Experimenter Publishing. It was published under various titles, including *Astounding Science-Fiction* and *Astounding Stories of Super-Science*, and by providing an outlet for a new breed of writers is credited with spawning an entirely new genre in the publishing industry. Over the years, many of the most famous names of science fiction appeared in its columns.

A. E. van Vogt's classic work *Rogue Ship* (1965) includes elements from a short story originally published in *Astounding Science-Fiction* featuring the kinds of relativistic effects that intrigued Berezin. In the book, a spaceship manages to exceed the speed of light. It returns to Earth on a collision course, but instead of being smashed to smithereens on impact, it burrows into the ground, barrels straight through, and reemerges unscathed! This, all thanks to those relativistic effects. The ship's owner, who had sent it on its way six years earlier, forces his way inside the spaceship, where he finds time slowed down to a near standstill and everything, people included, severely compressed in the direction of travel.

"Certainly, science fiction requires you, in Steve Jobs' phrase, to 'think different.'"

If college drop-out and lifelong hippy Steve Jobs makes an unlikely candidate for a twentieth-century computer scientist, Berezin's background isn't the obvious one either. Her parents were refugees from Russia who arrived and settled in New York at the start of the twentieth century as part of a Jewish exodus. Evelyn would be born in poverty in the Bronx in 1925, with two brothers, seven and five years older respectively. Her father was a furrier, and neither parent could read or write English, nor were they much better in any other languages. He worked thirteen hours a day, six days a week, which was the standard experience of workers of the time.

At her junior school, called rather grimly Public School 6, Evelyn had to walk in a line determined by height. Every week included a test. School 6 was not a place where creativity was encouraged. However, being hardworking and precocious, by age fifteen she had progressed to a newly opened high school called Christopher Columbus. This school was as exciting and innovative as the previous one was dull and traditional. And it was here that her interest in science and things technical grew to become her lifelong passion. The United States was still in the grip of the Great Depression, and jobs were hard to find; in this new school, her math teacher had a PhD from Princeton, and her physics teacher had a PhD from Chicago. And they were both young. The teachers were close to the students and set up laboratories for students to freely try things out. Evelyn would stay after school experimenting as if in a deluxe toy shop. For her, schools and the local library were the best places to be, as she recalled later.

But the spark that set her on the path that in due course would lead her to invent the first word processor and design the first digital booking system—which never crashed, not once—came not from school but from those short stories of science fiction.

When Evelyn was very young, she had read things like fairy tales, but she became fascinated by the alternative universes she discovered when her elder brother started buying a magazine called *Astounding Science*. Talking about her early influences as part of an oral history project on computers, she said, "I was fascinated by it, I thought it was marvelous. I used to steal them from him all the time. It was really the thing that got me interested in this."

In an extended interview on March 10, 2014, recorded in New York at her home, she went on to explain to the researcher Gardner Hendrie how, when she was only seven, she "started looking at these things" and how much of an impression they had made. "I wanted to study physics from the time I read about in *Astounding Science*." This was all the more remarkable as, at the time she was studying, girls just weren't supposed to do science. Indeed, she was often *obliged* to study other things.

One incident she describes is revealing. She went up to her science teacher in junior high and asked him about something she had read in the magazine. The question was about how when something goes very fast, near the speed of light, the object shrinks in size in the direction of travel. The teacher had said, "Oh no, that's impossible, they're making it up." As she recalled to Hendrie, "And I never forgot that, because I believed him."

Now, although "length contraction," as it is known, is a fairly well-established element of relativity theory, which dates from the early years of the twentieth century, perhaps the teacher can be forgiven this assumption, partly because the magazine was originally titled *Astounding Stories of Super-Science*, before being shortened to the dodgy sounding *Astounding Stories* and finally becoming *Astounding Science-Fiction* in 1938 under its new editor, George Campbell. However, Berezin's remembering it as *Astounding Science* is understandable. Campbell asked his writers to write stories that felt as though they could have been published as factual science stories in a magazine of the future; he also included regular nonfiction pieces with the goal of stimulating ideas. Berezin again: "In one of these *Astounding Science* articles, a lot of which used real physics—they were imaginative and all things but they actually had real science in them."

For SF aficionados, the period beginning with Campbell's editorship of *Astounding* is the golden age, and certainly the magazine had immense influence on the genre. Within two years, alongside pieces by established authors like L. Ron Hubbard, Clifford Simak, Jack Williamson, L. Sprague de Camp, Henry Kuttner, and C. L. Moore, all regulars in either *Astounding* or its sister magazine, *Unknown*, Campbell had published stories by new writers who would become iconic figures in the genre, including Lester del Rey, Theodore Sturgeon, Isaac Asimov, A. E. van Vogt, and Robert Heinlein. For these, publication in the magazine was a literary launchpad, just as for readers, like the young Berezin, their ideas were lifelong inspirations.

It is no coincidence that Asimov, Heinlein, and de Camp were all trained scientists and engineers because Campbell's cultivation of this new genre of writing emphasized scientific accuracy—sometimes even over literary style. And if her first teacher had poured cold water on the stories, more support came for the pulp science magazine when she moved up to high school and asked the physics teacher there about the same scientific claims. Now she found out that this first science teacher had told her something wrong indeed, "really wrong," as she still put it even so many years later.

Actually, to be fair to the offending teacher, although it was Einstein's work that was in those days popularizing the idea of relativistic effects, the *Astounding* article was specifically talking about the theories of George

Fitzgerald, offered as part of a nineteenth-century debate about the speed of light and whether or not it traveled through an invisible ether. So maybe "really wrong" is a bit unkind to the school's science teacher, who was presumably trying to arbitrate on this older scientific debate.

Either way, though, it did reveal to the young Evelyn the extraordinary access to cutting-edge ideas that the written word, in this case a two-dime magazine, can bring. "I was just dumbstruck by the idea that a teacher can be wrong," she recalled to Hendrie seventy years later.

Anyway, we shouldn't come down too hard on teachers because if one almost put Berezin off her destiny as a computer scientist, it was another who directly encouraged and even facilitated it. A very practical reason why she managed to follow her unlikely dream was that one day her high school teacher turned up at her home and told her about an opportunity at a new company called International Printing Ink. As her teacher explained that day, the company had its own research labs and would finance her future studies. Actually, part of the reason that the opportunity arose was because, at this time, the opening years of World War II, Evelyn Berezin's being female was actually an advantage as young men were subject to the call up for the army.

Other times, though, being female worked against her. Applying for a job to design a new computer system for the New York Stock Exchange, a job that she may well have been the only person in the country capable of implementing, she was turned down on the grounds that the work would have required her to mix with the traders on the floor and thus to have been exposed to "bad language." Of course this patronizing attitude really concealed a determination to protect a male bastion from infiltration by the fair sex. Talking to Hendrie for the history project, Berezin offers a characteristically wry footnote to that unfair decision, describing how the job that she eventually ended up taking involved supervising an early computer constructed out of hundreds if not thousands of vacuum tubes, technology that generated at the best of times enormous amounts of surplus heat. In the summer the building she worked in with her male engineering team reached temperatures of 100° Fahrenheit, and the men were in the habit of stripping down to nothing but a sort of apron that prominently displayed their buttocks. Her job required her to mix with them as if nothing was remarkable in the slightest. Which is, of course, exactly what she did.

5

See the World in the Wider Social Context

Jacob Riis and Mike Duffy

Books about imaginary worlds or grand philosophical theories or even great people can all inspire, but so too, perhaps perplexingly, can books about the grubby details of life, the seedy corners of the cities—or even the bloody details of scalping prisoners. Thus it is with Jacob A. Riis, journalist and photographer, who became famous for his tireless work in the late nineteenth and early twentieth century exposing corruption and public ills in the United States, who seems to have been set on his way by the novels of Charles Dickens, works like *A Tale of Two Cities*, which are equally divided between subtle psychological characterizations and polemical denunciations of the ills of public life in a world turned upside-down by industrialization. And so it is in recent years too, with Mike Duffy, founding CEO of CityBase, who says that the book that inspired him was a rather depressing tale of life when you are "down and out" in big cities: George Orwell's *Down and Out in Paris and London*.

It's not an immediately obvious connection. Duffy, after all, has a background in entrepreneurship and finance, including time at Northern Trust managing assets in short-term interest rate markets. But he developed his interest in behavioral economics over a decade working in capital markets, including as a Federal Reserve analyst at Northern Trust. He then concentrated in economics, econometrics and statistics, and entrepreneurship at the University of Chicago Booth School of Business before founding CityBase and "embarking on his mission for humanity" as his website today unabashedly puts it.

He explains that CityBase pulls together all his business interests—finance, behavioral economics, and government—and that the core idea is to use technology to "unlock" the opportunity to give each citizen their own experience. Today his website proudly declares that "Mike was driven to embrace local government's distinct operational challenge of serving every person, regardless of their needs or demographics."

All over the United States different municipalities are at different stages of implementing his ideas, with Chicago, for instance, busy installing a kiosk in every library, police station, and alderman's council to enable every citizen easy access to their services.

And all this, as Duffy revealed in a 2017 comment for Inc.com, drew in several crucial respects on Orwell's book; it had been for him "a gateway to . . . deeper exploration of behavioral economics and the struggle of the working class."

Duffy goes on to explain how the English writer, best known for the two dark political classics *Animal Farm* and *1984*, became a key influence, saying of *Down and Out*:

> This memoir is about his time living essentially as a tramp in the late 1920s, during a time when Europe—and the U.S., for that matter—was peaking in an economic boom fueled by the creative monetary policy that would soon lead to a global Depression. The associated asset inflation of the boom widened the gap between those who owned and those who earned: workers whose standard of living had eroded. Orwell captures the humanity and spirit of the downtrodden poor during this period, in 1929, at a peak of extravagance that we now know was in its twilight, on the cusp of the Great Depression and WWII.

And when asked to suggest his favorite George Orwell quotation, Duffy points to *Down and Out*, saying that one line sticks with him even today: "When you have a hundred francs in the world you are liable to the most craven panics. When you have only three francs you are quite indifferent; for three francs will feed you till tomorrow, and you cannot think further than that."

But let's go back to well over a hundred years ago and Jacob Riis. In 1891, one of his photo stories revealed sewage flowing unchecked into New York reservoirs and on its own is considered to have led to public health programs that saved tens of thousands of lives. It was feats such as this that led that grand political figure Theodore Roosevelt to describe him as "the most useful citizen of New York" and to history itself according him the honor of pioneering a vital, investigative kind of journalism, the variety nowadays called (if sometimes rather disparagingly) "muckraking."

One of Riis's images of "the other half": Brandt's Roost, in New York. (Jacob Riis, Preus Museum, n.d. https://www.flickr.com/photos/preus museum/5389939434/in/photolist-9dhRdf.)

It all came together for Riis when he wrote an article for an illustrated magazine that included engravings adapted from his photographs, and if it seems hard to imagine the effect it had now, in an age of cameras and indeed pretty shocking images everywhere, it was the visual representations as much as the words that had the power to shock readers to the extent that change became unavoidable and to upset convention to the extent that other magazines (or at least their proprietors) henceforth refused to deal with him. Nonetheless, the public debate led to an invitation to write a book that proved to be even more influential than features in the weeklies.

The book was called *How the Other Half Lives*, and it emerged just a year later, in 1890. Today, it is still counted as a classic work of photojournalism documenting the conditions of life in the slums and *bidonvilles* of New York in the closing decades of the nineteenth century as well as raising broader issues about the extent to which the rich lived completely parallel lives to their struggling neighbors, barely conscious of the everyday realities of life just around the corner.

HOW THE OTHER HALF LIVES:
STUDIES AMONG THE TENEMENTS OF NEW YORK
AUTHOR: JACOB RIIS
PUBLISHED: 1890

Long ago it was said that "one half of the world does not know how the other half lives." That was true then. It did not know because it did not care. The half that was on top cared little for the struggles, and less for the fate of those who were underneath, so long as it was able to hold them there and keep its own seat. There came a time when the discomfort and consequent upheavals so violent, that it was no longer an easy thing to do, and then the upper half fell to inquiring what was the matter. Information on the subject has been accumulating rapidly since, and the whole world has had its hands full answering for its old ignorance.

—*How the Other Half Lives*

Riis's pioneering account describes the living conditions in the New York slums in the late nineteenth century.

The book follows a standard pattern for works advocating social reform of the time: there is a section on crime, on the Protestant virtues and vices (including idleness and uncleanliness), on the miserable living conditions, on disease, and a lament for the loss of human dignity and the dissolution of the family.

Without doubt, it was the inclusion of images that gave the book its impact. The photos brought the squalid conditions to life and also increased sympathy for the individuals depicted in them. Riis told his readers that the poor were not so by choice and that the dangerous and unhygienic conditions in which they lived were a social evil that society needed to address rather than shun. Riis ends *How the Other Half Lives* with a plan for fixing the problem.

In 1891, the *New York Times* lauded its content, calling it a "powerful book" concerning "matters we ought to know." The *Christian Intelligencer* reviewed it, saying, "Books like this that lift the curtains and expose to public gaze the great evils of the system will hasten the day of reform." And so, indeed, it did.

The title of Riis's book is an inseparable part of its success and has a curious origin. It had, in fact, been adapted from a phrase in a classic French tale called *Pantagruel*. This is, on the surface of it, an absurd and not infrequently scatological (meaning plain rude) story about the adventures of two giants—yet underneath lurks a story about society too, one that the Russian philosopher Michael Bakhtin later dubbed "grotesque realism." What is more, the underlying theme and insight of the Frenchman's tales, according to Bakhtin, is that of social conscience and collective thinking—themes that are at the heart of Riis's work too. Take, for example, the way people feel and behave during carnivals in a town or village. These are precious moments when a special sense of time and space causes social divisions to fold away, and the individual becomes part of the collectivity, even to the extent that they cease to be individuals. At such special instants in time, a special form of free and familiar contact briefly reigns among people who may otherwise be divided by "the barriers of caste, property, profession, and age," as Bakhtin puts it. It's an idea that is also present in those writings of Charles Dickens that Mike Duffy mentions. Dickens, a writer usually more at home describing life in cities, particularly life in the slums of the big cities, sees in carnivals a kind of suspension of man-made time in favor of an alternative "festive time" that is rooted in nature and the seasons.

Time, and the perennial battle between nature and human plans, is one aspect of the complex social life that Riis describes and photographs. However, it is not with the multilayered novels of the likes of Dickens but with a very different, much more straightforward, set of stories that his own journey starts. It is in the ripping yarns of James Fenimore Cooper—sometimes called America's first novelist—that Riis found his inspiration. Cooper is best known today for *Last of the Mohicans*, not merely as a book but as a plotline for many TV dramas, but he was also the author of a book called *The Deerslayer*, and it is to this that Jacob Riis frequently refers.

This book is not only a fantastic tale of the adventures of a woodsman known as Deerslayer and his Indian friend Chingachgook but also, beneath the surface, a more profound study of the interface between wilderness and civilization and the clash of nature and human values. At the time that Cooper was writing, the American settlers were legislating the forced removal of the Native Americans from the lands described in the book to the bleaker landscapes of the Midwest. In real life, Cooper supported these cruel and frequently fatal removals, citing things such as the cultural and religious divisions between white man and Indian. It is for throwing light on these deeper issues that Riis owes Cooper an intellectual debt.

And surely without such books, Riis would have had no reason to contemplate such subtle things as the different social and cultural perspectives of two communities living side by side in the same land but with completely different experiences of it. For such concerns were truly remote for a child born in Ribe, a small town in Jutland, Denmark, the third of fifteen children. Indeed, only Jacob, one sister, and a foster sister would survive to see the twentieth century.

His father was the opposite of a woodsman, or indeed any kind of adventurer, being a schoolteacher and writer for the local newspaper, while his mother was happy to be a *hjemmegående husmor*, which is what the Danes call a housewife or homemaker. On the other hand, being himself a literary man, his father did urge Jacob to read and improve his English, particularly by tucking regularly into the much-admired writing of Charles Dickens via a magazine called *All the Year Round* that Dickens himself had founded and edited. If, in Riis's day, books were a luxury, his father's magazine was full of tales of the virtuous poor suffering from slum conditions and poverty, including serializations and extracts from Dickens's writings, such as the tearjerker of the orphan Oliver Twist asking for "more gruel from the master of the parish workhouse" and the drama of Monseigneur's carriage recklessly racing through the streets of Paris and running over a child. Indeed, the magazine included a serialization of *A Tale of Two Cities*, which included that sad story of the carriage accident as well as passages like this one: "The wives and mothers we have been used to see since we were as little as this child, and much less, have not been greatly considered? We have known their husbands and fathers laid in prison and kept from them, often enough? All our lives, we have seen our sister-women suffer, in themselves and in their children, poverty, nakedness, hunger, thirst, sickness, misery, oppression and neglect of all kinds?" (*A Tale of Two Cities*, book 3, chapter 3).

Such passages would, at the very least, have alerted the young Jacob to the huge issues of social justice. And *A Tale of Two Cities*, printed in full (naturally in little chunks) in the magazine, was Charles Dickens's sixteenth novel and a perfect example of why the English author was in his own lifetime a publishing phenomenon, read enthusiastically both in England and abroad. The "two cities" are London and Paris, and the tale weaves together chaos, espionage, and adventure in the two great European capitals against the backdrop of the terrifying French Revolution. In characteristic Dickens style, the social upheaval is mirrored too in the lives of the novel's two male leads, Charles Darney and Sydney Carton, and their battle for the attention of Lucie Manette, the woman they both love.

Dickens's influence was made evident by the fact that when still only age eleven or twelve, Jacob donated all the money he had to a poor family living in squalor in a house in Ribe—on condition that they clean it. Apparently the tenants accepted the help and the terms attached, and indeed when his mother learned of the project she went to help.

So, surely it is Dickens's social conscience that reappears in Jacob Riis's concern for the people of the hidden New York, but his actual decision to travel there in the first place and his fascination for exploring the darker side of the city owes more to his reading of the novels of a very different kind of author. It is from Fenimore Cooper, an American writer whose adventure stories offer an exciting and romantic picture of frontier life, that Riis borrows the framework that defines his investigations of the world between wilderness and civilization and of social life tugged in two directions by the laws of nature and the laws of man.

THE DEERSLAYER, OR THE FIRST WAR-PATH
AUTHOR: JAMES FENIMORE COOPER
PUBLISHED: 1841

"Point de quartier aux coquins!" cried an eager pursuer, who seemed to direct the operations of the enemy.

"Stand firm and be ready, my gallant 60ths!" suddenly exclaimed a voice above them; "wait to see the enemy, fire low, and sweep the glacis."

"Father! Father" exclaimed a piercing cry from out the mist. "It is I! Alice! Thy own Elsie! Spare, O! Save your daughters!"

"Hold!" shouted the former speaker, in the awful tones of parental agony, the sound reaching even to the woods, and rolling back in a solemn echo. "Tis she! God has restored me my children! Throw open the sally-port; to the field, 60ths, to the field! Pull not a trigger, lest ye kill my lambs! Drive off these dogs of France with your steel!"

This is an exciting moment drawn from *The Deerslayer*, the last of Cooper's so-called Leatherstocking Tales. "Exciting," at least, for generations of young readers. It is the last in the series, although its time period makes it the first installment chronologically in the lifetime of its hero, Natty Bumpoo, a frontiersman and "deerslayer" who objects to the practice of taking scalps, a confusing time reversal of the kind that not only annoys many readers but in Cooper's case left the logic of his tale lacking in many places. As to "scalping," though, this is indeed quite a thread in the book, often done while the victim was alive, and there is much warmongering and massacring to boot, which seems to have established the tall tales in the American imagination. Add to which that Fenimore Cooper starts the story by relating the rapid advance of "civilization" in New York State, and the action takes place around a lake that the author actually lived by, thus giving some of the descriptions of the landscape a genuine fondness.

Yet, stripped of its defense of being historically interesting, for many readers, as indicated by reviews on Goodreads, the book is a literary disaster on stilts. It seems it is exactly as Mark Twain put it in his famous essay "Fenimore Cooper's Literary Offenses": there are nineteen rules governing literary art in the domain of romantic fiction, and in *The Deerslayer* Cooper violated all but one of them. Unfortunately, Twain doesn't say specify the rule Cooper didn't break, and it's certainly not obvious.

If books like *The Deerslayer* appear on the surface, and indeed quite a long way down too, to be unsophisticated yarns built on an unconscious assumption of the white man's superiority, it is still true that Cooper was one of the first major American novelists to include African, African American, and Native American characters in his works. Perhaps that's the best thing about the so-called Leatherstocking, or frontiersman, tales of which *The Deerslayer* is the final installment.

However, not everyone appreciated the finer points. Cooper's older contemporary Mark Twain was no great fan of the stories. To be precise, he hated them. In a little essay directed at some professors who had the temerity to praise the author, entitled "Fenimore Cooper's Literary Offenses," Twain writes,

> Cooper's gift in the way of invention was not a rich endowment; but such as it was he liked to work it, he was pleased with the effects, and indeed he did some quite sweet things with it. In his little box of stage-properties he kept six or eight cunning devices, tricks, artifices for his savages and woodsmen to deceive and circumvent each other with, and he was never so happy as

when he was working these innocent things and seeing them go. A favorite one was to make a moccasined person tread in the tracks of a moccasined enemy, and thus hide his own trail. Cooper wore out barrels and barrels of moccasins in working that trick. Another stage-property that he pulled out of his box pretty frequently was the broken twig. He prized his broken twig above all the rest of his effects, and worked it the hardest. It is a restful chapter in any book of his when somebody doesn't step on a dry twig and alarm all the Reds and Whites for two hundred yards around. Every time a Cooper person is in peril, and absolute silence is worth four dollars a minute, he is sure to step on a dry twig. There may be a hundred other handier things to step on, but that wouldn't satisfy Cooper. Cooper requires him to turn out and find a dry twig; and if he can't do it, go and borrow one. In fact, the *Leatherstocking Series* ought to have been called the *Broken Twig Series*.

Twain also quotes, disparagingly, two examples of Deerslayer's mode of speech. In the first, talking as it were "normally," he has a strange dialect: "If I was Injin born, now, I might tell of this, or carry in the scalp and boast of the expl'ite afore the whole tribe; of if my inimy had only been a bear." But later, both his thoughts and his language are lifted to almost poetic heights by thoughts of his beloved. Then, as Twain notes, when someone asks Deerslayer if he has a sweetheart and if so, where she is now, this is the finely expressed response: "She's in the forest—hanging from the boughs of the trees, in a soft rain—in the dew on the open grass—the clouds that float about in the blue heavens—the birds that sing in the woods—the sweet springs where I slake my thirst—and in all the other glorious gifts that come from God's Providence!"

That's an example of literary inconsistency that could be said to nonetheless convey some emotional content. Not so with the many practical implausibilities that seem to enrage Twain in the way that some people are enraged by continuity errors in films. (I mean things like the scene in *Pulp Fiction* [1994] in which Jules and Vincent escape a hail of bullets fired at point-blank range, an implausible feat that is additionally marred when you look closely because there you can see bullet holes are already visible on the wall well before any shots have been fired.)

Yet even if Mark Twain hated the writing, another great writer, D. H. Lawrence, called *The Deerslayer* "one of the most beautiful and perfect books in the world: flawless as a jewel and of gem-like concentration." So back to Riis's favorite read; here's a passage describing how another character in the novel, Pathfinder, displays his awesome powers with a rifle, shooting not merely at a target but at a tiny nail placed on the target:

"Be all ready to clench it, boys!" cried out Pathfinder, stepping into his friend's tracks the instant they were vacant. "Never mind a new nail; I can see that, though the paint is gone, and what I can see I can hit at a hundred yards, though it were only a mosquito's eye. Be ready to clench!"

The rifle cracked, the bullet sped its way, and the head of the nail was buried in the wood, covered by the piece of flattened lead.

It is, to be sure, an unlikely kind of literary jewel, maybe more like a shiny trinket of a Boys' Own adventure.

But, well, you know, that too has its place sometimes, and certainly the book seems to have given Jacob Riis a thirst, a curiosity to travel to the Americas. And if it is not a logical or even a very literal connection that was made via these ripping yarns of Indian trackers and dead-shot settlers in the woods of the New World, it is still an important one.

A small defense can be mounted for literary stereotypes too, maybe. In ancient Greece, actors in plays wore masks painted with exaggerated expressions. The idea was that this enabled them to portray different roles without confusing the audience. In a similar way, crude stereotypes such as the "virtuous," beautiful girl and the suspicious man with a scar on his face can allow for the exploration of deeper ideas.

Thus, underneath the surface silliness of the Leatherstocking Tales can be discerned something more complex, a subtext that highlights the tenuous relationship between frontier settlers and American Indians. In *The Wept of Wish-ton-Wish*, for example, a captured white girl is taken care of by an Indian chief until, after several years, she is eventually returned to her parents—all of which, at least, hints at subtler notions of personal identity. Often, Cooper offers contrasting views of characters to emphasize the ancient message of the potential of individuals for good versus their tendency to produce mayhem. Thus, Cooper's most famous story, *Last of the Mohicans*, includes both the character of Magua, the Indian known as Cunning Fox, who is devoid of almost any redeeming qualities, as well as Chingachgook, the last chief of the Mohicans, who is portrayed as noble, courageous, and heroic.

Anyway, whatever Mark Twain may have thought, the French novelist Victor Hugo pronounced Cooper the greatest novelist of the century, meaning, of course, outside France. Another icon of French literature, Honoré de Balzac, while mocking a few of Cooper's novels as "rhapsodies" and expressing reservations about his portrayal of characters, enthusiastically called the first of the Leatherstocking series, *The Pathfinder*, a masterpiece and compared his portrayal of his portrait of nature to the work of the Scottish poet and playwright Sir Walter Scott, famous for his book *Ivanhoe*.

Praise for Cooper's depiction of women characters in his work is impossible to find though. Instead, as James Russell Lowell, a contemporary and a critic, wrote rhymingly:

The women he draws from one model don't vary.
All sappy as maples and flat as a prairie.

Notwithstanding any such literary weaknesses, Cooper was honored on a US commemorative stamp, the Famous American series, issued in 1940, and there is a gilded and red tole chandelier hanging in the library of the White House in Washington, DC, that is from the family of James Fenimore Cooper. It was brought there through the efforts of First Lady Jacqueline Kennedy in her great White House restoration. There is also a James Fenimore Cooper Memorial Prize at New York University that is awarded annually to an outstanding undergraduate student of journalism. And in 2013, Cooper was inducted into the New York Writers Hall of Fame. Mark Twain ain't there, but then he's not from New York.

Most effusive of all were the words of the renowned Russian literary critic Vissarion Belinsky, who even declared *The Pathfinder* to be "a Shakespearean drama in the form of a novel," a "triumph of modern art" in the form of "epic poetry." It seems that for Russians, the author's middle name, Fenimore, was exotic, and indeed it became a symbol of exciting adventures among that country's readers. For example, in the 1977 Soviet movie *The Secret of Fenimore*, a mysterious stranger known simply as Fenimore pays nightly visits to a boys' dorm in a summer camp and relates fascinating stories about Indians and extraterrestrials.

Perhaps Russians have a taste for action heroes. Oleg Konovalov, business guru, contemporary author, rated "#1 Global Thought Leader on Culture" by Thinkers 360 told me once that adventure stories read in his youth had an influence on his life well after his tastes changed

"For sure, Jack London and his *White Fang, The Sea Wolf, The Call of the Wild*, and others. I even reread some of Jack London's books again not long ago. What inspired me in Jack London—adventure, challenging own boundaries, being own self, focus on a goal whatever difficult it can be, and going for unexplored terrains."

Be that as it may, much as the young Jacob enjoyed Cooper's ripping yarns and was inspired by Dickens's morality-laden stories, and much as his father had hoped that he would head toward careers like his own involving writing, it turned out that all Jacob wanted to be was a carpenter. So he became an apprentice instead and promptly fell head over heels in love with Elisabeth, the (twelve-year-old!) daughter of the company owner, who did not approve of the apprentice's attentions. The result was that Jacob was obliged to finish learning his trade in Copenhagen. And then, at the end of his apprenticeship, unable to find a post, far less woo his beloved, Riis decided to travel to the New World and seek his future there instead.

The Australian writer and art critic Robert Hughes sums up the scene he would have found on arrival through the judicious use of statistics, saying, "In the 1880s, 334,000 people were crammed into a single square mile of the Lower East Side, making it the most densely populated place on earth. They were packed into filthy, disease-ridden tenements, 10 or 15 to a room, and the well-off knew nothing about them and cared less."

When Riis arrived in the United States in 1870, he was still just twenty-one years old and focused less on exploring the wilderness, let alone social do-gooding, and more on finding employment as a carpenter. He had arrived, after all, with just forty dollars donated by friends (having used up all his own savings to pay the fifty dollars for the passage), plus a gold locket with a strand of Elisabeth's hair given him by her mother and letters of introduction to Mr. Goodall, the Danish Consul. Actually, this letter, the result of his family's involvement in Goodall's rescue from a shipwreck at Ribe, gave Riis considerable advantages over the large number of migrants and immigrants seeking prosperity in a more industrialized environment in a society still recovering from the American Civil War.

The first thing Riis did with his meager resources was to spend twenty dollars, fully half of it, on a gun. It was doubtless a tribute to his literary tastes that he considered this an essential precaution, as he imagined, to ward off wild animals and human predators alike. Fortunately, an immigrant with a practical trade can usually find work, and within a week Riis had a new post as a carpenter at Brady's Bend Iron Works on the Allegheny River above Pittsburgh. However, barely had he started there than he was distracted by the news from Europe that France had declared war on Germany, news which to a Dane dangled an opportunity to join up and help avenge the Prussian seizure of Schleswig.

Indeed, Riis's enthusiasm for this warlike project led him to pawn all his possessions and attempt to enlist at the French consulate in New York, but there he was firmly told that there was no plan to send a volunteer army from the United States, and so instead he was left to try to walk home, which he did until he collapsed from exhaustion. He woke up at Fordham College with a Catholic priest serving him breakfast.

After a brief period working on a farm and performing other odd jobs, Riis found himself destitute, sleeping on a tombstone, and surviving on windfall apples. His only project remained joining in the war in Europe, so he set out again for New York. Again, he was unable to enlist and again he ended up living on scavenged food and handouts while sleeping on the streets or in a foul-smelling police lodging-house with only a stray dog for a companion. At last, one morning in a lodging-house, he awoke to find that his gold locket, with its more than precious strand of Elisabeth's hair, had been stolen. This was truly his lowest point.

Perhaps the experience triggered a new resolve. In any case, Riis now left New York and eventually reached Philadelphia, where he received vital help from the Danish Consul and his wife that letter proving the power of words again! They looked after him for two weeks, bought him a new suit, and put him in touch with an old friend who offered him a job—as a carpenter.

Set up thus, Riis was soon in much demand for his woodworking, but more for the low rates he charged than for any particular skills. Nonetheless, this success enabled him at last to return to the Big Apple, where he was able for the first time to find work as a journalist, ending up as a trainee at the New York News Association. It was this job that at last brought Riis back to his investigations of the lives of both the rich and successful and the struggling and impoverished immigrant communities. In due course, he become editor of one of the group's newspapers, the weekly *News*, and when the company struggled financially he even managed (partly with seventy-five dollars of his savings but mostly with promissory notes) to buy the *News* company itself.

Now fully independent, he was able to investigate and report freely on the politicians who had previously been his employers. And there was wonderful news from Denmark too: his childhood love, Elisabeth, had written to ask him to come to Denmark for her, saying, "We will strive together for all that is noble and good." Conveniently, the politicians offered to buy back the newspaper for five times the price Riis had paid; he was thus able to travel to Denmark, marry Elisabeth, and return to the United States to take up a series of positions on newspapers, including crucially one as police reporter for the *New-York Tribune*.

He was based in a press office across from police headquarters on Mulberry Street, nicknamed by the locals "Death's Thoroughfare." As Riis's biographer Alexander Alland writes, "It was here, where the street crooks its elbow at the Five Points, that the streets and numerous alleys radiated in all directions, forming the foul core of the New York slums."

And so it was as a reporter working alongside police officers that Riis really came to know the slums of the city. It was these experiences in the poorhouses, there as a neutral, careful witness, that led him to a new role as a pioneer of socially aware and committed reporting, always characterized by a precise and factual style that reflected the precision of the police he was working alongside and reporting on.

At the same time, Riis was aware of an element missing in these dry, clinical accounts and strove to find ways to make the reality of the slums more real to his readers. He tried sketching but soon found he had no talent for it. Photography was impractical as the cameras of the day relied on large photographic plates coated in emulsion that took many minutes to record an image—and that was under bright lights. In those days, the ability to snap moments from real life and in real conditions was limited to landscape photography. And then, in 1887, Riis read of a new way to take pictures using sharp flashes of light.

This was a German innovation called "flash powder," and it involved igniting a mixture of magnesium and potassium chlorate (with a dash of antimony sulfide for added stability) and firing a kind of pistol device fitted with cartridges.

Soon, equipped with this new weapon of truth, Riis and three friends, including Dr. John Nagle, chief of the Bureau of Vital Statistics in the City Health Department (who was also a keen amateur photographer), returned to photograph the slums. Their story, featuring pictures of Gotham's crime and misery "by night and day," was published in the *New York Sun* on February 12, 1888, under the tagline "The Other Half: How It Lives and Dies in New York." It caused a sensation.

What was actually printed in the newspaper, though, was not yet actual photographs but line drawings based on them. Riis's second innovation was to enthusiastically adopt new ways to screen black-and-white images into dots suitable for printing. He also adapted the flash technique so that it utilized not a pistol, which both looked dangerous and also *was* dangerous, but a kind of large frying pan.

Flash photography enabled him not only to work at night but also to photograph the dark streets, dingy tenements, and "stale-beer" dives by day and the faces of the people living and dying there.

This is when that all-important, eighteen-page article by Riis, "How the Other Half Lives," appeared in the Christmas edition of *Scribner's Magazine*, along with those nineteen photographs, still rendered as line drawings. The article attracted so much interest that Riis was invited to expand the material into an entire book. *How the Other Half Lives*, subtitled *Studies among the Tenements of New York*, was published a year later, in 1890, reusing the line drawings that had appeared in the *Scribner's* article but also including for the first time seventeen screened photographs. In fact, this was one of the first, maybe *the* first, extensive use of halftone photographic reproductions in a book.

How the Other Half Lives sold well and was favorably reviewed, although some critics accused Riis of oversimplifying and exaggerating. A sequel, called *Children of the Poor* (1892), describing the lives of children that he had encountered in the slums, also sold well. This starts, "The problem of our children is the problem of the State. As we mould the children of the toiling masses in our cities, so we shape the destiny of the State which they will rule in their turn, taking the reins from our hands."

Riis then, characteristically, offers some statistics—précised to two significant figures too!—noting that whereas at the beginning of the century the urban population of the United States was "3.97% of the whole" or "not quite one in twenty-five," that it had now become "29.12%" or "nearly one in three."

It is fortunate, then, that Riis mixes statistics with a more poetic flair with words, and so he also speaks of the slums "as a dumping ground" by which New York seeks to rid itself of helplessness and incapacity, leaving the procession of the strong and the able free to move on. "This sediment forms the body of our poor, the contingent that lives, always from hand to mouth, with no provision and no means of providing for the morrow." The slum, he says, "is the measure of civilization."

"In self-defence, you know, all life eventually accommodates itself to its environment, and human life is no exception."

A particularly important effort by Riis was his exposure of the condition of New York's water supply. His five-column story "Some Things We Drink," in the August 21, 1891, edition of the *New York Evening Sun*, included six photographs (later lost). Riis wrote, "I took my camera and went up in the watershed photographing my evidence wherever I found it. Populous towns sewered directly into our drinking water. I went to the doctors and asked how many days a vigorous cholera bacillus may live and multiply in running water. About seven, said they. My case was made."

And all the time, at the heart of Riis's writings are his early experiences in Ribe, which gave him a yardstick with which to measure tenement dwellers' quality of life. His own experiences as a poor immigrant lent authenticity to his news articles and larger works, whereas his themes of self-sufficiency, perseverance, and material success are archetypes that many other Europeans also used in describing the exceptional opportunities that seemed to exist in the United States.

Riis emphatically supported the spread of wealth to lower classes through improved social programs and philanthropy, but several chapters of *How the Other Half Lives*, open with his observations of the economic and social situations of different ethnic and racial groups via indictments of their perceived natural flaws—often prejudices that may well have been fueled by prevailing theories claiming scientific evidence for hierarchies of the races. Or maybe from reading too much Fenimore Cooper.

Recent critics like Professor Maren Stange have complained that Riis "recoiled from workers and working class culture" and appealed instead to the anxieties and fears of his middle-class audience. One contemporary economist, Thomas Sowell, even claims that the plight of many immigrants during Riis's time was not quite what it seemed but rather that the migrants were often choosing to live in unpleasant circumstances as a deliberate short-term strategy that allowed them to save more of their earnings both to help other family members come to the United States and in preparation for onward migration of the whole "clan" to more comfortable lodgings later.

Such slum dwellers, Sowell argues, were extremely unwilling to relocate to better housing as advocated by reformers like Riis, because other lodgings were too costly to allow for the high rate of savings possible in the tenements. Indeed, as Sowell points out, Riis's own personal experience had been to live in the tenements only temporarily before earning enough money to relocate to different lodgings. But such criticism is perhaps overdone. Riis, after all, is also criticized for suggesting that African and West Indian immigrants were happy with their lives in the "slums" of New York City, with accounts and images of them celebrating carnivals, for example.

That said, Riis tried hard to have part of the slums around Five Points in Lower Manhattan demolished and replaced with a park. His writings resulted in the Drexel Committee investigation of unsafe tenements and the Small Park Act of 1887. Riis was not invited to the eventual opening of the park on June 15, 1897, but went all the same, together with another journalist with a reputation as a "muckraker," Lincoln Steffens. In the last speech, the street cleaning commissioner credited Riis for the park and led the public in giving him three cheers of "Hooray, Jacob Riis!" When other parks were created, Riis was often popularly credited with them as well.

But let's fast-forward now to the twenty-first century and the parallel tale of Mike Duffy. On the surface, the two reformers' lives are worlds apart, but the founding CEO of CityBase, a database company based in Chicago with offices in San Francisco, does share one crucial thing with Riis which is an inspirational debt to a book.

Now, databases can sound like boring things, and, in fact, they can actually be rather boring things, but these days our lives revolve around them. We all use Google, which is one huge database, and when we go to the shop, the things we buy are there courtesy of another database. In fact, today, according to Duffy's company's website, more than a hundred government agencies and utility service providers across the United States use CityBase to handle payments and provide access to digital services. But what really links Mike Duffy across the centuries to Jacob Riis is a shared focus on people on the margins of society. As Duffy puts it, he wants his company to serve people who are unbanked and must pay a bill in cash just as well as those who want to complete a transaction using their credit cards and smartphones. Duffy says he brought to the design of CityBase lessons from over a decade working in capital markets, including as a Federal Reserve analyst at Northern Trust, and academic studies at the University of Chicago Booth School of Business, but there's also a deeper level of awareness of the problems of the socially excluded that comes, it seems, from reading Orwell's classic tale of life when you are "down and out" in the two great European capitals.

Orwell is one of my own favorite writers, who inspired me in a broad sense. For me, though, it was not so much the sociological aspects of his writing as the sheer elegance of his craft. But anyway, *Down and Out in Paris and London* was Orwell's first book, published in January 1933 by Victor Gollancz, who was a founder of Left Book Club Committee, and always had a political (and progressive) purpose.

DOWN AND OUT IN PARIS AND LONDON
AUTHOR: GEORGE ORWELL
PUBLISHED: 1933

This is actually Orwell's first book-length work, a personal memoir on the theme of poverty in the two cities. The first part of the book is an account of being a casual worker in restaurant kitchens in Paris, while the second part is a kind of travelogue describing London from a tramp's perspective, which majors on the hostel accommodation available and the often rather unsavory characters to be encountered within them. A curious historical detail of the book is that an early version was rejected by no less a literary figure than T. S. Eliot, then an editor for Faber and Faber. The manuscript was eventually published by Gollancz and favorably reviewed by literary icons including C. Day Lewis and J. B. Priestly. The former summed up the book as "a tour of the underworld, conducted without hysteria or prejudice," and the latter called it "an excellent book and a valuable social document."

Some readers, notably those in the restaurant trade, disputed his lurid picture. However, in his later, and I think rather better, book *The Road to Wigan Pier*, Orwell referred to the tramping experiences described in *Down and Out*, writing that "nearly all the incidents described there actually happened, though they have been re-arranged."

Orwell, whose real name, by the way, was Eric Blair, was actually born into quite privileged circles and went to some of the poshest British schools. It was only later, as a struggling writer in Paris, that Orwell discovered poverty in all its dimensions. He encountered it in the hotels, hospitals, and parks of the mean and degenerate Paris. In the book he describes how at one point he has to pawn all his clothes to save himself from starvation. He records the cruel behavior of a clerk at the counter of a pawnshop, where there is a long queue of people standing for the purpose:

> It was the first time that I had been in a French pawnshop. One went through grandiose stone portals (marked, of course, *"Liberté, Egatité, Fraternité"* they write that even over the police stations in France) into a large, bare room like a school classroom, with a counter and rows of benches. Forty or fifty people were waiting. One handed one's pledge over the counter and sat down. Presently, when the clerk had assessed its value he would call out, "Numéro such and such, will you take fifty francs?" Sometimes it was only fifteen francs, or ten, or five—whatever it was, the whole room knew it. As I came in the clerk called with an air of offence, "Numéro 83—here!" and gave a little whistle and a beckon, as though calling a dog.

Later, returning to London, Orwell lived in some of the cheap rented room of London but reported that they were better furnished than the lodgings of Paris. He also now realized that there was more going on in tramp behavior than met the eye: that they moved from one place to another in groups and stayed in "spikes," which were abnormally dirty and provided the worst kind of food. He reports of a bathroom in such a spike: "The scene in the bathroom was extraordinarily repulsive. Fifty dirty, stark-naked men elbowing each other in a room twenty feet square, with only two bathtubs and two slimy roller towels between them all. Bad food, dirty lodgings, have turned tramps almost into animals. It is most humiliating to watch when they are gathered up like cattle in a small passage in the spikes."

Orwell is shocked to see the animal-like looks of tramps in such a civilized place as London: "You can not conceive what ruinous degenerate curs we looked, standing there in the merciless morning light." And he adds, "A tramp's clothes are bad, but they conceal worse things, to see him as he really is, unmitigated, you must see him naked. Flat feet, pot bellies, hollow chests, sagging muscles—every kind of physical rottenness was there."

Orwell never loses sight of our common shared humanity. He writes, "They are worthy people capable of something but due to a lack of opportunity they have become mentally and physically wrecked."

Once, Orwell was among a hundred tramps who were given free tea and six slices of bread and margarine but in return had to sit for mass; the tramps behaved shamelessly, chatting, laughing, smoking, calling out, and "frankly bullying" the few elder women of the congregation to such an extent that Orwell commented, "It was our revenge upon them for having humiliated us by feeding us. A man receiving charity practically hates his benefactor—it is a fixed characteristic of human nature."

Orwell described in detail how hotels in Paris functioned, the hierarchy of employees, how each caste in the hierarchy tried to express pride in their job, and how the more expensive the dish the more frequent the cooks and waiters dipped their greasy and sweaty fingers in it so that there was a counterintuitive link between how expensive and fashionable the food was and how hygienic.

Orwell ends his manuscript with what he learned from these months living as a down-and-out tramp in London and Paris:

> I shall never again think that all tramps are drunken scoundrels (since they can't purchase drinks), nor expect a beggar to be grateful when I give him a penny, nor be surprised if men out of work lack energy (living on just tea and two slices of bread and margarine), nor subscribe to the Salvation Army (since they treat the hosted tramps as prisoners), nor pawn my clothes, nor refuse a handbill (so that the distributor of handbill can finish his job early), nor enjoy a meal at a smart restaurant. That is a beginning.

Here, in a nutshell, is the insight and philosophy that could inspire Mike Duffy. And though Orwell was writing well after Jacob Riis, it is surely one that he too would share. But for Duffy we don't need to speculate as, in fact, he specifically cites George Orwell as a key influence in that interview for Inc.com in 2017, saying,

> I was first exposed to George Orwell's writing through his famous works *Animal Farm* and *1984*. I was entertained by his wit (the "civility" of the Spanish Civil War) and absorbed by his commentaries weaving politics, economics, and sociology.

Duffy then goes on to make that evocative comparison of the "extravagance" of the 1920s and the twilight of the Great Depression that followed it as well as selecting that line about how absolute poverty can, in a way, make you less worried about money, "for three francs will feed you till tomorrow, and you cannot think further than that."

In these ways, Orwell's book provided for Duffy a new way, a new perspective on social relationships, just as the Leatherstocking Tales, superficially trivial or not, led Jacob Riis to develop not only a fascination with the characters of the slums and "forgotten corners" of New York but also a deeper understanding and empathy.

6

✝

Be Ready to Reinvent Yourself

Henry Ford and Jimmy Carter

D o successful people start out with a grand, sweeping life plan or do they just keep reinventing themselves—rebuilding themselves brick by brick, remaking themselves piece by piece, until they become great? Two American icons, one a titan of business, the other a former president, shed a little light on this question. Although they are in many ways opposites, they do share some things, among them a remarkable ability to harness the lessons of experience, a belief in human souls—and a debt to an inspirational book.

Take the extraordinary case of Henry Ford, perhaps the most iconic business success story as well as one of the very few people who can genuinely be said to have shaped the modern world. What's his special insight? "If you always do what you've always done, you'll always get what you've always got," he says. Nothing very mystical about that. And yet behind this brisk statement lurks a much longer and stranger tale. If most of us think of Ford putting workers on a production line to make his famous Model T cars, what lay behind that practical, manufacturing approach is less appreciated and is nothing less than a full-blown philosophical theory about life as a series of experiences. Because Ford, it turns out, was deeply influenced by a book written at the start of the twentieth century by a guru named Orlando Smith who believed in reincarnation. This throws a different light on another of Ford's favorite aphorisms: "It's what you do, not who you are."

Certainly, Henry Ford's life symbolizes this homely advice. He was born on a farm in Greenfield Township, Michigan. His parents, far from being wealthy and well connected, were poor immigrants. His father was an English settler who had come to the United States from Ireland; his mother was an orphan who had been brought up in Belgium. The only notable privilege in Henry's early life was his father's gift of a pocket watch that Henry, fascinated, took apart with tools—tools he made himself out of scraps of metal. At age nineteen, he was still living a very ordinary life on the family farm (not at university studying engineering, let alone business management), where he was in charge of a farm's Westinghouse portable steam engine used to run the sawmill. After all, he suffered from chronic dyslexia—or word blindness.

Yet two decades later, by 1903, Ford had reinvented himself and was about to leap into the future as chief engineer in his own Ford Motor Company—with $28,000 of capital to play with. To me, that sounds quite a tidy sum already, but actually at today's prices it was a whole lot more, one hundred times more—call it $3 million! In fact, just the most superficial change for this farmer's son was becoming a multimillionaire and amassing one of the greatest fortunes in the world. Much more importantly, and in just five years, the first Model T automobile would roll out from the new factory, while in another ten (that is, by 1918) half of all cars in the United States would be Ford's Model Ts. In the following decade, just over fifteen million cars would be produced and sold. All this, incidentally, without Ford ever allowing any accountants to audit his company.

No wonder that many people started to ask, "How did he do this? What's the secret ingredient?" As to that last, at least in newspaper interviews, Ford liked to explain things this way: "Enthusiasm is the yeast that makes your hopes shine to the stars. Enthusiasm is the sparkle in your eyes, the swing in your gait. The grip of your hand, the irresistible surge of will and energy to execute your ideas."

Enthusiasm. Yes, indeed, that was part of the story. But the business graveyard is full of schemes started with great enthusiasm (and no accountants). So was his success perhaps rather due to a particular insight into how the world works? Even perhaps to do with a very philosophical investigation of the nature of identity? By that, I mean an exploration of what makes someone (or something) into what it is?

Henry Ford is conventionally pigeonholed as a loyal disciple of the great Scottish philosopher Adam Smith, whose book *Wealth of Nations*, published in the year of American Independence, became one of the best-selling books of all time.

One of the key passages in Adam Smith's book concerns the advantages of production-line technology. Smith illustrates this with an extended example of a pin factory. A single man, setting out to make a pin from scratch, might spend a year making a single pin, Smith wrote in an early draft. He would have to find the ore, dig it up, refine the metal, forge it, split it into small rods, draw a rod into wire, and, finally, draw the wire into a pin. In a modern factory, Smith noted, ten men or more were involved in specialized operations. Thanks to their dexterity, the saving of time between operations, and the invention of specialized pin-making machinery, they could make twelve pounds of pins a day—around forty-eight thousand in all.

However, the link between Ford and Adam Smith, although pleasing to historians, is overplayed. Techniques of mass production, as based on the principles of specialization and division of labor first described in *Wealth of Nations*, had been employed in places like Eli Whitney's gun factory in the United States since the 1790s. Indeed, as the contemporary business analyst David Warsh says, Henry Ford didn't even need to actually invent much of the technology for his famous assembly line. Magpie-like, he borrowed the concepts of sheet-metal stamping and electric welding from the producers of bicycles and sewing machines; he took the idea of continuous-process manufacture from cigarette makers and distillers, refiners, and meat packers. At the same time, this "borrowing" and repurposing fitted very well another and much grander theory that seems to have captured Ford's imagination. This was one rooted in the idea of reincarnation and the existence of an eternal mind continually acquiring ideas and "experiences."

Most accounts of Ford's life don't imagine so. Quite the reverse. If you ask a social scientist or economist just what it was that made Henry Ford such a success, they will tell you it was the way he standardized car making with that famous assembly line that churned out Model Ts. Certainly, this was an innovation back in Ford's day, because at the time the strategy for manufacturing cars was more like the one for making expensive suits or maybe sophisticated furniture. The cost of producing a car meant that it was a rich man's game, and rich people don't want to own the same things as everyone else. All the car companies accepted that. Luxury shops were not places stuffed with goods waiting for buyers. They were workplaces for craftsmen waiting to fulfill orders.

But that was not Ford's vision. After initially experimenting with multiple varieties of cars with different configurations (each given a letter, such as Model A, Model F, etc.), Ford hit on the idea of combining the best to produce a car that would be so good that it would please everyone. He called this the "universal car," and it would become the Model T. Then he went further—saying that it would be the only car the Ford Motor Company would produce. The newspapers thought this was crazy and predicted he would be out of business in months.

Of course, they were wrong. But Ford wasn't swayed by their predictions anyway, because he was guided by intuitions about identity. He hinted at this in an interview with *Forbes* magazine: "We didn't start from Model T and attempt to improve that. We started from scratch. We brushed aside all preconceptions and simply asked ourselves the question: What is a car for? And what does a car have to have in order to fulfill its purpose? There were a thousand things, of course, which it had to have, and as we came to each one we asked: How can this part be made in fulfill its purpose better than it has ever been fulfilled before?" Note that phrase "What is a car for?" It is a philosophical question, even an existentialist question.

Ford, without any doubt, reinvented the motor car. In his engineering, he started from first principles and built on them confidently. The practical results for the "universal car," as Richard Bak put it in his book *Henry and Edsel: The Creation of the Ford Empire* (2003), were that "it had the steering wheel on the left, which every other company soon copied . . . The car was very simple to drive, and easy and cheap to repair. It was so cheap at $825 in 1908 ($22,470 today) that by the 1920s, a majority of American drivers had learned to drive on the Model T."

However, Ford wasn't satisfied just to reinvent the American car—he wanted to redesign the American people too. In part he did this by offering workers on the newfangled car assembly line the then unheard-of high wage of five dollars a day—at least double the going rate. He told everyone that he believed that the people making his automobiles should be able to afford to buy them, and indeed, it was estimated that the average worker at Ford Motor Company would only need four months' pay to afford one. "In underpaying men," Ford said, "we are preparing a generation of underfed children who will be physically and morally undernourished; we will have a generation of workers weak in body and spirit who, for this reason, will be inefficient when they come into industry. It is industry which will pay the bill."

Naturally, the transformation of the American worker required more than just financial carrots. And so, his much-trumpeted five-dollar rate was in reality about half pay and half bonus. The bonus came with character requirements that were enforced by something called, rather ominously, the Socialization Organization. This was a committee that was empowered to visit the employees' homes to ensure that they were doing things the American way! Committee members would check that workers were properly married, devoutly religious, maintained neat houses, kept away from alcohol, didn't gamble, and so on.

This was because there was a puritan aspect to Ford's philanthropy, and he made sure that the premium wage was only given to those who met strict standards. Among other things, the workers had to speak English, recent immigrants had to attend classes to become "Americanized," and, of course, they had to eschew social ills such as gambling and drinking. As for women, well, originally the Ford Motor Company would not even hire married women, and any single women who later on married were summarily dismissed. A ruthless streak was a key ingredient of Ford's success, along with the more presentable qualities of the willingness to "think different" and that dose of enthusiasm.

In short, Ford's wage policy was part of a drive for a new, controlled style of working-class life in which there would be increased consumption of consumer goodies and things like cars, but only of the "right" kind. Now he had reinvented himself again—as a kind of benevolent dictator. Aldous Huxley had very good reason to invoke Ford's name as the patron of the dictatorship in his classic tale *Brave New World*, written in 1931.

In Huxley's dystopia, or nightmare society, Ford's project of mass production made the vision of a "World State" possible. That sort of society could never function with craftsmen working on individual projects. Instead, with mass production, everything was streamlined and made on an assembly line. Even humans were to be mass-produced and decanted, with the citizens all created via genetic engineering and "hatched" to fill predetermined roles.

In his book, Huxley makes Ford into the symbol of a soulless community. Ford is a demigod and held up as a pillar of society in the World State. Time is no longer referred to as "the year of our Lord" but as "the year of our Ford," and history only starts in 1908—the year the first Model T rolled off the production line. On street corners the Christian cross has its top lopped off and is turned into a "T"—to remind the reader of Ford's automobile. Significantly, in *Brave New World*, Ford is revered not merely as the man who invented a faster process for building an automobile; the citizens worship him for the way that he changes or "transforms" them. This was no mere literary conceit; it was very much Ford's real-world plan too. Yet if Huxley's book presents a nightmarish society, transforming people is not a bad aim in itself. It all depends on how it is done, by whom, and of course for what reasons.

Whatever Huxley may have thought of him, Ford did have a big vision and plenty of ideas—philosophical ideas obtained via books. However, if historians have focused on the writings of the dour Scottish economist Adam Smith as an influence, it is another Smith altogether, one Orlando Jay Smith, that is really the unexpected source from which Ford drew his inspiration.

A SHORT VIEW OF GREAT QUESTIONS
AUTHOR: ORLANDO J. SMITH
PUBLISHED: 1899

Smith starts by stating, very methodically, that there are but three theories of "man's origin and destiny," and they can be expressed in a few words. First, there is materialism—the idea "that man's life begins with the birth and ends with the death of his body"; second, there is theology—"that man is created at his birth with an immortal soul which survives the death of his body"; and third and most importantly, he thinks, the "theory of Reincarnation, sometimes called Metempsychosis, or the Transmigration of Souls—that man has an immortal soul which existed before his birth and survives the death of his body." Most of the book is devoted to demonstrating the truth of the third hypothesis.

As to the obvious question—Why do we have so little recollection of our past lives?—Orlando Smith simply assumes that, well, it would be impractical for us to remember too many things. Nonetheless, he notes, some great figures, like Sir Walter Scott, have recorded strange moments when they did seem to have a feeling of preexistence, that famous sense of déjà vu. More generally, Orlando thinks that we recall little because the human spirit really lives in another world (a much nicer one than the earthly one, of course). He says enthusiastically of it:

> The Other world is a place of peace and order, while the earth, in the economy of Nature, is as a state of war, a hard school, a place in which conditions are adverse, harsh and rigorous, in which oppression may thrive, and greed fatten, and hypocrisy pass as holiness, and lies as truth in which the noble may be obscured and the vulgar exalted—all for a little time. After the death of the physical body, each soul returns to its real part in the land of Truth. In the Other-world, the more spiritual and noble are at peace and rest. They have returned home, as it were, after a weary pilgrimage in alien lands. In this home they may rest for a very long period, and the higher souls perhaps eternally.

The most significant thing, ultimately, about the book was the influence it would have on Henry Ford and perhaps some of his contemporaries, several of whom formed a small club of supposedly like-minded souls called The Vagabonds. The members were Thomas Edison, Harvey Firestone, Warren G. Harding, John Burroughs, and Ford himself, and their motto was that "great minds come together and true companionship is a treasure for life." Almost every year, they embarked together on lengthy camping trips, involving impromptu tree chopping and climbing contests that inspired them later (they said) to novel ideas, which they shared while sitting around the campfire.

Smith's book is called *A Short View of Great Questions*, and it was published in the last year of the nineteenth century—that is, just as Ford was looking for and exploring ideas. It was in its heyday a best seller and quite a talking point. Indeed, Orlando Smith was himself, at the time, a big cheese: a journalist who founded the American Press Association in Chicago and a philosophical authority on science and religion credited with developing a belief system called Eternalism. Ford states plainly that the book had a profound influence on him and "changed his outlook" on life. In a 1928 interview with the *San Francisco Examiner*, he told the newspaper reporter that he had adopted the theory of reincarnation from Smith's book when he was twenty-six, adding, "When I discovered reincarnation it was as if I had found a universal plan. I realized that there was a chance to work out my ideas. Time was no longer limited." What Ford means is that he realized that he had many future lives to continue developing his dream. That begins to seem a bit cranky, but wait! There's more. In another 1928 interview, this time with the *Detroit Times*' German American journalist George Sylvester Viereck (whose links to the Nazis led to him later being imprisoned in the United States), Ford even says that he owed any strokes of brilliance to a "Master Mind." Adding, "Somewhere is a Master Mind sending brain wave messages to us. There is a Great Spirit. I never did anything by my own volition. I was pushed by invisible forces within and without me."

In fact, far from being the soulless technocrat of so many economics texts, Ford was a kind of guru, and if his cult was not quite as bad as that depicted by Huxley, certainly there was something strange lurking not far below the surface. Charles M. Wood, associate editor of *Forbes* magazine, put it this way: "Mr. Ford not only believes, but he acts constantly upon who belief, that the Engineer of the Universe has placed each of the two billion or so human beings on this planet on the job of learning by experience the particular things each most needs to learn."

This view can be traced back to *A Short View of Great Questions*, where Orlando argues, by way of a vaguely scientific account of caterpillars becoming butterflies, for what we would now consider a kind of Buddhist notion of the transmigration of souls, although he is at pains to claim it fits with "all religions" and scientific thinking too. Plus, of course, Orlando insists his new philosophy is "good for man" as "it affords a powerful stimulus to the practice of morality, and to the study of the exact definitions of right and wrong in the affairs of individuals, of society, of the state, and between nations. It would ameliorate poverty, abolish caste and privilege, substitute peace for war, benevolence for conquest, and freedom for oppression."

That's not bad for one philosophy! And, he adds, in terms Ford would have instantly appreciated, "It strengthens and reinforces the noble doctrine of moral responsibility."

Orlando's book was, as I say, briefly very fashionable, but then it disappeared. Apart, that is, for its lingering influence on Ford. For him the theory of reincarnation was a perfect conceptual fit with his notions of mass production as it implied people themselves were a kind of robot into which reborn minds were fitted by the Great Engineer. Again and again, Ford insists that life is about gaining experience, and for him the factory workers were not repeating monotonous routines but rather being taught vital new skills as they changed from being agricultural laborers into assembly line workers.

It is revealing that Ford always vigorously rejected the claim that his assembly line was boring. This kind of criticism made him angry, as one interviewer inadvertently discovered. Talking to the magazine *The Literary Digest* in 1928, Ford denies with heat that his workers are "robots," saying that on the contrary, work on the assembly line is very skilled and provides for much new learning. "For what purpose do you suppose you are living on earth?" he demanded of his interviewer at one point. "Do you know what you are here for?" And then he answered his own question: "I'll tell you what every living person is here for, and that is to get experience. That's all we can get out of life" (*The Literary Digest*, January 7, 1928, "Henry Ford on His Plans and His Philosophy").

Similarly, in that 1928 interview with the *San Francisco Examiner*, Ford expands on a more ambitious theory by which the skills of many individuals become fused together into a more powerful, more intelligent production line. Human intelligence is still essential, but it has now left the individual's body to become something eternal! He goes on:

> I adopted the theory of Reincarnation when I was 26. Religion offered nothing to the point. Even work could not give me complete satisfaction. Work is futile if we cannot utilize the experience we collect in one life in the next. When I discovered Reincarnation it was as if I had found a universal plan: I realized that there was a chance to work out my ideas. Time was no longer limited. I was no longer a slave to the hands of the clock. Genius is experience. Some seem to think that it is a gift or talent, but it is the fruit of long experience in many lives. Some are older souls than others, and so they know more. The discovery of Reincarnation put my mind at ease. If you preserve a record of this conversation, write it so that it puts men's minds at ease. I would like to communicate to others the calmness that the long view of life gives to us.

Ford's comment about "no longer being a slave to the clock" might sound a rather duff note when we think of his practical legacy in terms of workers on assembly lines, of course. But the clock Ford has in mind is not a human one at all. Rather, it is the clock of human lifetimes.

Ford, then, was far from being just an engineer with rigid political views. He had another side that was highly spiritual, if not exactly moral—and this side of him was nourished and fed by Orlando Smith's book. Jimmy Carter, on the other hand, is usually considered a moralist and an idealist and maybe not so much a practical man. He is someone who seems in his own lifetime to have actually gone through several incarnations. This indeed has made him in the past, and in many ways still today, a confounding figure to understand. Just how did a "peanut farmer" rise to the US presidency anyway?

Writing in *Jimmy Carter, American Moralist*, his biographer, Kenneth Morris, reveals quite a bit about Carter from an examination of his upbringing in Plains, Georgia. And, first of all, he says people should know that Carter actually grew up in an even smaller town near Plains, called Archery. His father, James Earl Carter (called Earl by everyone), was not only a prosperous farmer but also a businessman who served in the Georgia legislature.

Morris doesn't offer many stories about the young Jimmy Carter, although elsewhere the man himself shares one that reflects that he was always a keen reader. He reveals that when he was twelve years old, he had a school principal called Miss Julia Coleman, who urged him (he says "forced him"!) to read the classics. And in some quantity. Carter recalls that she would give him a silver star when he had read five and a gold star when he read ten! That's books, not pages.

Anyway, one day Miss Coleman called him into her study and said, "Jimmy, I think it's time for you to read *War and Peace*." This is a heavyweight tome by a Russian intellectual about Napoleon's entry into Russia in the early years of the nineteenth century and is about 1,500 pages long. It's considered a timeless classic and, among many other things, is credited with inspiring Nelson Mandela while he was incarcerated in a South African prison cell. However, Carter didn't know any of that. Rather, he was, he says, "relieved" because he thought it might be a book about cowboys and Indians.

He dutifully went to the library, checked the book out, and found it was written by Tolstoy and was really "history." But it was also, Carter soon realized, a story about people—about, for example, Napoleon's conviction that since he had never been defeated, he was bound to win this war too and his underestimation of the severity of the Russian winter and the peasants' love for their land, with the result that, the next spring, he retreated in defeat. The point being, and this is where we see Carter genuinely making his own interpretation and drawing ideas, that "even the greatest historical events are controlled by the combined wisdom and courage and commitment and discernment and unselfishness and compassion and love and idealism of the common ordinary people."

Indeed, Tolstoy himself points out (in the epilogue) that he didn't focus in the book on Napoleon, the czar of Russia, or even the generals, but rather he wrote about the students, housewives, barbers, farmers, and privates in the army.

Carter's suggestion is that if it was true that history was really decided by ordinary people in the case of Russia where they had a czar and in France where they had an emperor, "how much more true is it in our own case where the Constitution charges us with a direct responsibility to determine what our government is and ought to be?"

It's a story that you could easily read psychological aspects into in terms of the Carter family, where Jimmy was at odds with his father because Earl was a strong supporter of Herman Talmadge, a Georgia governor and ardent segregationist. Earl was, like many Southerners of his era, a supporter of such segregation, although apparently he was personally kind to African Americans and was a good landlord to those who rented from him. However, he was not at all of the mind that they should share any sort of economic or political equality with whites. Jimmy, though, was sure that this was wrong. The result was, according to his biographer, that soon there was a son who didn't much like his father, even if he nonetheless wanted nothing more than his father's approval. The only solution for Jimmy was to leave Plains in 1943 and go to the US Naval Academy. In so doing he hoped to get away from the influence of a man whom he felt he could never satisfy and instead start out on a new phase of his life.

Morris spoke to many of the sailors that Carter served with, and none of them had any stories to tell about him except to say that he was a loner who almost always kept to himself, even on a submarine. And then in 1953, Earl Carter died of cancer. His eldest son immediately resigned his naval commission and headed back to Plains (that was where the family business was located) and, essentially, became his father, taking charge of the family business and reinventing himself as a peanut farmer. This reinvention was only successful up to a point because, as Carter says himself, his younger brother Billy was actually the better businessman. So in 1962, Carter decided to change role again and try for government office, this time as a senator for Georgia.

Initially he was far from successful and actually lost his first election for the state Senate seat. Fortunately, however, the results were thrown out because of voter fraud, and Carter soon found his feet, emphasizing education in his new role. People remarked how during his four years in the state Senate, Carter attempted to read every page of every bill he voted on. This, he said, was to show that he was not a machine politician who could be swayed by his lobbyists' suggestions. Carter apparently did keep to this promise, which likely required him to stay up pretty late some nights at the end of each legislative session. But then, we remember, this is a man who read classic books by the dozens while still at school.

By 1966, Carter was considering running for a House seat. He might well have managed it too except that, at the last minute, he decided to run for governor instead. This prize, however, he didn't win, and what's more, or rather less, he ended up splitting the Democratic primary vote in such a way that Lester Maddox, a segregationist who had a policy of not serving blacks at his restaurant, sometimes chasing away potential black customers by waving an axe handle at them, won instead.

After this setback, Carter underwent another reincarnation. With time on his hands, he returned to books and began in particular to read the works of notable philosophers and theologians. He soon became especially enamored with the work of the American pastor and ethicist Reinhold Niebuhr. It was a fellow Democrat politician, Bill Gunter, who made the introduction when he lent Carter his copy of *Reinhold Niebuhr on Politics*, a collection of excerpts from his writings. The book made an immediate impression, and its influence can be seen clearly in many of Carter's own writings and speeches, notably his 1974 Georgia Law Day Speech, where he describes Niebuhr as one of two important influences and echoes Niebuhr by saying, "It is the sad duty of politics to establish justice in a sinful world."[1]

Actually, his biographer, Kenneth Morris, says rather dismissively of Carter that he misread much of Niebuhr, instead searching his writings for pessimistic conclusions that corresponded with "the sentiments of his own evangelical tradition." On the other hand, he allows that Niebuhr reinforced Carter's social ethics along with its emphasis on compassion.

In his 1974 speech to Georgia's law students, Carter gives a powerful and simple example of why he agrees with Niebuhr that politicians have to be prepared to not merely ensure governments play by the rules but also that they change those rules when circumstances warrant it.

I was in the Governor's mansion for two years, enjoying the services of a very fine cook, who was a prisoner, a woman. And one day she came to me, after she got over her two years of timidity and said, "Governor, I would like to borrow $250 from you." And I said, "What could you possibly want with

---

1. Slightly bizarrely, the other source for Carter's understanding about what's right and wrong in society is Bob Dylan. He writes: "After listening to his records about 'The Ballad of Hattie Carol' and 'Like a Rolling Stone' and 'The Times, They Are a-Changing,' I've learned to appreciate the dynamism of change in a modern society."

$250 as a prisoner?" I said, "I'm not sure that a lawyer would be worth that much." And she said, "I don't want to hire a lawyer, I want to pay the judge."

And I thought it was a ridiculous statement for her. I felt that she was ignorant. But I found out that she wasn't. She had been sentenced by a superior court judge in the state, who still serves, to seven years or $750. And she had finally raised, earlier in her prison career, $500. She had been in prison five years and couldn't raise the other $250. I didn't lend her the money, but I had Bill Harper, my legal secretary, look into it. And he found that the circumstances were true. And she was quickly released.

It's an extraordinary, very human story. Indeed, Karl Paul Reinhold Niebuhr (1892–1971), to give him his full citation, was considered to be one of America's leading public intellectuals in the mid-twentieth century. *Time* magazine even put him on its cover in 1948 with the cryptic caption "Religion: Faith for a Lenten Age" (presumably "Lenten" being a link to the Christian period for self-control and abstinence), and his status was publicly confirmed by his presentation of the Presidential Medal of Freedom in 1964. The honor was marked by President Lyndon B. Johnson with the words, "He has invoked the ancient insights of Christianity to illuminate the experience and fortify the will of the modern age."

Niebuhr's best-known books are *Moral Man and Immoral Society* and *The Nature and Destiny of Man*. However, another one, called *The Irony of American History*, described as "the most important book ever written on U.S. foreign policy" by Andrew J. Bacevich, a Boston university professor, seems to have influenced Carter too. In this, Niebuhr questions simpleminded narratives in which "the consequences of an act are diametrically opposed to the original intention" and strikes a note almost like that of a rousing song—or is it a prayer?

"Nothing worth doing is completed in our lifetime, therefore we are saved by hope. Nothing true or beautiful or good makes complete sense in any immediate context of history, therefore we are saved by faith. Nothing we do, however virtuous, can ever be accomplished alone, therefore we are saved by love. No virtuous act is quite as virtuous from the standpoint of our friend or foe as from our own, therefore we are saved by the final form of love which is forgiveness."

Much the same feeling seems to be conveyed by Carter too, when he says, "I have one life and one chance to make it count for something . . . I'm free to choose what that something is, and the something I've chosen is my faith. Now, my faith goes beyond theology and religion and requires considerable work and effort. My faith demands—this is not optional—my faith demands that I do whatever I can, wherever I am, whenever I can, for as long as I can with whatever I have to try to make a difference."

MORAL MAN AND IMMORAL SOCIETY
AUTHOR: KARL NIEBUHR
PUBLISHED: 1932

In June 1978, Carter referred directly to Niebuhr in support of what he evidently considered a very important political concept: that the expectations for behavior for individuals and collectives (such as society itself) were very different. Individuals should have as a goal "complete agape love," but the most that could be expected from society was "to institute simple justice."

And when he retreated to Camp David in the depths of political crisis, Jimmy Carter hardly needed to reread *Moral Man and Immoral Society* as he could almost quote it by heart.

"Reason is not the sole basis of moral virtue in man. His social impulses are more deeply rooted than his rational life."

It is this book that contained what many believe is one of Niebuhr's most important insights: individuals are capable of overcoming sin, he argued, but groups are not. Only individuals can be moral because they "are endowed by nature with a measure of sympathy and consideration for their kind." Groups of people, organizations, and nations necessarily lack this empathy. In consequence, Niebuhr wrote, man was destined to live in an immoral society.

It is a profound insight and one pregnant with political implications, as Niebuhr well understood. A reviewer wrote in 1933 of *Moral Man and Immoral Society*, "To call this book fully Christian in tone is to travesty the heart of Jesus' message to the world." The reviewer particularly rejected Niebuhr's implication that Christians could sometimes resort to violence when acting as and dealing with groups.

Niebuhr defended his thesis vigorously though. In 1940, at the height of the battle with Nazi Germany, and with homosexuals, gypsies, and, of course, Jews being herded into concentration camps, he wrote in response to criticism from the Christian pacifist movement, "If modern churches were to symbolize their true faith, they would take the crucifix from their altars and substitute the three little monkeys who counsel men to 'speak no evil, hear no evil, see no evil.'"

Discerning Niebuhr's influence on Carter is complicated by the fact that, around the same time as Carter was discovering Niebuhr, his sister, Ruth, had become a minister, and she sought to bring about a religious reawakening in her older brother. It was as part of this, really, that Carter would begin to identify himself as a born-again Christian. If, fifty years earlier, Henry Ford had been content to imagine being reborn in later lives, Carter grabbed the opportunity to restart his existing one.

Curiously, Niebuhr connects Carter to Henry Ford as he was an outspoken critic of the industrialist and even allowed union organizers to use his pulpit to expound their message of workers' rights. He attacked poor conditions created by the assembly lines and erratic employment practices, writing (in his diary),

> We went through one of the big automobile factories today. . . . The foundry interested me particularly. The heat was terrific. The men seemed weary. Here manual labor is a drudgery and toil is slavery. The men cannot possibly find any satisfaction in their work. They simply work to make a living. Their sweat and their dull pain are part of the price paid for the fine cars we all run. And most of us run the cars without knowing what price is being paid for them. . . . We are all responsible. We all want the things which the factory produces and none of us is sensitive enough to care how much in human values the efficiency of the modern factory costs.

This is a very different picture to that offered by Ford, but indeed social scientists accept that out of all the workers, those in car factories and the like seem to be pretty well treated. The historian Ronald H. Stone thinks that Niebuhr never actually talked to the assembly line workers (many of whom were skilled craftsmen) but projected feelings onto them after discussions with Samuel Marquis, an Episcopalian minister who was also the head of the sociology department at Ford Motor Company. Marquis wrote his own book on Ford, called *Henry Ford: An Interpretation,* but if it is only an interpretation, it is still not a very nice one. Instead of a history of Ford Motor Company or a simple retelling of Ford's life story, Marquis described his book as an effort to analyze the "psychological puzzle such as the unusual mind and personality of Henry Ford presents."

According to some accounts, Henry Ford was greatly pained by the criticism in some of Marquis's essays and attempted to suppress the wide distribution of the volume. It is also said that so many copies of *Henry Ford: An Interpretation* were borrowed from the Detroit Public Library and never returned that the library was forced to remove the volume from its shelves! However Niebuhr came about his views on Ford, his criticism of big business resonated with Democratic politicians and progressives generally and helped make Carter's adoption of his views successful beyond his Christian base.

As part of his religious transformation, he also restarted his political career and prepared for another run at being state governor. First of all, he carefully studied voting patterns for each one of Georgia's 159 counties to map out a strategy that would make this possible. From now on, it seemed, there wouldn't be merely one new "Jimmy Carter" but lots of them! With multiple new versions of "Jimmy Carter," one would appeal to just about everyone in the state of Georgia. The tactic paid off, and Carter assumed the governor's job in 1971.

And then, almost as soon as Carter was elected governor, he started to prepare for a presidential run. Carter was one of the first declared candidates for the Democratic nomination in 1976, and most political pundits assumed that the election was in the bag for the Democrats in the wake of Watergate and President Ford's pardon of Richard Nixon. This time, however, Carter almost blew a huge lead in the polls and eventually barely edged out Ford by a little more than 2 percent of the popular vote.

Nor would Carter's four years in office be a time that many Americans would look back on with much fondness. The "stagflation" of the Nixon and Ford era continued with double-digit inflation alongside interest rates of well over 15 percent. People's standards of living declined. And then there were sporadic energy shortages.

Carter's response, as Kenneth E. Morris puts it in *Jimmy Carter: American Moralist*, was to try to find the perfect middle road on every issue—to the fury of his political base. There were estimates that Carter had over 250 different position papers on separate subjects. People sniped that the only thing he was really in favor of was Jimmy Carter!

The criticism was really overdone. After all, Carter was not himself responsible for the stagflation or the energy shortages. Meanwhile, in foreign policy, he had several notable successes. He managed to return the Panama Canal to Panama, a task that had evaded many previous administrations, albeit doing so used up quite a bit of his own political capital. And in 1978, Carter made his first big mark on history when he persuaded the two sworn foes of the Middle East, Israel's prime minister Menachem Begin and Egypt's president Anwar Sadat, to come to Camp David and sign a peace treaty.

However, by the end of the 1970s, that area of the world was attracting popular attention for a different reason. In the early years of the decade, the OPEC cartel, comprised mostly of Middle Eastern countries, had cut oil production, and, in the late 1970s, it declined again. Coupled with high global demand, this generated an energy crisis that saw gasoline prices shoot up by over half in the first six months of 1979.

High gas prices make for angry voters. On June 25, the *New York Times* reported that a state of emergency was declared in Bristol Township, Philadelphia, following two nights of rioting by two thousand residents who had joined a protest by truck drivers and were setting bonfires and hurling rocks at police. Carter's approval rating sank to 30 percent. An anxious Carter cut short his overseas trip to Vienna, where he was holding nuclear-arms talks with the Soviet Union's Leonid Brezhnev.

After a brief stop in Washington, the president retreated to Camp David for ten days. Here, as he considered the many problems facing his administration, he consulted books for guidance, including the Bible (of course), *The Culture of Narcissism* by the historian Christopher Lasch, and *Small Is Beautiful*, a meditation on the value of local community and the problems of excessive consumption by the economist E. F. Schumacher.

He also continued to reflect on the ideas contained in *Moral Man and Immoral Society* by Karl Niebuhr. After what at the time was considered an unprecedentedly long retreat, the president emerged from Camp David with great fanfare on July 15, 1979, to deliver his conclusions. In a nationally televised speech watched by sixty-five million Americans, Carter offered an intense and almost evangelical warning about "the crisis of the American spirit."

He said that in a nation that was proud of hard work, strong families, close-knit communities, and faith in God, "too many of us now worship self-indulgence and consumption." And he specifically talked about identity—both of individuals and of the nation itself: "Human identity is no longer defined by what one does, but by what one owns. But we've discovered that owning things and consuming things does not satisfy our longing for meaning. We've learned that piling up material goods cannot fill the emptiness of lives which have no confidence or purpose."

Although the speech is often considered something of a sermon to the American public, even dubbed "the Malaise Speech," at the time it was well received, and Carter's poll ratings shot up a whopping 11 percent. One man wrote to Carter, "You are the first politician that has said the words that I have been thinking for years. Last month I purchased a moped to drive to work with. I plan to use it as much as possible, and by doing so I have cut my gas consumption by 75%."

It seemed Carter was reborn again—politically speaking. But then on November 4, 1979, Islamic militants took fifty-two Americans hostage in the US embassy in Tehran. This was first in protest of Carter allowing the deposed Shah to come to the United States for medical treatment, but the crisis continued past the Shah's death. Carter retreated into the White House and seemed to offer little hope for the hostages' return. Not that finding their release would be easy as the Iranian government was in flux and it was difficult to find anyone who had any authority. Also, decades of anti-American attitudes were being played out in this event.

Eventually, Carter ordered a commando-style rescue of the hostages, but it ended up in disaster with two American helicopters crashing in the desert, the hostages still in Tehran, and Secretary of State Cyrus Vance resigning in protest.

In the 1980 presidential election, Carter had to face one of the most polished campaigners in American politics in Ronald Reagan. Compared to "the Gipper," the earnest, moralizing Southern farmer seemed politically outclassed by a slick opponent who simply kept asking if people felt better

off than they were four years ago. Since the answer to that was almost always "no," Reagan won by a landslide of 440 votes in the Electoral College.

The crushing defeat brought about a final reinvention of Jimmy Carter.
Now, he would become Mr. Humanitarian. He flew round the world
spreading democracy, serving as an election observer in countries like
Haiti and Nicaragua. He set up a health fund that helped dramatically
reduce deaths from unfashionable but deadly health concerns like Guinea
worm. He went to Jerusalem to bring the Israelis and Palestinians together for a historic peace accord. (He won the Nobel Peace Prize in 2002.)
He devoted himself to building bridges with world figures (Fidel Castro,
Daniel Ortega, Hafez Assad, Kim Il Sung, and Yasir Arafat) that made
conservatives blanch in horror. After so many reincarnations, this final
role of global do-gooder seemed to be the authentic fit for Carter at last.

What is the ingredient that has made the ideas of Karl Niebuhr so attractive to many politicians? It seems to be the political shift from idealism to
realism. The cover story for the 1948 *Time* magazine on Niebuhr described
his influence like this: "To the mass of untheological Christians, God has
become, at best, a rather unfairly furtive presence, a lurking luminosity, a
cozy thought. Reinhold Niebuhr's new orthodoxy is the old-time religion
put through the intellectual wringer. It is a re-examination of orthodoxy
for an age dominated by such trends as rationalism, liberalism, Marxism,
fascism, idealism and the idea of progress."

Strange Subtext: The story was written by one Whittaker Chambers,
an American writer-editor whose revelations about Russian networks of
spies played a key role in the postwar "Red Scare." Chambers spoke with
considerable authority on shifts from idealism to realism—he himself had
at one time been successfully recruited by the Russians. Repositioning
God as a "lurking luminosity" is part of this shift and an aspect of what
Jimmy Carter once summed up as "the sad duty of the political system . . .
to establish justice in a sinful world."

Among other American politicians to have acknowledged the influence
of Niebuhr's ideas on them are Martin Luther King Jr., Hillary Clinton,
and Barack Obama. In the "Letter from Birmingham Jail," for instance,
Martin Luther King Jr. wrote, "Individuals may see the moral light and
voluntarily give up their unjust posture; but, as Reinhold Niebuhr has
reminded us, groups tend to be more immoral than individuals."

King even invited Niebuhr to participate in a march in 1965, and
Niebuhr responded by telegram: "Only a severe stroke prevents me from
accepting . . . I hope there will be a massive demonstration of all the citizens with conscience in favor of the elemental human rights of voting and
freedom of assembly." When, two years later, the black civil rights leader
was criticized for speaking out against the Vietnam War, Niebuhr defended him, saying, "Dr. King has the right and a duty, as both a religious

and a civil rights leader, to express his concern," adding that in his own view, the war made him for the first time feel ashamed to be American.

Obama, who says in his autobiography that generally he has no time for philosophy, considering it on a par with reading the back of cereal boxes, struck a very different note in response to *New York Times* journalist David Brooks's inquiry about whether he had ever read any Niebuhr: "I love him. He's one of my favorite philosophers."

Obama the community organizer would have particularly latched on to passages like this in *The Children of Light and the Children of Darkness* (1944), where Niebuhr says, "Social improvement arises not from the reasonableness of groups, which, contrary to individuals, are unlikely and perhaps unable to act other than in self-interest. Rather, it emerges out of conflicts over power."

Individuals are flawed, Niebuhr continues, but they can occasionally overcome their egoism and "consider interests other than their own." Not so groups of individuals, relations between which are "determined by the proportion of power which each group possesses and not by grand and idealistic notions."

One key lesson advanced by Obama is very much drawn from Niebuhr's writings. As Obama told Ryan Lizza for an article published in the *New Republic*, "The key to creating successful organizations was making sure people's self-interest was met and not basing it on pie-in-the-sky idealism. So there were some basic principles that remained powerful then, and in fact I still believe in."

Two "not quite presidents," John McCain and Hillary Clinton, also both reference Niebuhr in their books: in *Hard Call*, McCain admires Niebuhr's expression of the "moral ambiguity that is inescapable for the soldier who must kill to defend his country," and in *Living History*, Clinton writes that Niebuhr "struck a persuasive balance between a clear-eyed realism about human nature and an unrelenting passion for justice and social reform."

And finally, *Slate* magazine columnist Fred Kaplan characterized Obama's 2009 Nobel Peace Prize acceptance speech as a "faithful reflection" of Niebuhr. In this way, one book actually lies behind the programs of three presidents and two Nobel Peace Prizes!

7

✛

Set Your Thinking Free

Thomas Edison and Harry Kroto

Where do scientists obtain their inspiration? Is it from investigating nature and peering through microscopes? Or is it from philosophy books? Well, you might be surprised to know that sometimes it actually is the latter.

Take two examples: one is an American icon often described as that nation's greatest inventor; the other is a British academic who played a key role in the discovery of a new kind of carbon chemistry. Both are scientists—Thomas Edison and Harry Kroto—and both combine the spark of imagination with the power of invention. Edison seems to have obtained from his reading of the revolutionary philosopher Tom Paine a kind of humanist zeal, writing, "The world is my country; to do good my religion." Kroto was an eclectic reader who took inspiration from ideas he came across in many different works, from the speculations of Plato to the imaginary worlds explored by J. R. R. Tolkien, and, to be sure, from some science books, too, notably the popular accounts of quantum physics by Richard Feynman.

Let's start with the monumental figure of Thomas Edison, who is famous for his extraordinary output of new ideas and inventions. He made important contributions in fields as diverse as electric power generation, mass communication, sound recording, and even moving pictures. As he would later say, "Inventors must be poets so that they may have imagination."

Growing up in Michigan, Edison's teachers thought he was an incredibly stupid, stubborn, and disobedient boy, perhaps because childhood illness had left him with acute hearing difficulties. His mother, however, had different thoughts on the matter. Rejecting the school's verdict, she attempted to educate the young boy at home. Central to her approach was introducing him to books, including ones at a far higher level than recommended for his age. Thanks to his mother's approach, Edison's horizons were immensely broadened with a rich tapestry of human achievement not limited just to science but also including English, history, and philosophy. In terms of science, the books kindled Edison's curiosity to such an extent that by the time he was eleven, he had created his own laboratory in his basement, where he would make new discoveries and develop new skills.

At the age of twelve, Edison was obliged to start a job instead of studying. He sold food, sweets, and newspapers to the passengers on the Grand Trunk Railway that made daily runs between Port Huron and Detroit. Later on, taking advantage of access to the news coming in via the station telegraphs, he wrote and sold his own newspaper, called the *Grand Trunk Herald*. In Detroit he visited the Free Library and systematically worked his way through its entire stock of books.

Years later, Edison even wrote a special essay on one of his early fascinations, entitled "The Philosophy of Thomas Paine." Apart from what it reveals about Paine, the essay shows Edison to have had a strong sense of humor and a ready wit. It starts by noting sadly that "Tom Paine" had become unknown to the average citizen and thus had almost no influence on contemporary thinking in the United States. For Edison this was "a national loss" made all the worse by the peddling of unkind myths about the philosopher. Theodore Roosevelt, he recalls, coldly dismissed Paine as "a dirty little atheist" who spent his last days drinking in pothouses. The truth, Edison asserts, is quite the contrary: "We never had a sounder intelligence in this Republic," he said, adding, "I consider Paine our greatest political thinker."

Edison focuses on Paine's most revolutionary pamphlet, the one entitled *Common Sense*: "an anonymous tract which immediately stirred the fires of liberty." The pamphlet was written with a terse power that inspired readers to make an immediate choice between their current, secondary status as a mere colony and full-scale revolt and freedom from British rule.

"It flashed from hand to hand throughout the Colonies. One copy reached the New York Assembly, in session at Albany, and a night meeting was voted to answer this unknown writer with his clarion call to liberty."

Edison does not exaggerate. Within just a few months, the pamphlet had sold more than half a million copies. In proportion to the population of the colonies at that time (two and a half million souls), it had the largest sale and circulation of any book published in American history. He reflects the view of orthodox political commentators in saying that in *Common Sense*, "Paine flared forth with a document so powerful that the Revolution became inevitable."

Born in Norfolk, England, the young Thomas Paine worked variously as a staymaker (a tailor who makes corsets, which sounds trivial but actually involves some structural engineering!), a civil servant, a journalist, and a schoolteacher. It was while working in the second capacity for the Excise Board in Lewes, Sussex, that he became interested in politics, serving on the town council and hosting political discussions of the celebrated English philosopher John Locke's ideas in the White Hart Inn. Actually, Paine downplayed his debt to his political forbear, even saying rather disgracefully that he had "never read any Locke, nor ever had the work in my hand," but it was certainly Locke's ideas on liberty and human dignity that made the running in those political debates.

However, it was only when Paine left quiet, sleepy Lewes for the New World, on the recommendation of no less a figure than Benjamin Franklin himself, whom he had met in London (Franklin was then a diplomat) and discussed scientific matters with, that his political activity became serious. On settling in Philadelphia, he immediately began to set out his ideas on paper: equal rights for men and women and for people of different races and even if not full rights at least fair treatment for animals. Paine was one of the first in the United States to press for the abolition of slavery, and his more substantial book *The Rights of Man* is rightly considered a political classic.

Befitting his own background, Paine was also interested in the details of government, even working out neatly, in double-entry bookkeeping form, exactly how much the kind of democratic government he was proposing would cost, which was not to be very much. In fact, when finances are done his way, there is, happily, enough money to actually pay something to all the poor people of the country! This was truly an idea far ahead of its time. Indeed, in the lead-up to the 2020 presidential election, it was still revolutionary when Democratic hopeful and computer whiz Andrew Yang proposed something similar. Such payments to citizens are, Paine points out, no more than remission of their own taxes from hidden taxation imposed by duties on imports and so on.

But it was the novel issue of national self-determination that made the name of Thomas Paine historically significant—the issue that John Adams, second president of the United States, once described as a dreadful "hobgoblin . . . so frightful . . . that it would throw a delicate person into fits to look it in the face." Indeed, Paine's nationalistic pamphlet *Common Sense* started a fire that would eventually destroy the English claim to America. It was with the brisk, efficient language of a journalist that Paine urged in *The Rights of Man* (1791), "It is time that nations should be rational, and not be governed like animals, for the pleasure of their riders."

COMMON SENSE
AUTHOR: THOMAS PAINE
PUBLISHED: 1776

Originally a mere forty-nine pages, *Common Sense* was a pamphlet rather than a book, written by Thomas Paine just at the beginning of the American Revolution in 1775–1776 to advocate independence for the then "Thirteen Colonies" from Great Britain. Writing in clear and persuasive prose, Paine presented powerful moral and political arguments on behalf of the colonies. The pamphlet was read aloud in taverns and at meeting places and made a phenomenal impact. In proportion to the population of the country at that time, the book had the largest sale and circulation of any book published in American history! And it is still in print today.

Paine made a case for independence that previously had not been given serious intellectual consideration. He also linked independence with the freedom of Protestants to pursue their religion, structuring his account almost as if it were a sermon. The historian Gordon S. Wood has described *Common Sense* as "the most incendiary and popular pamphlet of the entire revolutionary era."

Part of speaking common sense is speaking plainly, and Paine wrote his pamphlet in a straightforward, simple style, ignoring the then almost obligatory literary pretensions of philosophical references and Latin terms, while sprinkling into the text instead well-known biblical references that would "speak to the common man," as it were, in the manner of a sermon by a small-town preacher. Within just a few months, the pamphlet had sold more than five hundred thousand copies, or one for every five colonists at the time, and, more than any other single publication, it is credited with paving the way for the Declaration of Independence on July 4, 1776, just a few years later.

Edison goes on to explain he had long been fascinated by Thomas Paine. His father had had a set of Paine's books on the shelf at home, and he says he thinks he must have "opened the covers" about the time he was thirteen, adding, "I can still remember the flash of enlightenment which shone from his pages. It was a revelation, indeed, to encounter his views on political and religious matters, so different from the views of many people around us. Of course I did not understand him very well, but his sincerity and ardor made an impression upon me that nothing has ever served to lessen."

The young Edison was, of course, no political activist. Nor was he searching for a philosophical hero. Rather, right from the start, he saw in the Englishman a role model and a practical guide as to how to live. This was because (although it is not widely remembered) Paine was himself something of an engineer and experimenter. Edison writes, "I was always interested in Paine the inventor. He conceived and designed the iron bridge and the hollow candle, the principle of the modern central draught burner. The man had a sort of universal genius. He was interested in a diversity of things; but his special creed, his first thought, was liberty."

The editors of biography.com recall Paine's remarkable "other" life, noting that if many of his ideas and inventions never developed beyond the "planning stage," there were several notable exceptions that did. There was his invention of a crane for lifting heavy objects, a smokeless candle, and the idea of using gunpowder as a method for generating power. It sounds like a dangerous idea, but something similar goes on at the heart of the ubiquitous internal combustion engine, and anyway, Paine survived years of "tinkering" with it.

Above all, though, Paine possessed a fascination with bridges. After the end of the Revolutionary War, he made several attempts to build them in both England and America. At a time when conventional wisdom said bridges were made either of stone or wood, Paine experimented with iron. He worked out a plan for bridging the Harlem River, which General Lewis Morris, founder of Morrisania on the farther shore, was to have financed. Alas, the money failed to appear, and so instead his most impressive achievement was to be the Sunderland Bridge across the Wear River at Wearmouth, England.[1] His achievement here was to construct a wide single-span bridge (with no additional supporting piers), and in 1796, a 236-foot span bridge was completed. It was at the time the largest in the world as well as only the second iron bridge ever built. For pioneering the use of iron and steel like this, it is not too much to say that Thomas

---

1. The bridge was demolished in 1929. There is only one bridge in the United States that really embodies Tom Paine's idea, the Dunlap Creek Bridge in Pennsylvania, which stands as the first cast-iron arch bridge in America, built between 1836 and 1839, long after Paine's death.

Paine is an important inspiration behind later iconic bridges such as San Francisco's Golden Gate or New York's Brooklyn Bridge. All of this goes some way to explain why George Washington was as much a fan of Paine for his bridges as for his revolutionary prose.

However, for Edison, it was the other way around. He was most inspired by Paine's famous declaration, already mentioned, that "the world is my country; to do good my religion" and his reputation as the man "who helped to lay the foundations of our liberty," as he puts it at the end of his observations. And yet, more than this, Paine provided Edison with an inspirational model and the evidence that here was a kindred spirit.

In due course, among Edison's many inventions would be included the telegraph, the universal stock ticker, the phonograph, the first practical electric light bulb, alkaline storage batteries, and an early kind of moving image projector that he called the kinetograph. Edison, though it is rarely appreciated, was truly a disciple of the revolutionary Englishman that he first came across in some leather-bound books.

It should be emphasized that, at the time Edison was reading these, Paine's reputation was grim. He had died alone on June 8, 1809, and it was recorded that only six mourners were present at his funeral—three of them former slaves. The only status the press gave him was as a political rabble-rouser, with the *New York Citizen* printing the following line in Paine's obituary: "He had lived long, did some good and much harm."

All of this emphasizes another quality of books: that they are also a kind of time capsule, whose contents are sealed up when written but can be rediscovered decades, even centuries, later. So it was with Edison. When he says that you can't realize your dreams unless you have one to begin with and that his desire was "to do everything within [his] power to free people from drudgery and create the largest measure of happiness and prosperity," he is actually echoing the political manifesto of Thomas Paine for the American Revolution.

Edison was dyslexic and almost deaf since his early childhood and only received three months of formal education before he was requested to leave school at the age of seven due to his behavior. Fortunately his mother continued to believe in his rare abilities and intelligence and devoted herself to providing education at home. Edison later remembered lovingly, "My mother was the making of me. She was so true, so sure of me. And I felt I had something to live for, someone I must not disappoint."

Under his mother's guidance, a whole new world was opened for the young boy, and he became a passionate reader of world history, English literature, poetry, and the works of the great English scientist Isaac Newton.

Edison realized how lucky he was to have had this sort of education. He wrote later, "The most necessary task of civilization is to teach people how to think . . . The trouble with our way of educating is that it does not give elasticity to the mind. It casts the brain into a mold. It does not encourage original thought or reasoning, and it lays more stress on memory than observation."

As mentioned above, Edison continued his education at home by creating a kind of laboratory in the basement; his parents had to tolerate occasional explosions caused by his experiments into the properties of chemicals. This was the forerunner for what later would be the world's first R&D lab created by Edison at Menlo Park in 1876 and intended to be an "invention factory." Outside the lab, Edison made extraordinary engineering progress too, in particular by designing and constructing the world's first central power station. Testament to this, in 1882, the streets of Manhattan were for the first time lit up at night. Following a merger led by his friend the financier J. P. Morgan, the Edison Illuminating Company became the world's best-known energy company: General Electric.

Edison was not just an inventor but also an entrepreneur who focused on what he saw as society's need for innovation and betterment. He once said, "Anything that will not sell, I do not want to invent. Its sale is proof of utility, and utility is success." He was a careful investor and built up a diversified portfolio of companies, including electric lighting systems, battery supplies, manufacturing, cement products, mining, and motion pictures. Explaining what he thought were the ingredients of success, he said, "The three great essentials to achieve anything worthwhile, are first hard-work; second, stick-to-itiveness, third, common sense."

Thomas Edison and Tom Paine show the power of minds that are able to draw inspiration from diverse sources. This is also essentially the secret of the twentieth-century chemist Harry Kroto. While you may not know the name, you've probably already benefited from many of Kroto's inventions—be they in medicine, space technology, or nanotechnology (that's science conducted on the tiniest scale)—without realizing it. Kroto's co-discovery of a new form of carbon, the so-called Fullerenes, earned him, together with the American scientists Robert Curl and Richard Smalley, a Nobel Prize in 1996. Their new way of seeing the universe affected science across areas ranging from cosmology to drug delivery and solar panels to light-emitting diodes.

However, that's just the business-speak. I find his story appealing on many levels. Here is a scientist who was also an artist and a humanist who used his Nobel Prize to create educational opportunities. His arguments in favor of scientists having freedom and opportunities to pursue research that may not yet have a practical application mesh with my interest in promoting reading as a way of broadening horizons. Harry Kroto also praises philosophy as our tool to make sense of the world and distinguish truth and error. And last but not least, for twenty years we both lived in the same small town—Lewes in East Sussex on the south coast of England, the town where Thomas Paine first became interested in politics too. Small world!

Most importantly, Harry Kroto was a voracious and wide-ranging reader. In his home library, all the art, design, and photography books were always carefully filed away by category, but philosophy and science were allowed to mix. Hidden among thousands of other books are at least ten on Einstein with similar numbers for other people Kroto was particularly interested in. But then, a line he often liked to quote from J. R. R. Tolkien's epic tale *The Lord of the Rings* is evocative: "Not all those who wander are lost," and in such spirit he freely switches between references to philosopher Bertrand Russell's writings and those of the physicist Richard Feynman's "small and interesting book," *The Meaning of It All.* His wife, Margaret Kroto, told me how Harry liked to refer to such texts when talking to young people and encouraging them to find out more about science. A favorite quote from Russell that he often used (actually a popular re-rendering of what Russell actually said) was, "The whole problem with the world is that fools and fanatics are always so certain of themselves, but wiser people so full of doubt."

THE LORD OF THE RINGS
AUTHOR: J. R. R. TOLKIEN
WRITTEN IN STAGES BETWEEN 1937 AND 1949

The Lord of the Rings is certainly a great book. For one thing, it is a great big book. At about half a million words long, it is at least five times the length of the average novel. No wonder that Tolkien originally both presented and published it as three separate chunks, but they are nowadays invariably bound into one hefty tome.

It is also a rather odd book, written not just in English but in fifteen different "Elvish" dialects made up by the author, not to forget new languages for the Ents, the Orcs, the Dwarves, and the Hobbits, among others. Tolkien's fascination with the workings of language even led him to create a separate sign language for the Dwarves—necessary because the forges they worked with were too loud.

Whether for its length or its obscurity, I suspect that Harry Kroto, like myself and many others, never actually read the whole book; that's not really the point. *The Lord of the Rings* is more like an exotic alternative universe, carefully crafted by Tolkien from a range of surprisingly obscure academic sources.

Tolkien, you see, was a professor with a specialty in Anglo-Saxon and Old English. His first civilian job, after a period as a soldier in World War I, was at the Oxford English Dictionary, where he worked mainly on the history and etymology of words of Germanic origin beginning with the letter W, but he soon moved on to teaching and researching English in a university. This meant that he was familiar with works no one else was, such as the Old Norse Völsunga saga and the Old High German Nibelungenlied, both of them ancient texts featuring tales of magical golden rings and broken swords that become whole. Even the details of the characters in Tolkien's book come from these earlier works. Gandalf, the wise old wizard, is particularly influenced by the Norse deity Odin, who is described in the ancient texts as an old man with one eye, a long white beard, a wide-brimmed hat, and a wooden staff. However, *The Lord of the Rings* manages to move beyond being just dusty references to long-obscured epic poems to become a series of tales about friendship, loyalty, sacrifice, and compassion.

Whether it was science or philosophy, for Kroto it was always underpinned by a love of mystery. Actually, like many of us, and not just scientists, Harry Kroto didn't have the time to actually plough stolidly through the works of many philosophers, but he did enjoy snippets or potted versions of them. One such source for him was Paul Strathern's biography *Spinoza in 90 Minutes*. The philosopher Spinoza is popular with scientists as he saw the whole of creation as containing an element of mind. In other words, he did not think that mind and matter were two distinct things but rather that both were aspects of the same thing. For Spinoza, this something had many aspects, including that of existing as rocks, as animals, and above all, as God. For scientists, this idea helps solve the mystery of the incredible complexity and precision of nature.

That's full-blown metaphysics, but Kroto was also fond of skeptical quotes from literary figures such as Walt Whitman, who he reminded audiences had once said, "I like the scientific spirit, the holding off, the being sure but not too sure, the willingness to surrender ideas when the evidence is against them. This is ultimately fine—it keeps the way beyond open."

As to what might be his favorite saying, though, a website he created himself called Kroto.info mentions two philosophers: Confucius and Plato. It was Confucius who wrote long ago, "I seek not the answer—but to understand the question," but both philosophers could be summed up by this motto, which is also a fine general principle for all scientists. However, there is also a mystical side to the ancient Green, and this seems to have intrigued Kroto even more than the standard, textbook one. Where most mainstream philosophers hurried by, Kroto paused to look with great curiosity into Plato's theory of geometrical solids.

TIMAEUS
AUTHOR: PLATO
WRITTEN AROUND 360 BCE

Timaeus, named after a leading character, is one of a series of short books recording supposed conversations between the ancient Greek philosopher Socrates and various members of the Athens elite. The dialogues, which are almost like mini-plays, albeit with more emphasis on conversations than "events," have had a profound effect on the development of Western culture and influenced many later thinkers.

Each dialogue has its own special themes, with today the most famous dialogue being the one called the *Republic*, which deals with the nature of government and justice. However, in the dialogue known as *Timaeus*, Plato explores the *geometry of matter* and starts by describing Socrates's invitation to Timaeus to consider the four elements that the ancients believed were the building blocks of the universe: fire, earth, air, and water.

First of all, Timaeus says, "To earth, then, let us assign the cubical form (or *hexahedron*); for earth is the most immoveable of the four and the most plastic of all bodies, and that which has the most stable bases must of necessity be of such a nature."

Next, he explains that the shape of a pyramid (*tetrahedron*) is given to fire with part of the justification being that the shape is pointed and fire feels like being pricked or stabbed; the complicated-sounding, and indeed complicated-looking, *icosahedron* corresponds to water. The idea seems to be that water flows like little balls, and that is the effect of the geometry of icosahedra. Finally, air is made of *octahedra*, the explanation being that its minuscule components are so smooth that you can barely feel it.

There is, in fact, a fifth geometrical solid, the *dodecahedron*, concerning which Timaeus obscurely remarks, "The god used it for arranging the constellations on the whole heaven." Now, okay, in one sense this is all nonsense. But it appears very technical and thus impressive. And at least Plato is right on the money when he says that symmetry defines structure and when, in general, he lent dignity and grandeur to the study of geometry and greatly stimulated its development. Scholars speculate that Euclid planned the classic work of mathematics, *The Elements*, to culminate with a proof supporting Plato's ideas. In this sense, incredibly, Plato's dialogue created most of what we know as mathematics—and foreshadowed atomic chemistry too.

Plato's text, which is, remember, nearly 2,500 years old, and what is more is reporting the views of even older thinkers, such as Pythagoras, is quite extraordinarily prescient in terms of the geometry of chemical elements. In the *Timaeus* dialogue, named after an even older, Pythagorean thinker called Timaeus who (naturally) seems to have been interested in math, the central intuition is that the hidden structure of the elements creates their actual properties. This leads Plato to go on to describe three-dimensional structures too, supposing that "the solid body which has taken the form of the pyramid—tetrahedron—is the element and seed of fire; and the second in order of generation—octahedron—let us say to be that of air, and the third—icosahedron—that of water."

Fire, earth, air, water, and ether (which Aristotle added later, meaning whatever it was that filled up the space between the stars and planets): all together making the building blocks of the universe for the philosophers. These ingredients were arranged, they intuited even back then, according to the laws of mathematics. Indeed, today's atomic microscopes reveal that dull, soft graphite has the carbon atoms arranged in hexagons, whereas the crystal structure of hard, sparkling diamonds is octahedral with the carbon atoms arranged in little pyramids.

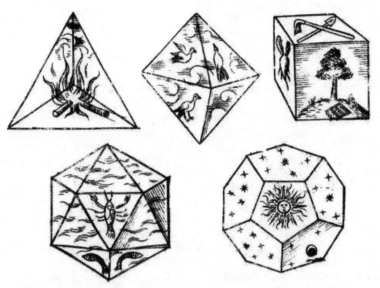

In the dialogue known as the *Timaeus*, written around 360 BCE, Plato explores the geometry of matter. In this engraving, Plato's five geometrical solids are imaginatively linked to the five ancient elements: earth, water, fire, air, and ether or empty space. (Johannes Kepler, *Harmonices Mundi*, 1619. http://geometricism.com/c/renaissance-geometricism.)

But calling these shapes the "Platonic solids" is a bit of a shortcut. Instead, they seem to belong to an even more ancient Greek philosopher called Pythagoras, who seems to have in turn been reporting discoveries made in his travels in North Africa and the East. However, maybe due to a Eurocentric cultural bias, these roots are often neglected in discussions of Plato's writing, with the result that a lot of what was really being said is distorted and stripped from its cultural context. Introductions to philosophy, for example, often breathlessly relate that inscribed over the door of Plato's Academy were the words, "Let no one who is ignorant of geometry enter," yet it seems likely that it was not geometers who Plato invites in but geometrikoí. A small difference in spelling but a great difference in sense as this is the term for followers w the Great Path (also called the Parmenidean Path to Truth) in search of equality and justice. As the contemporary German physicist Peter Hubral, author of a book called The Socrates Code, say, such a shift in understanding would seem to make a great deal more sense.

Nonetheless, in both medieval and recent popular editions of Plato's writings, the ancient dialogue is invariably accompanied by more recent line drawings of the elements themselves, showing them as complex geometrical solids constructed of simpler shapes and entitled "The Platonic Solids." Kroto particularly focused on the illustrations that accompanied books and articles, and these line drawings bring the theory to life.

Likewise, well before him, Plato's foray into the geometry of matter had inspired Renaissance artists such as Leonardo of Pisa to create sophisticated drawings of spherical solids intriguingly similar to the "buckyballs" that Kroto and his colleagues would later identify as a new class of carbon compounds, while craftsmen likewise adopted the potentials of the strange geometry to create striking wooden inlay panels like the one at the church of Santa Maria in Organo, Verona (northern Italy), in the closing years of the fifteenth century.

Wooden inlay panel by Giovanni of Verona, from the Church of Santa Maria in Organo, Verona, c. 1494–1499. Note in particular the very striking "buckyball" at the top of the image. (Fra Giovanni of Verona, *Intarsia*, wooden inlay, c. 1503–1506. http://geometricism.com/c /renaissance-geometricism.)

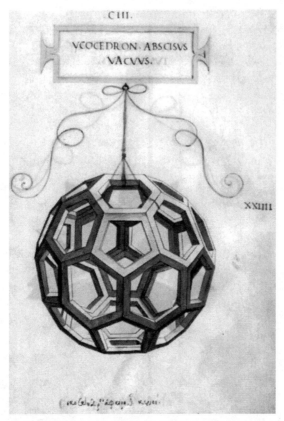

An illustration by Leonardo da Vinci, from Luca Pacioli's book *De divina proportione (On Divine Geometry)*,
1509 edition. (Leonardo da Pisa, *Skeletised polehyrdon,
for Luca Pacioli's De Dvina Proportione* woodcut, 1509.
http://geometricism.com/c/renaissance-geometricism.)

Nonetheless, the most extraordinary legacy of Plato's book is the very
powerful idea that elements are composed of a few basic geometrical
shapes that combine to allow new possibilities. And the key aspect of
Kroto's new carbon compound, Buckminsterfullerene, is a ball of carbon
atoms created out of the fusing of simpler carbon shapes. Yet where and
how could such fusing have taken place? Kroto favored the idea of compounds being created in the fire of red giant stars, an intuition that may
again have been fueled by his reading of Plato, who says,

When earth meets with fire and is dissolved by the keenness of it, it would drift about, whether it were dissolved in fire itself, or in some mass of air or water, until the parts of it meeting and again being united became earth once more; for it never could pass into any other kind. But when water is divided by fire or by air, it may be formed again and become one particle of fire and two of air: and the divisions of air may become for every particle broken up two particles of fire. And again when fire is caught in air or in waters or in earth, a little in a great bulk, moving amid a rushing body, and contending with it is vanquished and broken up, two particles of fire combine into one figure of air: and when air is vanquished and broken small, from two whole and one half particle one whole figure of water will be composed. (Section 57a, Tr. R. D. Archer-Hind, *The Timaeus of Plato* [1888] pp. 203–05)

For whatever reason, Kroto suggested to his two key American collaborators, Robert Curl and Richard Smalley, that they should simulate the atmospheric conditions of red giant carbon stars. He hypothesized that the mysterious molecules had been created in the atmospheres of carbon-rich red giant stars, and he wanted to use a piece of equipment invented by Smalley in order to investigate. Smalley's apparatus fired pulsed laser beams at chemical elements, achieving temperatures hotter than the surface of most stars and vaporizing the target element.

As the vapor began to cool, the atoms would align in clusters. A second laser pulse ionized the clusters, pushing them into a mass spectrometer, where they could be analyzed. These experiments revealed the existence of a strange new kind of molecule made up of sixty carbon atoms. This was amazing as carbon had long been known to exist as diamond or graphite, or in impure form as grubby but essential coal, but carbon as a small molecule required completely new thinking.

In fact, when first approached by Kroto in 1984, Smalley and Curl had been reluctant to interrupt the cluster research that they had been conducting on metals and semiconductors to make the device available. But they ultimately conceded, and Kroto arrived at Rice University in September 1985. The first results of their carbon experiments, conducted with the assistance of graduate students James Heath, Sean O'Brien, and Yuan Liu, spawned the long carbon snakes that Kroto had sought. Harry was working with one student when the unusual peak was first noticed, and it is in his handwriting that the results are noted on this historic first printout—showing extraordinary peaks in the mass spectra of the clusters formed, indicating the presence of molecules composed of carbon 60 (and also carbon 70) atoms.

But what was this mystery molecule? A love of investigating mysteries was built into Kroto's professional genes. Right from the start of his career, as a postdoctoral researcher at the National Research Council in Ottawa, Canada, in 1964, he was able, he says, to follow his intuitions; indeed, he

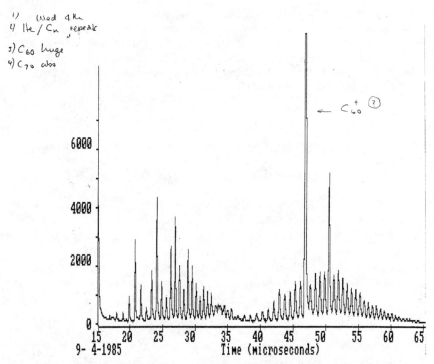

A scanned copy of the historic first printout from the mass spectrometer showing two unusual peaks indicating molecules composed of sixty carbon atoms. The results are noted in Kroto's handwriting.

describes an atmosphere in the laboratory that was "quite exhilarating." Kroto started out as one of the more junior members of a team of highly distinguished people; however, there was no pecking order at Ottawa—rather, everyone was encouraged to share their ideas freely. Kroto later wrote that "the encouraging atmosphere was, in my opinion, the most important quality of the laboratory . . . it was a fantastic, free environment."

The philosophy at Ottawa was to make the state-of-the-art equipment available and let the young scientists do almost whatever they wanted. The emphasis was on freedom to explore. Reflecting on this later, Kroto, whose own discoveries were as valuable as they were unexpected, always regretted that although it seemed obvious that unexpected discoveries must be intrinsically more important than predictable advances, it had become more and more difficult for scientists to obtain support for speculative, exploratory research—research, for example, such as attempting to reproduce the conditions that might have existed in the early universe by vaporizing graphite in an atmosphere of helium to generate clusters of carbon molecules.

Of course, the flip side of unexpected discoveries is that they can be hard to make sense of. In this case, though, a breakthrough came when Kroto realized that the atoms were bonding together in a symmetrical hollow structure resembling a sphere.

This is perhaps where Kroto drew not only on his artistic side and knowledge of graphic design but his reading of that ancient philosophical theory too: he proposed that the carbon 60 molecule was made up of a mixture of pentagons and hexagons. Not only had such geometrical patterns been explored even in ancient times but they had also had a contemporary life both in the steel-framed geodesic domes created by the American architect Richard Buckminster Fuller and in the mix of pentagons and hexagons created by the stitching of modern soccer balls. Kroto himself emphasized more the former, recalling seeing some of the domes at the Montreal World Exhibition.

One way or another, the discovery of the unique structure of fullerenes, or buckyballs, opened up an entirely new branch of chemistry. Kroto, along with Curl and Smalley, jointly received their Nobel Prize in Chemistry in 1996 for it. At first, though, no one could prove the existence of these new spherical molecules, and indeed many were openly skeptical.

Undeterred, Smalley speculated that the buckyballs might actually be not only one of the most common molecules in the universe but one of the oldest. If they were indeed created in the seething heat of red giant stars ten to twenty billion years ago, he suggested, then they might have served as the primordial nuclei around which the first solid objects coalesced: interstellar dust particles, then rocks, asteroids, comets, planets, and finally the opportunity for life on earth. It's enough to make you very philosophical.

Indeed, in the following years, Kroto's work on these large and unstable molecules included a detailed study of carbon chains with David Walton, a Sussex colleague with a knack for making long snakes of these, with whom he had been sharing ideas about carbon atoms for many years. This led to a radio astronomy program that uncovered that the newly discovered molecules existed in vast amounts throughout interstellar space and in the gas ejected from carbon stars.

Kroto's background in graphic design and his long-standing interest in architecture are the first and most obvious factors regularly cited for his arriving at a possible structure for the mysterious carbon 60 atoms ahead of his colleagues, but ideas grow from subtler inputs.

Indeed, when asked, he usually insisted that pictures spoke more for him than words. As a young child he had cut out and collected images from publications such as the *Radio Times* (the British TV listings magazine) and also visited travel agents on Saturday mornings to pick up brochures, which in those days used drawings rather than photographs. He had also bought *The Eagle*, the illustrated British comic magazine that featured Dan Dare and re-created many drawings of airplanes and other images from it. His school biology book had beautiful and intricate drawings, notably one of a frog.

Even as a young chemist, he still devoted considerable time to a student magazine called *Arrows*, specializing in designing its covers and posters. However, it's worth restating, Kroto's passion for art still has a lot to do with books, not least because book covers are part of the magic of reading. In fact, Harry Kroto's first major award was for a book jacket design. And it was with a mix of grand ideas and an artist's eye that he visited the 1967 Universal Exposition and saw there the ultramodern geodesic domes of Robert Buckminster Fuller.

Writing for a German science blog, the writer Ashutosh Jogalekar has described Kroto's life story as one of serendipitous scientific discovery, adding that "the trick in science consists of seeing what everyone sees, and thinking of what nobody thinks." Indeed, in this case, literally so. Because, in fact, other research chemists, including a team working for the oil company Exxon in the United States led by Andy Kaldor, had seen very similar results about two years earlier but not grasped the significance. Thus the question of why Kroto was the first to understand what he was seeing is a very real one. And although Kroto himself talks of seeing the Montreal Expo dome as the key experience that permitted the later insight into the chemistry, I think the visual observation itself fitted into a larger, more philosophical mindset nourished by books.

A UNIVERSAL MOLECULE

Carbon 60 is now firmly fixed in the textbooks as a third allotrope or physical form of carbon and is being applied to everything from superconductors to solar cells. In a special reprint of a 1991 cover story on Kroto from 2016, in honor of his passing, Edward Edelson described how Kroto's idea upturned the world of chemistry: "In California, Robert Whetten fired buckyball molecules into a stainless steel wall at 15,000 miles an hour. They bounced back unharmed. 'It's resilient beyond any particle that's been known,' Whetten exclaimed to Edelson, adding that the newly discovered material was resilient enough, maybe, to be used as rocket fuel, which must withstand enormous pressures."

For IBM's Don Bethune, though, that was just the beginning. "This molecule looks like something some genius engineer sat down and designed. . . . There's the possibility of making molecular Christmas trees. We can decorate them with all sorts of functional groups. It's a Swiss army knife of a molecule."

With transistors the size of single molecules, for example, electronic devices can become dramatically smaller. Molecular electronics is a subfield of nanotechnology, the broader effort to view, measure, and manipulate materials at the molecular or atomic scale, approaches anticipated by Richard Feynman in 1959 when he became interested in DNA and the mechanisms of genetics.

Perhaps the most significant fullerenes to emerge since the buckyball are the carbon nanotubes, often dubbed "buckytubes," discovered in Japan. They are excellent conductors of heat and electricity and extremely strong. Applications in electronics, structural materials, and medicine beckon. You already benefit from them in the form of LED (light-emitting diode) displays. It is this kind of molecular flexibility that seems to have given the carbon 60 molecule a vital role in the formation of the universe and the creation of matter itself.

Following his Nobel Prize, Kroto devoted himself to visiting schools and colleges and campaigning for what he called "an astute analytical approach to all aspects of life." In general lectures he would stress that natural philosophy, meaning the search for the rules and underlying principles governing nature and the universe, "is the only philosophical construct we have devised to determine truth with any degree of reliability" and that "the ethical purpose of education must be the schooling of young people in the ways of deciding what they are being told or what they believe is actually true."

With this focus in mind, it is the words of another philosopher, Bertrand Russell (from the book *Unpopular Essays*), that he would frequently recite to young people: "Man is a credulous creature and without good reasons to believe he is satisfied with bad ones." In like spirit, Kroto would recall President Kennedy's dictum that "the great enemy of the truth is very often not the lie, deliberate, contrived, and dishonest, but the myth, persistent, persuasive, and unrealistic. Belief in myths allows the comfort of opinion without the discomfort of thought."

The moral of this seems to be that we cannot always be sure that what we take as factual will always be true. It has even been said that the *majority* of information in textbooks today will be revised within two generations. Samuel Arbesman, a mathematician at Harvard, calls this "the half-life of facts" and compares this churn of knowledge to radioactive decay. You cannot predict which individual fact is going to succumb, but you can be pretty sure about how long it takes for half the facts in a discipline to become obsolete.

Nonetheless, the idea that science is a grand edifice constructed "brick by brick" persists, with the result that complex issues from climate change to gender roles are often reduced to misleading simplicities by people claiming access to a universe of unchanging, monolithic facts.

All of which is why Kroto would sometimes close a session or talk with a phrase of Don Marquis: "If you make people think they're thinking, they'll love you but if you really make them think, they'll hate you." More than this, though, it was Tolkien's words in the epic novel *Lord of the Rings* that sum up Kroto's way of doing science: "Not all who wander are lost." This wonderfully quotable line directly connected to his way of working: if the result he was expecting didn't come, he looked for the reasons why, often saying, "I think there's something interesting there." And that is exactly the spirit that governed his reading too.

ANOTHER SIDE OF *THE LORD OF THE RINGS*

J. R. R. Tolkien's son, Christopher, offers a curious insight into "the story behind the story." He says that it was actually in Yorkshire during a yearlong convalescence from trench fever, contracted in the hellish landscape of World War I in France, that J. R. R. found the spark of inspiration for both *The Hobbit* and *The Lord of the Rings*.

At this time, even as the war raged on a country away, Tolkien and his wife, Edith, found peace and beauty in a small woodland glade not far from the sanatorium. It seems that here Edith began to dance for Tolkien among the trees, creating a moment fixed powerfully forever in his mind. Tolkien imagined her as a kind of Elvish princess and likened her to Princess Lúthien, one of the figures in the ancient texts, and himself to Beren, a mortal onlooker. "In those days her hair was raven, her skin clear, her eyes brighter than you have seen them, and she could sing—and dance," Tolkien wrote in a letter to Christopher long after, on July 11, 1972.

And some of the descriptions of journeys draw upon his own real-life experiences too. Bilbo Baggins, for example, the title character and central figure of *The Hobbit* and a supporting character in *The Lord of the Rings*, follows a route in the book across the Misty Mountains, including a "glissade down the slithering stones into the pine woods" that is based on Tolkien's recollections of his real-life adventures as one of a party of twelve hikers exploring the foothills and mountains of Switzerland.

The plot centers on an ancient ring, called the One Ring, with mysterious powers, forged by Sauron, the Dark Lord, that happens to fall into the hands of a hobbit called Bilbo Baggins. For some, but perhaps rather confusingly not all, the ring confers the power of invisibility, echoing Plato's ancient description of the Ring of Gyges, and just as Plato warned, the price paid by the wearer is a slow corruption of character. Such a thing would not worry Sauron, of course, who, from his base in the Dark Tower of Mordor, searches far and wide for the ring to complete his dominion, but in vain.

Eventually Bilbo reaches his "eleventy-first birthday" and disappears, but not before bequeathing to his young cousin Frodo the task of undertaking a perilous journey across Middle-earth, traveling deep into the shadow of the Dark Lord to destroy the One Ring by casting it into the Cracks of Doom.

Well, that's the plot, and whether or not people actually read the thing, *The Lord of the Rings* is indisputably one of the best-selling novels ever written, with over 150 million copies sold worldwide, not to forget entirely the three very popular film adaptations.

8

Make a Huge Profit— and Then Share It

John Rockefeller and Warren Buffett

M ost of the books here so far have been either fiction or broad-brush factual works, particularly philosophical ones. The readers I've described seem to have chanced upon ideas in them that either captivated or inspired them and sent them off on a new line of thinking.

But of course there's another kind of reader who has a pretty precise idea already of what they want, and this kind looks through the library shelves for books on precisely that. They're not in search of new ideas as such but rather are looking for facts, methods, and details. If fictional works attract the gushing reviews in the Sunday papers, the grand prizes, and the excited media chatter, it is in more workmanlike volumes in reference libraries that many readers first found a crucial guide, a fellow spirit that would channel their intuitions and shape their destiny.

The American stock market guru Warren Buffett is just such a case in point. Here is a man who seems to have always had a pretty precise idea of what he wanted to do and achieve in life (essentially following in his father's footsteps) and, as a young man, had already taken certain career steps to effect that. Yet of all the people I looked at while researching this book, Buffett is the one to most firmly declare that books shaped his life.

We already saw a little bit of this conviction in the introduction, where I recalled him pointing at a pile of books in his office and offering as advice to entrepreneurs of all kinds that they read "500 pages like this every day." Five hundred pages! This directive turns books into a kind of raw material that might be dug out of the ground and sold on the stock exchanges that Buffett's life revolves around. Plus, to me, it's absurd to imagine that plowing through pages and pages of texts chosen like this will give you anything other than tired eyes and maybe a headache. But of course that's not what Buffett is really urging. I think that he is more likely saying that time invested (and "investments" is the word that defines this man) in reading is well spent because books are like brain multipliers. It might take you a decade to match an author for background knowledge in their chosen field; how much smarter to just read their books and let them share their insights.

NONFICTION FAVORITES OF CEOS

Warren Buffett's advice to anyone who wants to become a successful entrepreneur can be summed up in three words: read a lot. And here are the favorite books of three such businesspeople who seem to think the same thing.

First of all, consider Narayana Murthy, the Indian cofounder of Infosys, who has been listed as one of the twelve greatest entrepreneurs of our time by *Fortune* magazine. (Infosys is a global brand specializing in cutting-edge digital services.) Murthy has never shied away from sharing his love for reading. Like Buffett, his favorite book is a practical guide directly relevant to his work—in his case, Jon M. Huntsman's story of how he built a $12 billion company from scratch. The book is called *Winners Never Cheat Even in Difficult Times*, and its core message is that although it can sometimes seem tempting to take shortcuts to get to the top, it is always best to build your company with integrity, and doubly so when times get tough.

Then there's Bill Gates, cofounder of Microsoft and one of Buffett's personal friends. Indeed, Gates shares with Buffett many things, the most superficial being that he is fabulously rich, but a second being that he is a dedicated philanthropist who seeks to use his wealth for the benefit of humankind. The third similarity is a real love of books. As discussed in the introduction, Gates recommends many authors from different genres, but it seems that in his own case it is really a business book that is his preferred beach read, *Business Adventures: Twelve Classic Tales from the World of Wall Street* written by John Brooks. The book, which is also one of Buffett's favorites, seeks to explain why some businesses, like Xerox and General Electric, are successful and why others, like Ford's Edsel venture, fail. If these twelve tales are given a new spin by the publisher, some reviewers nonetheless saw them as being rather dated tales of corporate life in America.

Facebook founder Mark Zuckerberg has spoken time and again, though to my mind less convincingly than Gates or Buffett, of his love for books. Perhaps that's because Zuckerberg names *Why Nations Fail: The Origins of Power, Prosperity, and Poverty* as his favorite book. This joint effort by Armenian American economist Daron Acemoglu and British political scientist James Robinson uses institutional economics, development economics, and economic history to understand why nations develop differently, with some succeeding in the accumulation of power and prosperity and others failing along the way. Zuckerberg, rather sanctimoniously, credits this book with helping him better understand the origins of global poverty.

Warren Edward Buffett (born August 30, 1930; he's a Virgo, the sign astrologers consider a "natural" fit for investments!) is an American tycoon with a net worth of nearly $90 billion, making him the third-wealthiest person in the world. Buffett is the second of three children and the only son of Congressman Howard Buffett, who was himself an investor with a small private firm. Buffett displayed an interest in business and markets at a young age. How young? When he was just seven, he borrowed a book called *One Thousand Ways to Make $1000* from the Omaha Public Library.

Entrepreneurial ventures punctuated much of Buffett's early childhood years: selling chewing gum, Coca-Cola bottles, golf balls, and magazines door to door. On his first income tax return in 1944, Buffett claimed a thirty-five-dollar deduction for the use of his bicycle and watch on his paper route. In 1945, as a high school sophomore, Buffett and a friend spent twenty-five dollars to purchase a used pinball machine, which they placed in the local barber shop. Within months, they owned several machines in three different barber shops across Omaha. The business was sold later in the year for $1,200.

In high school, he invested in a business his father owned and purchased a forty-acre farm worked by a tenant farmer. He bought the land when he was fourteen years old with $1,200 of his savings. By the time Buffett had finished college, he had already saved up the equivalent of

$100,000 today. He might even have become *the* richest person in the world if he hadn't also turned out to be splendidly disinterested in money for himself, favoring instead numerous philanthropic ventures.

And so Buffett's interest in the world of business and investing was well established even as a teenager. In fact, he would have preferred to skip university in order to focus on his business ventures; he only enrolled at university at his father's insistence. After a spell at Pennsylvania, he transferred to Nebraska, from where he graduated at only nineteen years of age. It was at this point that he happened across a newly published book called *The Intelligent Investor* by one Benjamin Graham. Buffett liked the book so much he says he read it about half a dozen times. What is more, seeing that Graham taught at the Business School of Columbia University, he made a beeline there to continue his studies after all. In due course, he would not only complete a master of science in economics at Colombia but also develop an investment philosophy rooted in Graham's ideas.

THE INTELLIGENT INVESTOR
AUTHOR: BENJAMIN GRAHAM
PUBLISHED: 1949

Buffett learned the art of investing from a number of books by Benjamin Graham, but first and most importantly, he came across *The Intelligent Investor*. The book came out in 1949 and soon became a standard reference work on value investing—an approach Graham developed while teaching at Columbia Business School in the late 1920s.

At the heart of the book is the allegory of Mr. Market, an obliging fellow who turns up every day at the shareholder's door, offering to buy or sell his shares at a different price. Often, the price quoted by Mr. Market seems plausible, but sometimes it is ridiculous. The investor is free to either agree with his quoted price and trade with him or ignore him completely. Mr. Market doesn't mind being ignored, though, and will be back the following day to quote another price.

The point of this anecdote is that the investor should not regard the whims of Mr. Market as a determining factor in the value of the shares the investor owns. And Buffett freely credits Graham's book as guiding his own business strategies: first, that smart investors should profit from market folly rather than participate in it, and second, to concentrate on the real-life performance of companies and dividends rather than be too concerned with Mr. Market's behavior.

Graham's allegory offers the figure of Mr. Market as someone who is iras-
cible and moody. Indeed, the more manic-depressive he is, the greater the
spread between price and value, and therefore the greater the investment
opportunities he offers. In his book *The Essays of Warren Buffett: Lessons for
Corporate America* (1997), Buffett reintroduces Mr. Market, emphasizing how
valuable he finds the allegory for disciplined investing. Another debt to Graham that Buffett is quick to acknowledge is in the margin-of-safety principle.
This practical piece of wisdom holds that one should not invest unless there is
a good reason to believe that the price being paid is substantially lower than
the value being delivered.

Since the work was published in 1949, Graham has revised it several times,
the last time being in the early 1970s for the fourth revised edition, which
features a preface and several appendices by Buffett himself. (Any editions produced since 1976 are necessarily without Graham's input as he died that year.)

Buffett unambiguously credits the book as his big inspiration. In an interview,
he said of it, "It not only changed my investment philosophy, it really changed
my whole life . . . I'd have been a different person in a different place if I hadn't
seen that book," adding, "It was Ben's ideas that sent me down the right path."

Soon after (with a segue to study economics at the New York Institute
of Finance), Buffett set up several business investment companies, including one with Graham himself. He created Buffett Partnership Ltd. in 1956
(the key "partners" being a company that made maps for the fire insurance industry and another that made windmills), and this firm in turn
became Berkshire Hathaway in 1970 after it absorbed a textile manufacturing firm and became a diversified holding company.

Ever since Buffett became the chairperson of Berkshire Hathaway, he
has been noted for holding firmly to two principles. The first is pretty
much one that anyone might hold to: he says his company only invests in
firms that he believes have long-term value and prospects. But the second
principle goes much wider and relates to the responsibilities of wealth.
The flamboyant lifestyle and baubles of luxury are not for Warren Buffett.
Even today, he still lives in a five-bedroom stucco house in Omaha that he
bought in 1957 for $31,500. Not for him the gilded palaces or architectural
extravagances of other members of the superrich club.

Instead, despite his immense wealth, he concentrates on ways to put
his money to good use. This strategy means that Buffett has pledged to
give away not a measly 10 percent, as per traditional religious injunctions,
but *99 percent* of his fortune to philanthropic causes! How do you give
away vast sums of money, though, without wasting it? Buffett's off-the-
peg ("ready to wear") solution is to do so primarily through the Bill &
Melinda Gates Foundation. Cynics might note that this is a very unusual
charity in that it regularly returns a substantial profit!

Addressing Colombia University's centennial celebrations (in 2015), Buffett put it like this: "Leaders who use their talents not only to do something for themselves, but for others. Leadership that is creating ideas, creating products, creating whatever it may be that will benefit millions of people."

In his philanthropy, as in his investing, Buffett follows Graham's overarching principle that true investing is based on an assessment of the relationship between price and value. Buffett says, "You can gain some insight into the differences between book value and intrinsic value by looking at one form of investment, a college education. Education's cost is its 'book value' and what is clear is that book value is meaningless as an indicator of intrinsic value."

This is a big idea with political and social ramifications. Buffett warns that strategies that do not employ this comparison of price and value do not amount to investing at all but rather to speculation. A key principle of Buffett's called the *circle of competence* principle follows naturally from this and is the third leg of the Graham/Buffett school of intelligent investing. This commonsense rule advises investors to consider investments only in businesses that they are capable of understanding.

Commenting once on why his investment company had bought a large shareholding in the *Washington Post* newspaper company at a time when such things were being generally shunned by the market, he said, "Most security analysts, media brokers, and media executives would have estimated WPC's intrinsic business value at $400 to $500 million just as we did. And its $100 million stock market valuation was published daily for all to see. Our advantage was our attitude, *that we had learned from Ben Graham*, that the key to successful investing was the purchase of shares in good businesses when market prices were at a large discount from underlying business values" (emphasis added).

Likewise, in the annual letter for his company's investors written in 1987 (starting with a reference to his vice president, Charlie Munger), Buffett follows Graham's lead, saying,

Whenever Charlie and I buy common stocks for Berkshire's insurance companies (leaving aside arbitrage purchases, discussed) we approach the transaction as if we were buying into a private business. We look at the economic prospects of the business, the people in charge of running it, and the price we must pay. We do not have in mind any time or price for sale. Indeed, we are willing to hold a stock indefinitely so long as we expect the business to increase in intrinsic value at a satisfactory rate. When investing, we view ourselves as business analysts, not as market analysts, not as macroeconomic analysts, and not even as security analysts.

This, of course, is the cue for Mr. Market to come in.

Ben Graham, my friend and teacher, long ago described the mental attitude toward market fluctuations that I believe to be most conducive to investment success. He said that you should imagine market quotations as coming from a remarkably accommodating fellow named Mr. Market who is your partner in a private business. Without fail, Mr. Market appears daily and names a price at which he will either buy your interest or sell you his. Even though the business that the two of you own may have economic characteristics that are stable, Mr. Market's quotations will be anything but. For, sad to say, the poor fellow has incurable emotional problems. At times he feels euphoric and can see only the favorable factors affecting the business. When in that mood, he names a very high buy-sell price because he fears that you will snap up his interest and rob him of imminent gains.

But sometimes Mr. Market gets depressed and can see nothing but trouble ahead for both the business and the world. Investors should seek to insulate themselves from "the super-contagious emotions that swirl about the marketplace," and, Buffett says, remember Graham's dictum that in the short run, the market is a voting machine, but in the long run it is a weighing machine. Or we might paraphrase to say that in the short run it is guided by opinions, in the long run by facts.

Such was certainly the case with the global subprime crisis of 2008 that ripped through the United States like a whirlwind, forcing tens of thousands of homeowners and firms to the wall and leaving whole national economies worldwide in tatters. For Buffett, it illustrated what happens when people invest hopefully in things they don't actually understand. "Charlie and I are of one mind in how we feel about derivatives and the trading activities that go with them: we view them as time bombs, both for the parties that deal in them and the economic system."

The problem, Buffett says, is that essentially such instruments call for money to change hands at some future date, with the amount to be determined by one or more reference items, such as interest rates, stock prices, or currency values. However, events such as the subprime crisis of 2007–2009 showed that many CEOs (or former CEOs) at major financial institutions were "simply incapable" of managing huge, complex books of derivatives. "Include Charlie and me in this hapless group," Buffett acknowledges ruefully, adding that it took five years and more than $400 million in losses to "close up shop" on the complex web of 23,218 derivatives contracts with 884 counterparties that they ended up with after purchasing General Re (General Reinsurance Corporation) in 1998.[1]

Buffett's other tips for investors are to beware weak accounting, to distrust unintelligible footnotes as indicative of untrustworthy management,

---

1. In financial dealings, every transaction must have a "counterparty" in order for the transaction to go through. Specifically, every buyer of an asset must be paired up with a seller who is willing to sell and vice versa.

and finally to be suspicious of companies that trumpet earnings projections and growth expectations. Instead of such things, Buffett says what needs to be reported is plain vanilla data that helps financially literate readers answer straightforward questions about how a company is actually doing and what is likely to be its competition in the future.

Judging the future, Buffett quickly acknowledges, is itself a dangerous game and "an expensive distraction for many investors and businessmen." During the darkest days of the subprime crisis, for example, in an op-ed for the *New York Times*, he wrote that if you imagined how the world must have looked to people in the 1960s, no one would have predicted or foresaw the enormity of the Vietnam War, wage and price controls, two oil shocks, the resignation of a president, the dissolution of the Soviet Union, a one-day drop in the Dow of 508 points, or Treasury bill yields fluctuating between 2.8 and 17.4 percent. The point being, he added, that a completely different and equally unpredictable set of major shocks was sure to occur for us in the next thirty years. "We should neither try to predict these nor to profit from them. If we can identify businesses similar to those we have purchased in the past, external surprises will have little effect on our long-term results."

It is because future gazing is so prone to error that Buffett and his company avoid making predictions and tell their managers to do the same. They think it is a bad managerial habit that too often results in faulty reports.

Buffett just gives a simple set of commands to his CEOs: run your business as if you are its sole owner, it is the only asset you hold, and you can't sell or merge it for a hundred years. Short-term results matter, of course, but his investment company's approach avoids any pressure to achieve them at the expense of strengthening long-term competitive advantages. Buffett warns against friendly salespeople promising that their special portfolios of high-yield high-risk bonds can produce greater returns than more humdrum portfolios of safer bonds offering lower returns. As part of his skepticism of elaborate and complex schemes, he even recommends—boringly—that investors simply invest their money in an index fund that doesn't require them to select anything because it simply tracks mainstream stocks. In this way, the smart investor can simply ignore the excited gesticulations of Graham's imaginary Mr. Market. Buffett's tip to investors, following as ever Graham's book, is that their goal should simply be to purchase at a rational price a small stake in an easily understandable business with good prospects not for the next day or week but for five, ten, or even twenty years on. Oh, and if you aren't willing to own a stock for ten years, he says, don't even think about owning it for ten minutes.

In fact, in his own quiet way, Buffett is a champion of the public or, let us say, the small shareholder, against the investing elite, CEOs, and bosses. Indeed, surveying the wreckage of the subprime disaster, he commented unambiguously, "It has not been shareholders who have botched the operations of some of our country's largest financial institutions. Yet they have borne the burden. The CEOs and directors of the failed companies, however, have largely gone unscathed. It is the behavior of these CEOs and directors that needs to be changed: If their institutions and the country are harmed by their recklessness, they should pay a heavy price—one not reimbursable by the companies."

It is for this reason that Buffett, unlike many CEOs who desire their company's stock to trade at the highest possible prices in the market, prefers Berkshire stock to trade at or around its intrinsic value (calculated by considering underlying fundamentals)—neither materially higher nor lower.

If you wonder whether all this stuff about ignoring Mr. Market seems a bit too obvious to really be an inspirational insight, Buffett notes that he is really quite a radical departure from standard economic thinking, in which "efficient market theory" (often abbreviated to EMT) became highly fashionable indeed, "almost holy scripture," in academic circles during the 1970s. Buffett explains, "Essentially, it said that analyzing stocks was useless because all public information about them was appropriately reflected in their prices. In other words, the market always knew everything. As a corollary, the professors who taught EMT said that someone throwing darts at the stock tables could select a stock portfolio having prospects just as good as one selected by the brightest, most hardworking security analyst."

To which Buffett says plainly, "We disagree," and warns again against the academics who like to define investment risk by employing vast databases and statistical skills. The bottom line is whether EMT (the idea that markets know best) or the Mr. Market model (the idea that they don't) is right. As to that, Buffett's reading of Graham's little book insisting the latter seems to have been a very good investment. Here is Buffett summing up his investment company again: "Our net worth has increased from $48 million to $157 billion during the last four decades. No other corporation has come to building its financial strength in this unrelenting way. . . . That's what allowed us to invest $15.6 billion in 25 days of panic following the Lehman bankruptcy in 2008."

Another socially progressive aspect of Buffett is that he prefers productive investments to merely profitable ones. This is a core idea in Adam Smith's pioneering work on early economic theory, *Wealth of Nations*, where Smith describes the flow of cash in the economy as a great wheel of circulation and warns that simply buying gold and putting it in the ground deprives the economy of its lifeblood. As Buffett says,

Today the world's gold stock is about 170,000 metric tons. If all of this gold were melded together, it would form a cube of about 68 feet per side. (Picture it fitting comfortably within a baseball infield.) At $1,750 per ounce—gold's price as I write this—its value would be $9.6 trillion. Let's now create a pile B costing an equal amount. For that, we could buy all U.S. cropland (400 million acres with output of about $200 billion annually), plus 16 Exxon Mobils (the world's most profitable company, one earning more than $40 billion annually). After these purchases, we would have about $1 trillion left over for walking-around money (no sense feeling strapped after this buying binge). Can you imagine an investor with $9.6 trillion selecting pile A over pile B? My own preference is investment in productive assets, whether businesses, farms, or real estate.

Buffett's notion of what is "productive" is quite generous, as over the years he has invested in media companies like ABC and in The Coca-Cola Company, things that Adam Smith would have run a mile from. Nonetheless, the fizzy drink company has turned out to be one of his most lucrative investments—at least up to 1998, when it peaked at eighty-six dollars a share. But then, knowing when a good thing has had its day is always the investor's challenge. Buffett discussed the difficulties of knowing when to sell in the company's 2004 annual report: "That may seem easy to do when one looks through an always-clean, rear-view mirror. Unfortunately, however, it's the windshield through which investors must peer, and that glass is invariably fogged." Likewise, in June 2010, Buffett defended the credit-rating agencies for their role in the US financial crisis, claiming, "Very, very few people could appreciate the bubble. That's the nature of bubbles—they're mass delusions."

During the subprime crisis of 2007–2009, Buffett ran into criticism because he called the downturn "poetic justice," but he was also purposefully scolding himself. His own company suffered a 77 percent drop in earnings in the third quarter of 2008, and several of his later deals suffered large losses.

One time, during a presentation to Georgetown University students in Washington, DC, in late September 2013, Buffett compared the US Federal Reserve to a hedge fund and stated that the bank was generating between $80 and $90 billion a year in revenue for the US government. Buffett also advocated further on the issue of wealth equality in society: "We have learned to turn out lots of goods and services, but we haven't learned as well how to have everybody share in the bounty. The obligation of a society as prosperous as ours is to figure out how nobody gets left too far behind."

In December 2006, it was reported that Buffett did not carry a mobile phone, did not have a computer at his desk, and drove his own automobile, a Cadillac DTS. In 2013, he had an old Nokia flip phone and had sent one email in his entire life. In contrast to that, at the 2018 Berkshire Hathaway shareholder meeting, he said he uses Google as his preferred search engine. However, Buffett is not entirely frugal. As well as that modest stucco house in Omaha bought in the 1950s, he also owns a $4 million house in Laguna Beach, California. Oh, and he spent nearly $6.7 million of Berkshire's funds on a private jet wryly named *The Indefensible*.

Buffett has written several times that in a market economy, the rich earn outsized rewards for their talents. His own children will not inherit a significant proportion of his wealth. Instead, he says, "I want to give my kids just enough so that they would feel that they could do anything, but not so much that they would feel like doing nothing."

Buffett has stated that he only paid 19 percent of his income for 2006 ($48.1 million) in total federal taxes (due to their source as dividends and capital gains), while his employees paid 33 percent of theirs, despite making much less money. "How can this be fair?" Buffett asked, regarding how little he pays in taxes compared to his employees. "There's class warfare, all right, but it's my class, the rich class, that's making war, and we're winning."

Buffett favors the inheritance tax, saying that repealing it would be like "choosing the 2020 Olympic team by picking the eldest sons of the gold-medal winners in the 2000 Olympics." In 2007, he testified before the Senate and urged them to preserve the estate tax so as to avoid a plutocracy. A final ethical conviction of Buffett's is that he insists that government should not be in the business of gambling, or legalizing casinos, activities he calls taxes on ignorance.

All of this paints a picture of an all-too-rare creature—someone who has managed to retain their principles even while becoming rich enough to be tempted to ignore them. This aspect of Buffett has caused some sniping from the sidelines. In an article called "The Church of Warren Buffett: Faith and Fundamentals in Omaha," for example, published by the liberal-leaning *Harper's Magazine* in 2010, Matthias Schwartz describes Buffett as a man who "sits alone in a room, on the fourteenth floor of a gray building."

"The man is the richest in the world," Schwartz continues, more poetically than precisely, "except for certain years when he is the second richest." If he wanted to, he could hire ten thousand people to do nothing but paint his picture every day for the rest of his life, Schwartz recalls is the example Buffett once gave of how much his money could buy, if what he wanted was money to spend. Of course he doesn't do this because, as Schwartz says, I think both unkindly and inaccurately, "the man would rather stay in his room and watch his heap of money grow." Thus he visits the same restaurant and orders the same steak. He goes home to the same house. He plays bridge on the Internet. Every other week he rides the elevator down to the basement of the gray building, where, in a tiny barbershop, he receives the same haircut.

Yet all the time, Schwartz says, Buffett is "living proof" that you can get rich without employing dubious means or borrowed money. He closes his piece by saying that the Buffett method is simply to sit in a room and think, but here too I think he is seriously off base, not least because, as we've seen, Buffett's method, as the man himself makes plain to anyone who will listen, is actually to sit in his room *and read*.

As an investment guru, Warren Buffett is a unique case. It's not really necessary to compare him to anyone else except, perhaps, in the sense of being a great philanthropist—a category there are regrettably few competitors in anyway. But there is one other fabulously rich businessperson whose life story echoes Buffett's and who certainly believed in putting his wealth to good use, and this is the oil magnate John D. Rockefeller. At his peak, at the start of the twentieth century, Rockefeller's net worth was around 1.5 percent of the entire economic output of the United States! Call it around $300 billion today. In his lifetime, Rockefeller donated more than $500 million (hundreds of billions of dollars in today's money) to various philanthropic causes. He funded scientific pioneering of vaccines for meningitis and yellow fever. He set up the schools of public health at Harvard and Johns Hopkins universities to lead the case for public sanitation and supported international efforts to tackle scourges like hookworm and malaria. And he vigorously made the case for providing nationwide public education, without distinction of sex, race, or creed.

With his money Rockefeller created two great research universities, helped the American South out of chronic poverty, educated legions of African Americans, and dramatically improved health around the globe. It is not surprising that his biographer Ron Chernow concluded that Rockefeller "must rank as the greatest philanthropist in American history."

Doing good works is not exactly straightforward either. Initially Rockefeller, as he noted later in his 1909 memoirs, distributed money in a "haphazard fashion, giving here and there as appeals presented themselves." But by the early 1880s he was receiving thousands of letters a month, and most were "requests of money for personal use, with no other title to consideration than that the writer would be gratified to have it."

The need to put his charity on a more methodical, indeed a businesslike, footing became crucial. At this point, a book seems to have helped guide his thinking. *Extracts from the Diary and Correspondence of the Late Amos Lawrence* describes the life of a cotton baron who had made his fortune in New England in the early nineteenth century and devoted his later years to giving it all away again. Upon Lawrence's death in 1852 in Boston, his fortune was estimated at $8 million, or about $250 million in today's dollars.

If Warren Buffett consumes books at the rate of two a day, Rockefeller seems to have barely managed that many in a decade. There are pointers to his interest in only a handful of texts, including those by Artemus Ward, Mark Twain, and Ella Wheeler Wilcox—apart, that is, from the Bible, a book he even led close readings of in his church community. On the other hand, the few books he read seem to have exerted all the stronger an influence, and none less crucial than William Lawrence's summary of his millionaire father's life.

One point the account makes, which surely spoke to Rockefeller as a loyal servant of the Baptist Church, was that Lawrence considered the Christian banner to cover *many* denominations and directed his charities to build up institutions under the influence of a wide range of sects "differing from that under which he himself was classed."

The end result was that Lawrence was "renowned in his generation for a munificence more than princely." He was "one of those rare men in whom the desire to relieve distress assumes the form of a masterpassion"; his benevolence was as "unsectarian as his general habits," and "he stood ready to assist a beneficent design in every party, but would be the creature of none." Lawrence gave not only largely but also wisely. The detailed accounts he kept of his work were not for ostentation, far less "the gratification of vanity," but to make the most "of every pound he gave. With him, his givings were made a matter of business, as Cowper says, in an elegy he wrote upon him: *'Thou hadst an industry in doing good, Restless as his who toils and sweats for food.'*"

Books, themselves largely but not exclusively religious texts, were a key part of Lawrence's charitable giving, both to colleges and individuals, and his son notes warmly that old and young, rich and poor shared equally in his distributions, and he rarely allowed an occasion to pass unimproved "when he thought an influence could be exerted by the gift of an appropriate volume."

In his biography of Rockefeller, John Thomas Flynn says that the youthful Rockefeller was fascinated in particular by the book's description of how Lawrence would instruct his secretary to bring him several hundred dollars in crisp one-, five-, and ten-dollar bills, adding that although he was not well enough to go out, he expected to have "some visits from my friends." As to this, Flynn says that the "sober-faced boy [Rockefeller] thought 'how nice that was' and how, when he was rich, he would like to be able to give out nice, crisp bills." Flynn says that although neither as a boy nor a man an avid reader, Rockefeller remembered this book and often spoke of it. Lawrence's edited diary recounts how he converted several rooms in his house to coordinate the charitable giving process and how he first of all identified libraries and academic institutions, a children's hospital in Boston, and the completion of the Bunker Hill

Monument (where Lawrence's father had fought during the Revolutionary War) as priorities. He also gave to many good causes on a smaller scale and took delight in giving people books from a bundle he kept in his carriage as he drove!

EXTRACTS FROM THE DIARY AND CORRESPONDENCE
OF THE LATE AMOS LAWRENCE;
WITH A BRIEF ACCOUNT OF SOME INCIDENTS OF HIS LIFE
EDITOR: WILLIAM R. LAWRENCE
PUBLISHED: 1856

Three strategies from this book seem to have influenced Rockefeller's own decision to devote much of his energy not to the task of making money but to giving it away effectively and ethically. The book starts by describing these: the first is that it is not enough for a rich man to leave money to good causes in his will; it is necessary that it be given away in his lifetime. "By his course," the book says reverentially, "Mr. Lawrence put his money to its true work long before it could have done anything on the principle of accumulation; and to a work, too, to which it never could have been put in any other way. He made it sure, also, that that work should be done; and had the pleasure of seeing its results, and of knowing that through it he became the object of gratitude and affection. So doing, he showed that he stood completely above that tendency to accumulate which seems to form the chief end of most successful business men; and which, unless strongly counteracted, narrows itself into avarice, as old age comes on, almost with the certainty of a natural law."

The second strategy that made his charitable giving remarkable was "the personal attention and sympathy" with which he directed it.

"He had in his house a room where he kept stores of useful articles for distribution. He made up the bundle; he directed the package. No detail was overlooked. He remembered the children, and designated for each the toy, the book, the elegant gift. He thought of every want, and was ingenious and happy in devising appropriate gifts. In this attention to the minutest token of regard, while, at the same time, he could give away thousands like a prince."

The importance of this expenditure of his own time lay in the fact that "man does not live by bread alone, but by sympathy and the play of reciprocal affection, and is often more touched by the kindness than by the relief." Only this care and consideration for others creates the right relationship between the rich and the poor. If, Lawrence says, it is "a great and a good thing for a rich man to set the stream of charity in motion, to employ an agent, to send a check, to found an asylum, to endow a professorship, to open a fountain that shall flow for ages," it is not the same thing as showing this kind of humanity and personal consideration. And so, his son writes, by Amos Lawrence, "both were done."

The third very important thing Rockefeller clearly absorbed was that Lawrence's daily actions were "guided by the most exalted sense of right and wrong; and in his strict sense of justice." In this way, he demonstrated "the possibility of success, while practicing the highest standard of moral obligation."

This, then, was the model for John D. Rockefeller when he retired from Standard Oil in 1897. He determined to step up his philanthropy with targeted assistance for his favorite educational, religious, and scientific causes. In 1913, the man who was now the United States' first billionaire endowed the Rockefeller Foundation, which had the ambitious goal "to promote the well-being of mankind throughout the world." The foundation contributed to achievements such as development of a yellow fever vaccine and the successful eradication of hookworm disease in the United States.

Despite this, Rockefeller is today often viewed with suspicion, not to say disapproval, as a proponent of social Darwinism who held the belief that the "growth of large business is merely a survival of the fittest." Business books skip over his philanthropism and study only his careful strategies of anticipating market needs and developing timely new products. Here, like Buffett, he took a down-to-earth approach with one of his sayings being the schoolteacherly advice, "The secret to success is to do the common things uncommonly well." However, in work matters, Rockefeller seems to have been a particularly ruthless operator.

John D. Rockefeller still ranks as one of the richest men in modern times and one of the great figures of Wall Street. Remarkably, he started life with almost no advantages. His father, William Avery Rockefeller, had to travel the country selling goods while his mother stayed home with the children. At least Rockefeller received a proper, indeed unusually good, education for his time and found work straight after leaving school as a commission house clerk at age sixteen. Within a few years, he left this to form a business partnership with oil driller Maurice Clark. The partnership would later become Rockefeller, Andrews & Flagler, a company focused on new products made in oil refineries rather than discoveries made by drilling.

The thing that distinguished Rockefeller from his competitors was his understanding of risk—something central to Warren Buffett's success as well. Rockefeller realized that companies looking for oil had the potential for huge profits if they hit a deposit but that they steadily lost money when they didn't. So Rockefeller focused on the certainty of income from the oil refining business instead. The profits were smaller but more reliable.

Disliking the way oil by-products were discarded during the refining process, Rockefeller invested heavily in research to find ways both to make the refining process more efficient and to find uses for the by-products—as lubricants, grease, and later as Vaseline, paint, and many other useful products.

By 1890, Rockefeller's company, Standard Oil of Ohio, was well ahead of the industry and enjoying a high profit margin. And Rockefeller used these profits to buy out competitors. When a competitor did not want to be bought out, Rockefeller used ruthless means of persuasion, including buying up essential materials, such as oil barrels or replacement parts, and causing shortages that crippled smaller companies; orchestrating price wars; and monopolizing essential transport by using his close relationship with the railroad companies.

Many competitors were forced to accept any offer Rockefeller made rather than try to fight against the tide of Standard Oil.

So where did Rockefeller catch the philanthropy bug? References to his idealistic, spiritual side seem to be secondhand and largely unreliable. For example, it is often claimed that under the influence of his mother, a devout Christian, Rockefeller had always tithed one tenth of his income to the local Baptist Church. However, a ledger of his gifts published by himself in 1897 tells an entirely different story.[2]

In the first year of his earnings, it notes his charitable contributions at a penny in the Sunday School plate every Sunday, far less than 10 percent of his fifty dollars annual income. The next year (1856), again according to his ledger, Rockefeller received a raise in his salary and earned $300. Following this, he made a raise in the Sunday School plate: he gave a dime a week instead of a penny.

Rockefeller spoke about his first few years' earnings at the Young Men's Bible Study Class at Fifth Avenue Baptist Church in 1897. Not once in his message to those young men did he say that he ever tithed his money to the church, nor did he tell the young men that they could be tithing their money to the church.

Here again, there is a popular myth that seeks to explain it. This starts by saying that the businessman met Swami Vivekananda, a charismatic spiritual leader and visionary from India, when he delivered a keynote address to the Parliament of World Religions in Chicago in 1893.

Vivekananda is said to have enhanced Rockefeller's perception of philanthropy and inspired him to view himself as a channel for sharing his

2. The ledger is preserved by Colombia University Libraries Preservation Division and can be viewed online at https://archive.org/stream/mrrockefellersle00rock/mrrockefellers le00rock_djvu.txt.

wealth with the world. The guru's message was that each soul is poten-
tially divine and that the goal of life is to manifest this divinity within by
controlling nature, external and internal. This can be achieved through
work, worship, mental discipline, or philosophy—that is, by one, or more,
or all of these—and in this way enable the soul to become free again. This
is the whole of religion. Doctrines, dogmas, rituals, books, temples, and
forms are but secondary details.

Vivekananda is even supposed to have admonished Rockefeller for expecting to be consulted about the selection of a new president for Denison
University, a college to which he had given many donations. One much-
repeated account, purporting to be of Rockefeller's first meeting with the
Indian mystic, as "told by Madame Emma Calvé to Madame Drinette
Verdier," describes how one day, Rockefeller was "pushed by impulse"
to meet the "Hindu monk" who was visiting one of his friends. The account continues,

> The butler ushered him into the living room, and, not waiting to be an-
> nounced, Rockefeller entered into Swamiji's adjoining study and was much
> surprised, I presume, to see Swamiji behind his writing table not even lift-
> ing his eyes to see who had entered. After a while, as with Calvé, Swamiji
> told Rockefeller much of his past that was not known to any but himself,
> and made him understand that the money he had already accumulated was
> not his, that he was only a channel and that his duty was to do good to the
> world—that God had given him all his wealth in order that he might have
> an opportunity to help and do good to people.

Madame Calvé goes on to say that Rockefeller was annoyed that anyone dared to talk to him that way and to tell him what to do. He left the
room in irritation, not even saying good-bye! But about a week after,
again without being announced, he marched into Swamiji's study and,
finding him there exactly the same as before, threw on his desk a copy
of plans to donate an enormous sum of money toward the financing of a
public institution.

"Well, there you are," he said. "You must be satisfied now, and you can
thank me for it."

But it seems Swamiji didn't even lift his eyes, did not move. Instead,
taking the paper, he quietly read it, saying, "It is for you to thank me."
That was all.

A put-down to a man with a monstrous ego? Was this the real reason
why, some twenty or so years later, America's first billionaire endowed
the Rockefeller Foundation, with the ambitious goal "to promote the well-
being of mankind throughout the world"?

Madame Emma Calvé's catchy tale appeals to our innate suspicion
of other people's natures. However, the original source seems to have

been an article published by one M. L. Burke in a magazine called *New Discoveries*—along with the caveat that it was, *ahem*, not authenticated. Naturally, the caveat has been long forgotten, while the story itself has been repeated so many times that it has become part of standard Vivekananda history.

In this, a central part of the Indian guru's greatness is that he was the one who persuaded Rockefeller to become a philanthropist. However, like much else said about Rockefeller, it is definitely not true. Curiously, it is not so much Rockefeller's biographers but members of the Vedanta Society of Kansas City, with a particular interest in the study of Vivekananda, who have attempted to reclaim Rockefeller's reputation and put the facts straight.

First of all, Rockefeller was already documented as a great philanthropist well before 1894. (For example, one of Rockefeller's donations to the University of Chicago is detailed in the December 28, 1892, *Chicago Daily Tribune*.) Second, the assumption that Vivekananda gave Rockefeller the idea that "God had given him all his wealth in order that he might have an opportunity to help and do good to people" is incorrect—Rockefeller had long had that conviction. Third, the claimed incident could not have taken place in Chicago in 1894 as Rockefeller's first visit to the university there would only be in July 1896 on the occasion of the dedication of the Haskell Oriental Museum. A trivial slip in the date for a meeting that did take place? But when Rockefeller really was in Chicago, Vivekananda was far away in Europe. Finally, there are the "psychological" aspects: Madame Calvé's story offers a conceited and short-tempered Rockefeller, and even Vivekananda himself was not exactly polite. Neither portrayal seems accurate.

So how to explain the appearance of such a story? It turns out that Madame Calvé, the original source, was a theatrical diva in the negative sense of a star always seeking more limelight. It's a fine piece of fiction, but as we have seen, the checkable details do not match the historical record, and it probably was never intended to become part of such.

Instead, the real moral impetus for Rockefeller's philanthropic behavior seems to be more straightforward. The book that inspired Rockefeller to donate in today's money hundreds of billions of dollars to good causes seems to have been . . . the Bible. Never underestimate that book. And as we have seen, the practical text that seems to have helped him to settle on the form his philanthropy should take was Amos Lawrence's *Extracts from the Diary and Correspondence of the Late Amos Lawrence*.

Rockefeller is a rare figure in history, not only because of his wealth but also due to his lasting influence on the world in both the oil sector and philanthropy. He is sometimes presented as the antithesis to Henry Ford, who essentially did to the auto industry what Rockefeller did for oil, yet

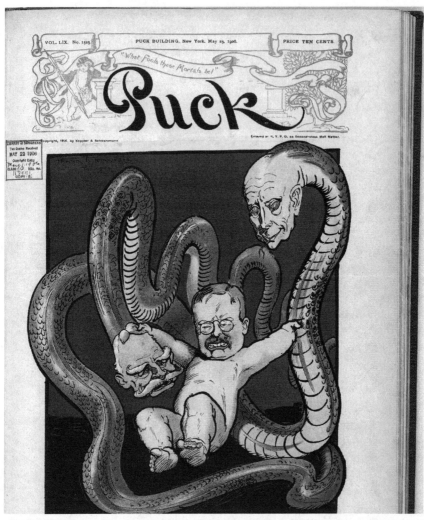

The power of the written word? Despite, by all accounts, being highly scrupulous and despite redefining the limits of philanthropy, Rockefeller has always attracted a hostile press. This cartoon, published in *Puck* magazine in 1906, depicts him as a dangerous snake, threatening US president Theodore Roosevelt (who the magazine supported). Five years later, Rockefeller's company, Standard Oil, would be forcibly broken up after the Supreme Court ruled it was an illegal monopoly. (Frank A. Nankivell, Prints and Photographs Online Catalog, Library of Congress, n.d. https://www.loc.gov /pictures/item/2011645893/.)

in their lifetimes Ford was applauded while Rockefeller was frowned upon and treated as controversial.

Despite being so tough-minded in business matters, Rockefeller did not stint with his philanthropic efforts. He threw himself behind business and charity with the same vigor. Moreover, his path of building a fortune and then giving it away has become a template for wealthy individuals such as Bill Gates and his eponymous foundation.

Through Rockefeller's own foundation, more wealth has been dispersed than Rockefeller personally earned during his lifetime. He inspired others like him to give even more. Some people might fault him for how he built his fortune, but his business practices and his philanthropy have ultimately benefited millions of people.

Many of us start life idealistic, with dreams of being a doctor saving lives, entering politics to win change directed at helping others, or maybe saving the environment as a green activist. Few of us actually end up following those dreams, but what Rockefeller illustrates very powerfully is that there are an infinite number of ways to do good in the world, and sometimes the most effective route is not the most direct one. And he obtained that inspiration from William Lawrence's book about his father.

9

✛

Recognize the Power of Symbols

Malcolm X and Clarence Thomas

Most of the work of a judge sitting on the US Supreme Court is conducted in writing. So shouldn't lists of the favorite texts read by the judges be particularly revealing? For example, it turns out that Justice Stephen Breyer points to a worthy list of classics from Proust to Montesquieu as his inspirations, while Anthony Kennedy loves Shakespeare, Solzhenitsyn, and Trollope. Well, okay, such classic selections sound impressive but are a little too orthodox to really tell us much.

At least Justice Ruth Bader Ginsburg took a small step toward reading-as-we-know-it because her favorite author was Vladimir Nabokov, the professor of literature who rocked the literary world with his acclaimed but controversial novel *Lolita*. Dealing with dangerous themes of a girl's emerging sexuality, the book was described as "shocking" in the original 1958 *Time* review, which also endorsed it as "a major work." Ginsburg said Nabokov changed the very way she looked at the written word. However, even more revealing is the choice of the Supreme Court's sole black member, and only the second ever to serve on the court, the so-called silent judge, Clarence Thomas, because the book that inspired him is *The Autobiography of Malcolm X*.

When you think about it, Malcolm X is far from being suitable reading for a judge, considering that Malcolm X was, above all, an outlaw. But don't get me wrong. I don't mean by this someone who breaks the law, although in his youth he certainly did do that too, but rather to say that Malcolm X was someone who wanted to create an alternative society under different rules. His very name is a rejection of the social order, a denial of his family and social roots, which he describes as irretrievably contaminated by "white rapists" and centuries of injustice. He says he came to hate his lighter skin as revealing "the white rapists' blood in me" and adopted the X to symbolize the true African identity stolen from him long ago. This Malcolm X is no kind of civil rights leader but, on the contrary, condemns notions of such rights *and the law itself* as chains continuing the oppression of "negroes," or "the original men" as he calls them, and reinforces centuries of servitude.

THE MAN WHO DIDN'T WRITE MALCOLM X'S AUTOBIOGRAPHY

Alex Haley (whose real name is actually Will Palmer) came from a very different background to Malcolm X—his father was even an Ivy League graduate. As a child, Haley loved stories, especially adventures and moral tales from the Bible. His grandparents' house, where he lived as a young child, "was the only one in Henning with a library, and it was well stocked. A black traveling bookseller would come around, especially in the fall, when people had money from the cotton harvest," notes Robert Norell in his biography of Haley, adding that books usually cost one dollar, except if they were Bibles, which were more expensive.

One evening, during the Great Depression, when Haley was living with his parents, a white man knocked at his parents' door and asked his mother if she had any work for him. This was doubly unusual, as in those days the shadow of Confederate massacres, lynchings, and official disenfranchisement were the backdrop for most black families. At this time, however, his parents had no income and were themselves being paid with food vouchers. "No," she answered, but she could give him a plate of food. Sometime later, as Norell recounts, the Haleys were driving through Oklahoma on their way to Tennessee when his mother, Bertha, became very sick. In desperation, his father knocked on the door of a strange house in the dark and asked for shelter. The owner of the house was none other than the man who years before had eaten with them. For Haley, the coincidence not only recalled the Bible stories he had read so avidly as a child but made them real.

Underneath the hate-filled radicalism (for which he is still condemned by many) there's another Malcolm X—a young man who aspires one day to be a lawyer. His teachers had told him "with a kind of half-smile" that becoming a lawyer wasn't a "realistic goal for a nigger"—just before advising him to consider instead something "practical" like carpentry. Now, carpentry was Jesus's humble profession, of course, but the idea was clearly received very badly by Malcolm.

But then the Christian—the "White Man's religion"—virtue of humility was never a trait in abundance with Malcolm X, even if he was obliged to feign something like it in jobs ranging from being a shoeshine boy to fourth cook (or glorified dishwasher, as he called it) on a train. Later, as a waiter, he began to exaggerate a humble attitude, including plenty of what he calls the "Uncle Tom-ing," to get better tips, having observed that white people would pay liberally for the impression that they were considered important. Such "Uncle Tom-ing" was an early use as well as recognition of the power of symbols, as was the decision to put a significant proportion of his earnings into buying a smart bright green suit. He made this investment, he writes, because "in order to get something, you had to look as if you already had something."

So the suit was an effort to stand out in the anonymous, mostly desperately poor, black underclass he was surrounded by, but it was also an effort to elevate himself a little bit above them. Just as when, in due course, he did become a respected figure, a community leader for at least part of the community, in the form of a minister in a church, it was as one unambiguously preaching from on high to the unenlightened.

Politics and religion have always mixed freely in Harlem, uptown Manhattan, and the combination can sometimes be pretty toxic. In the course of writing this book, I visited Malcolm X Boulevard, a key thoroughfare there named in Malcolm's honor, and couldn't avoid seeing a thirty-foot-high illuminated sign for the ATLAH World Missionary Church that uncompromisingly advises passersby (in block capitals):

HAD YOU FOLLOWED ME INSTEAD OF OBAMA
YOU WOULD BE MILLION DOLLAR HOME
OWNERS. OBAMA TURNED YOU
HOMO AND HOMELESS.

It's not a very progressive message and all the more aggressive when you recall that President Obama, the United States' first African American president, was supported by the great majority of black voters—a pretty comprehensive 96 percent. Perhaps the Reverend James David Manning was aiming his message at *non*voters, otherwise it would have seemed likely to fall upon deaf ears.

On the reverse side of its illuminated sign, the Church of ATLAH continues:

WHITE LGBTQ MISFITS TELL NEGROS ATLAH
IS A HATE CHURCH. BOOTLICKING COONS
HELPING WHITE MAN TEAR
DOWN A BROTHER.
ALL ATLAH MEN ARE HOMEOWNERS, BUSINESS OWNERS,
LEADERS IN THEIR HOMES. LEADERS IN THE CHURCH,
AND LEADERS IN THE COMMUNITY.

A local resident, Jackie, told me that everyone considered the pastor to be a bit mad but added that he also did a lot of good work within the community. Such are the contradictions of Harlem.

Malcolm X was accused, on the face of it quite fairly, of preaching hate. Indeed, in later years, he himself pretty much disowned his early views and teachings. Yet that is to read his words perhaps too literally. Within the Harlem community, congregations seem quite relaxed about what, in other contexts and other communities, would seem to be nothing less than hate speech. The rhetoric is one thing; the actions are another. It's a pragmatic approach to life sometimes lost on those from outside the community.

Anyway, as minister of Temple No. 7 in Harlem, the largest and most prestigious temple (after the Chicago headquarters) in the American church called the Nation of Islam,[1] he taught that the United States represented not so much "life, liberty, and the pursuit of happiness" as "slavery, suffering, and death." These uncompromising words, he recalls, were painted on a board in Temple No. 1. On the other side of the board were the three qualities of the new church: freedom, justice, and equality.

And yet, at the same time (as the book makes subtly clear) Malcolm X retained something of a philosopher's mindset. If in public he was rarely

---

1. The American church called the Nation of Islam was founded by Wallace Fard, also known as Wallace Fard Muhammad, in 1930.

prepared to allow any divergence of view, in private he acknowledged gaps in his theories and uncertainty as to their foundations.

THE AUTOBIOGRAPHY OF MALCOM X
AUTHOR: ALEX HALEY
PUBLISHED: 1965

The central thread running through his autobiography, combining theory and countertheory, thesis and antithesis, is that of identity or, perhaps we should say, social status. Malcolm X's account starts with intimate examples of the various pecking orders in the mean, poor, and crime-ridden streets of Harlem, what he calls "the ghetto," before it expands into a full-blown theory of racial prejudice and a shocking narrative of how inferiority was forced onto the "original people" by the treacherous and evil white man.

Malcolm X was fascinated by the ghetto. For him it was a place with two aspects: daytime squalor and "nighttime opulence in its back alleys and on its avenues" as another biographer, E. Victor Wolfenstein, has put it. It was a place of contrasts and contradictions, which only reflected the wider realities of the world. Haley's book charts Malcolm X's remarkable passage from the ghetto to the international stage and his personal journey from an angry preacher of racially framed simplicities to a more reflective statesman, but the journey in all the crucial personal and psychological aspects could have taken place simply on the streets of Harlem.

The book has been hugely popular, selling over a million copies in its first two years. Over the years notable readers have included Spike Lee, film director, producer, writer, and actor; James Baldwin, novelist, playwright, and activist; and Oprah Winfrey.

During the course of the biography, reflecting the development of his ideas over the years of his life, Malcolm begins to acknowledge that this figure of the enemy white man is something of a mythical construct and that the truth is more complex. Nonetheless, Malcolm X uses the evil white man as a symbol to argue against integration. Separating out "original man," the African negroes, he set the scene for a battle not merely for recognition but for supremacy in a eugenic hierarchy. Written in the early 1960s, *The Autobiography of Malcolm X* addressed a society in upheaval, so much so that merely listening to Malcolm X was a political, even radical, statement. Indeed, it still is, and doubly so for a black Supreme Court justice.

But perhaps Atallah Shabazz, Malcolm X's son (Shabazz, supposedly the name of a long-ago but great African leader, is one of the names that Malcolm adopted in preference to his birth name of Little), puts his finger on what connects the Supreme Court justice and radical church preacher best with a comparison to another famous personal history: *The Diary of Anne Frank*. Shabazz explains that his father shared a belief with the young Jewish girl hiding from the Nazis in a Dutch attic. They believed "in the power of words to influence and transform lives." This is a principle that Clarence Thomas also holds closely in his work in the grand, marbled halls of the US Supreme Court.

Likewise, at the heart of Malcolm X's book is the conviction that in order to understand the power of words, they need to be reinterpreted as operating on many levels, one of which is as a more fundamental kind of communication that uses the power of symbols.

Indeed, *The Autobiography of Malcolm X* is packed with symbolism. Starting in chapter 1, the welfare visits his mother received from city officials brought vital resources and advice but also a second and less welcome message: that the family was dependent and inferior. Malcolm X recalls that the welfare staff who visited the family "acted as if they owned us, as if we were their private property."

Similarly, when, as a teenager, he artificially straightened his natural hair, his "conk," to look more like the white man, he says his hairstyle was intended to raise him above the other black youths, to be a kind of rite of passage to the adult world, but was in reality marking his "first really big step towards self-degradation."

And then there was the status symbol of a good-looking white girl-friend. At the time, Malcolm X was incredibly proud to go out with one of the best-looking white girls in black downtown Roxbury, saying even that it seemed he had really begun to "mature into some real status," but later on he despised and regretted his own hypocrisy and insincerity.

Not to forget, of course, status also came from carrying guns. "Red," as he now called himself, soon packed a gun. "I saw how when the eyes stared at the big, black hole, the faces fell slack and mouths sagged open." Malcolm X even took to carrying three guns at once, in various holsters. Sure enough, he ends up in prison, but if that is where many people end their stories, it was really where Malcolm X's truly began. Norfolk Prison Colony had a remarkable feature: it contained a very substantial library, donated by "a millionaire named Parkhurst" who'd collected hundreds of old and rare books, many of which were on history and religion.[2]

---

2. Of course, New York City itself has many superb and completely free public libraries, like the palatial one on Fifth Avenue guarded by two massive stone lions. However, in Malcolm X's youth, not only did state and local racial segregation laws flatly deny African Americans access to public facilities across the US South, informal barriers deterred them elsewhere too. Even today, grand libraries can be a little *too* grand sometimes, while smaller ones can serve a different purpose and reach different people.

Malcolm X quickly overcame illiteracy, spending days looking up words in an illustrated dictionary. The word "aardvark'" particularly stuck in his mind: "a long-tailed, long-eared burrowing African mammal" that eats insects.

"I suppose it was inevitable that as my word-base broadened, I could for the first time pick up a book and read and now begin to understand what the book was saying. Anyone who has read a great deal can imagine the new world that opened."

For Malcolm X, the books made the prison bars melt away.

The first books he read, and the ones that impressed him most, were collections of scientific and historical facts, particularly one called *Wonders of the World*, along with Will and Ariel Durant's *The Story of Civilization* and H. G. Wells's *Outline of History*. An introduction into a lost inheritance of black culture came from W. E. B. Du Bois's *Souls of Black Folk* and Carter G. Woodson's *Negro History*. He also read the novel *Uncle Tom's Cabin*, a best-selling tale of a long-suffering black slave who is resold and sent off on a Mississippi riverboat. In fact, it seems this is almost the only novel that he did read.

Malcolm X read avidly about Gandhi's campaign to push the British out of India, about the history of China and the opium wars, and about the signs put up by the "vicious, arrogant white man: 'Chinese and dogs not allowed.'" These books provided him with "indisputable proof that the collective white man had acted like a devil in virtually every contact he had with the world's collective non-white man." At this stage in his life, he did not appreciate that the vicious treatment of the nonwhite man was also a feature of relationships within the white races, riven by innumerable other divides, be they religious, social, or ethnic, his failure particularly highlighted by casual and cold remarks about Hitler's treatment of the European Jews.

In these history books, Malcolm X looked for—and found—stories and parallels that enabled him to make sense not only of the world but also of himself. This is why *The Story of Civilization* made such a profound impression.

"Civilization is a stream with banks," Will Durant once said. "The stream is sometimes filled with blood from people killing, stealing, shouting and doing the things historians usually record, while on the banks, unnoticed, people build homes, make love, raise children, sing songs, write poetry and even whittle statues. The story of civilization is the story of what happened on the banks. Historians are pessimists because they ignore the banks for the river."

The Durants' approach was looked down on by conventional historians, who particularly accused them of seeking to personify processes and events, a charge to which they admitted. "We believe that in the last hundred years history has been too depersonalized," Will Durant once said, "and that statistics have replaced men in the story of mankind. History operates in events but through persons; these are the voice of events, the flesh and blood upon which events fall, and the human responses and feelings are also history."

And the Durants worked hard on their project. The research for each of the series of books was time-consuming and required from the mid-1930s on that the Durants follow a strictly observed regimen of work and study. They studied seven days a week, from eight in the morning to ten at night, reading and carefully noting information from about five hundred books for each of their own volumes.

The economic freedom to devote years of work like this was provided by the success of Will Durant's first book, *The Story of Philosophy*, a brisk account of the ideas of the world's greatest thinkers, from Plato to John Dewey. First published in 1926, *The Story of Philosophy* has sold three million copies. (Even many decades later, when I look at Amazon to see how my own humble introduction to philosophy, *101 Philosophy Problems*, is doing, I find that, as Amazon likes to put it, my customers have "also bought" Will Durant's venerable book.) *The Story of Philosophy* was aimed at the general reader and sprinkled with anecdotes and personal comments in a manner that made it far more readable than the standard philosophy book. And it was very much the template for the later *Story of Civilization*.

Will and Ariel Durant put it like this: "To those of us who study history not merely as a warning reminder of man's follies and crimes but also as a remembrance of generative souls, the past ceases to be a depressing chamber of horrors; it becomes a celestial city, a spacious country of the mind, wherein a thousand saints, statesmen, inventors, scientists, poets, artists, musicians, philosophers and lovers still live and speak, teach and crave and sing."

THE STORY OF CIVILIZATION
AUTHORS: WILL AND ARIEL DURANT
WRITTEN BETWEEN 1927 AND 1975

Malcolm X is not the first and won't be the last person to be enticed into the world of reading not by fiction but by facts and factoids. Indeed, it is a cliché of everyday life that encyclopedia salesmen used to visit suburban homes offering their wares to families who may well have had few other books. No one could read the twenty-three volumes of the *Britannica*, even if many explorations might start there. However, *The Story of Civilization* is a little bit more than a mere compilation of facts. It is, as the title claims, very much a story, and a grand one at that. The writing alone took up most of Will Durant's life (he started in 1927 and completed it, with the help of his wife, Ariel, in 1975), by which time it spanned more than five million words and eleven volumes.

Durant himself was led to his task by a book, *An Introduction to the History of Civilization*, which had been started but never completed by the nineteenth-century British historian Henry Thomas Buckle. Durant threw aside the British nationalism and determined instead, as he said in the preface to the book, "to tell as much as I can, in as little space as I can, of the contribution that genius and labor have made to the cultural heritage of mankind. . . . It may be of some use," he went on, "to those upon whom the passion for philosophy has laid the compulsion to try to see things whole, to pursue perspective, unity and understanding through history in time." The aim, he said, was "to portray in each period the total complex of a nation's culture, institutions, adventures and ways." The first volume, *Our Oriental Heritage*, traced the beginnings of civilization to the East, while the tenth volume, *Rousseau and Revolution*, found in the French philosopher's notion of universal rights a kind of logical closure even as the Durants allowed that chronologically there were two more centuries to document.

Rousseau and Revolution won the Pulitzer Prize for general nonfiction in 1968 and like all the other ten volumes was a best seller. The series managed total sales of more than two million copies in nine languages, a readership, as the *New York Times* noted in its obituary for Will Durant, enjoyed by few historians. The *Times* went on to suggest that one explanation for the success of *The Story of Civilization* was "the clarity and wit of its prose" (something no one has ever said of the *Britannica*), while another key ingredient was its emphasis on man's achievements in art, literature, science, and philosophy "rather than on the follies and crimes of mankind or on military, political and economic events." Or ideas, not statistics, we might say.

One way or another, the result was that, while in prison, Malcolm X explored philosophy. In his autobiography, he recalls, rather randomly, the German philosophers "Schopenhauer, Kant and Nietzsche" but quickly dismisses them, saying that they spent their time arguing over useless things and probably laid the ground for the rise of Hitler too. Spinoza impressed him, though, all the more because Spinoza was black—a black Jew, actually. Ultimately, Malcolm X says the whole of Western philosophy "wound up in a cul-de-sac" determined to hide the black man's greatness. He says that of Western and Eastern philosophies, he came to prefer the latter, seeing Western philosophy as essentially unacknowledged borrowings from the East. Even "Socrates, for instance, traveled to Egypt," he notes, ironically missing that any such visit would have been at the time that Egypt was conquered by the Greeks and becoming part of the classical (Hellenic) empire—and thus a poor example of non-Western influence.

He clearly found a chord with philosophy's great iconoclast Friedrich Nietzsche. In his sermons, directly following Nietzsche, Malcolm X denounces Christianity as a religion fit only for slaves, a slave ideology. Islam, instead, for Malcolm X, was a liberation theology.

Indisputably, reading in prison changed forever the course of his life. It awoke in him a craving to be mentally alive no less. He told one correspondent that his alma mater was books. "If I weren't here, every day, battling the white man, I could spend the rest of my life reading, just satisfying my curiosity, because you can hardly mention anything that I'm not curious about."

Alex Haley, the indispensable interviewer and editor behind the *Autobiography*, notes in a personal epilogue that closes it that any interesting book Malcolm X read could get him going about his love for reading books. "People don't realize how a man's whole life can be changed by one book," Malcolm X told Haley and returned again and again to the books he had first come across while in prison.

And yet, even if Malcolm X loved reading books, he was not really made of the stuff of a true author. Rather Malcolm X was a speaker, a fount of fiery words, who thundered out sermons and relished the cut and thrust of debate. His nature is revealed in his second life as an Islamic preacher. He notes that when he spoke at rallies he would draw "ten or twelve times as many people as most other so-called Negro leaders" and claims that the ghetto masses had "chosen him as their leader." Add to which, as Alex Haley notes, he was "clearly irked" by the newspapers reporting a poll that found that it was Martin Luther King, and not himself, who was "doing the best work for New York negroes."

Fard's Nation of Islam gave Malcolm X a platform that he used to develop and publicize a radical politics built on a theory of racial identity—and conflict. Yet Islam also later brought him to a very different view, one in which racial divisions began to melt away. This later vision came at a time when he was already in the process of falling out with Fard.

The turning point came on a pilgrimage to Mecca, when he was astonished that all the pilgrims were dressed the same. "You could be a king or a peasant and no one would know." But more importantly, he began to see that the color of people's skin was not important either. "Packed in the plane were white, black, brown, red and yellow people, blue eyes and blond hair, and my kinky red hair,—all together, brothers! All honoring the same God, Allah."

Now, for the first time in his life, Malcolm says, he considered it possible that a white man could be good to him without any hidden, selfish motive. "Always in my life, if it was a white man, I could see a selfish motive," he recalls with honest if appalling ungraciousness.

Asked what his feelings were after his pilgrimage, he tells reporters that what he has been struck by most is the brotherhood, "the people of all races and colors from all over the world coming together AS ONE!" Most significantly of all, he now says that he sees the earth's "most explosive and pernicious evil" as racism.

This reformed Malcolm X even says that Islam erases distinctions of race, but this is an optimistic assertion, clearly not borne out by actual societies, such as Saudi Arabia itself, where a small elite defined by race oppresses and exploits a foreign "worker" population. On his return to the United States, he tries to stress in all his public pronouncements that he is not condemning white people as such but rather white racists. In other respects, though, his position remains radical: he wants the negro to fight not for a place in the existing system but to overturn the system itself. Likewise, toward the end of the book, Malcolm talks of the origins of the United States in the genocide of indigenous American Indians, condemning the United States as the only nation that tried, "as a matter of national policy, to wipe out its indigenous population." More shameful still, he writes, even today "our literature, our films, our drama, our folklore all exalt it." He adds, "Our children are still taught to respect the violence which reduced a red-skinned people of an earlier culture into a few fragmented groups herded into impoverished reservations."

Here is a Malcolm X who has progressed far beyond simplistic notions of race toward ideas of indivisible human rights and universal values—the kind of values that the US Supreme Court, in fact, is tasked to uphold. Perhaps that is why, at the end of the biography and the close of one of history's most extraordinary personal journeys, Malcolm X talks of his days as a fiery Muslim preacher in New York as "a bad scene" and regrets the "sickness and madness of those days" before noting, rather plaintively, "I do believe I might have made a good lawyer."

Actually, I'm not so sure of that, but what is clear is that, a decade later, his story helped transform the frustration and anger at what seemed to be all-pervading racism of American life of another young, black, and struggling American, Clarence Thomas, into a more focused bid to become a kind of alternative Malcolm X, one who really did become a lawyer.

In his own autobiography, Thomas, like Malcolm X, starts by crisply mentioning shocking, jarring childhood experiences, invariably rooted in racial prejudice, that seem to have regularly marked his journey. *My Grandfather's Son* is in many ways a compelling read all on its own, detailing Thomas's extraordinary rise from poverty in rural Georgia in the bitterly divided American South to his bitterly fought promotion to the nation's highest court. Throughout, as with Malcolm X, the shadow of racial prejudice is always present. Thomas's career, life, and family's well-being were continually threatened by vicious accusations that fed off a seam of racism lurking just beneath the surface of the nation.

Yet the references to personal struggles are made tersely, even brusquely, and without elaboration or further comment. Because, with Judge Thomas, not only is there a line between fact and comment, but the latter is generally not wanted.

As Jan Crawford Greenburg, a journalist for ABC News who interviewed him at length, says, ever since Clarence Thomas joined the Supreme Court in 1991, he has largely remained silent, and his silence has become part of his mythology. "He rarely speaks from the bench. He hasn't responded to legions of critics. His judicial opinions reveal a powerful voice, but his story had been written by others." However, there she is not quite right. Because there is his autobiography.

MY GRANDFATHER'S SON: A MEMOIR
AUTHOR: CLARENCE THOMAS
PUBLISHED: 2007

It is surely notable that Clarence Thomas says that the pages of Malcolm X's autobiography became grubby and worn because he studied them so closely. But one other effect seems to have been on how the future Supreme Court judge later approached his own autobiography. Malcolm X starts with a plainly delivered account of his early childhood brought abruptly to an end by his father's suicide and his mother's subsequent institutionalization, while Thomas's story starts with a plainly delivered account of his early childhood in the Deep South ended by his mother's decision to send him and his brother to be raised by his grandparents as she felt unable to care for them. Indeed, the two men seem to have shared many key experiences and anxieties in their formative years.

But where Malcolm X eventually found himself as a fiery orator, Clarence Thomas always seems to have been something of an egghead, dedicated to nothing so much as getting the best grades. Indeed, the superficial heart of his autobiography is rather a self-serving tale of academic excellence, and you have to look behind that to find a more compelling, personal narrative that includes emotional distress over divorcing his first wife, his awkward embrace of conservative politics (seen as "anti-black"), and above all the drama of the confirmation hearings for his appointment to the Supreme Court.

It is this ostensibly very civilized process that is titled "Invitation to a Lynching." Here in this very public drama, Thomas's bitterness at the roles forced on African Americans in a white man's world is laid bare. Mind you, Thomas himself received rather better treatment in that world than many others, with a $1.5 million advance for his book and a wide readership, which saw the book hit number one on the *New York Times* nonfiction best-seller list.

In his book, Thomas combines a lawyer's grasp of detail with a deft storyteller's instinct. "Nothing about my childhood seemed unusual to me at the time," he explains early on before continuing matter-of-factly that he was born in 1948 in Pinpoint, a coastal community in southern Georgia. His father abandoned the family three years later, but even so Thomas has fond memories of his earliest years, which he calls idyllic.

"Sometimes I heard the grown-ups talk about the white people for whom they worked, but I took it for granted that they were all rich. Photographs in newspapers and magazines gave me fleeting glimpses of an unreal existence far from home, but Pinpoint (a saltwater creek not far from the town of Savannah) was my world and until I started going to school, the only sign that there might be another one was the occasional airship or blimp I saw flying overhead."

In fact, books were one of the few things that traveled between the two worlds. And books are central to Clarence Thomas's story: he notes that Savannah would be known to most people through reading *Midnight in the Garden of Good and Evil*, a nonfiction work later made into a film that presents the town as an "architectural wonderland full of well-heeled eccentrics." Yet, he says, if such a world ever existed, it was certainly not the deprived and ramshackle Savannah he knew.

He lived with his mother and siblings in the "ramshackle house" of an aunt and uncle, until the house burned down when he was seven. After this, his mother moved Thomas and his younger brother to a flat in a house in Savannah that lacked indoor plumbing or beds for the children. Thomas slept in a chair. "Overnight I moved from the comparative safety and cleanliness of rural poverty to the foulest of urban squalor," Thomas wrote, recalling a time of "hunger without the prospect of eating, cold without the prospect of warmth."

And then, one Saturday, Thomas wrote, his mother told Thomas and his younger brother Myers that they were going to live with their grandparents: Myers and Tina Andersen. The boys were sent out the front door with all their belongings hastily stuffed in a pair of grocery bags.

The Andersens were comparatively well off, but to say that his grandfather was stern would be an epic understatement. "The damn vacation is over," his new "father," or "daddy" as Clarence Thomas always refers to him, said as the two boys arrived, before setting out the rules of his new home, the most important of which was that his grandparents were always right. On one occasion Thomas answered back to his grandfather and was immediately slapped round the face—so hard it knocked him to the floor. And yet if "Daddy" was strict and unbending, the home was comfortable (and of course well regulated), and Thomas soon accepted the new routine.

Thomas went to all-black church schools through the tenth grade, although even then he was conscious of distinctions based on class and skin color. He was enrolled at Florence Street—"one of the finest public schools in Savannah built specifically for black students." Throughout the book, perhaps paradoxically, Thomas defends segregation, not obviously as an end in itself but as an acceptable feature of a world in which so many other factors divide. He insists, for example, that what black children need is good schools, not necessarily to be bused into white neighborhoods to sit alongside white children in rundown city schools.

Even in his segregated black school, he recalls being insulted by black classmates "because of the darkness of my skin" and says he was referred to as "ABC," code for "America's Blackest Child." Whites lived in a parallel world: his only real encounter with them was as nuns and priests.

"We didn't consider them white. They were nuns. You had white priests and white nuns, but they were considered nuns and priests," Thomas says. "That's sort of like thinking of angels. You didn't think of angels as white or black. They were angels."

Their example inspired Thomas, as did (more subtly) the fact that among his classmates were the children of professionals: teachers, doctors, and businesspeople. "The sisters taught us that God made all men equal, that blacks were inherently equal to whites, and that segregation was morally wrong." If, today, schools run by nuns seem to many secular educationalists as anachronistic, at the time they offered a crucial alternative to the state system.

Before long, Thomas decided he wanted to become a priest too. A Catholic boarding school prepared boys for the seminary, so at age sixteen Thomas "dared to leave the comfort zone of segregation," he wrote, and transferred there, enrolling in tenth grade and becoming one of the school's first black students.

Thomas recalls his feelings of panic and anxiety—the price his generation paid for moving out from behind the wall of segregation. He survived the many blows to his self-esteem, but his grades were excellent and he made swift progress as a diligent student. He was already determined to succeed, not only for himself but also for his race. When he returned home on weekends, Thomas says his proud grandfather would take him to the local NAACP (National Association for the Advancement of Colored People) meetings so he could report on his grades. He became one of the school's top students and was applauded at his grandfather's meetings. He realized that he himself had become a symbol—a symbol of hope and pride for them.

At the same time, however, he relates how he had become increasingly disillusioned with the Catholic Church's acceptance of the treatment of blacks in the United States, saying that its silence began to haunt him. To use the language of the church, he lost his vocation, a fact brought home to him one day when he walked into his school dormitory and heard someone shout that Martin Luther King Jr. had been shot, followed by the crude response of one of his fellow students: "That's good, I hope the son of a bitch dies." Thomas explains, "His brutal words finished off my vocation and my youthful innocence about race."

Thomas had begun to mature in his views, and in particular he began to see the church as an institution complicit in the racism of the era. "When I went to church back in the '60s, there was no focus on ending segregation, except from the nuns, who were adamant from day one," Thomas told a television interviewer later. "The Church wasn't. It seemed to be more accommodating, again, at least from where I stood. And I just thought that had they been as principled as the nuns or as forceful as they are on the issue of abortion now, I would have gone on and become a priest."

This was part of a political awakening that *The Autobiography of Malcolm X* in particular was instrumental in guiding and forming. At Holy Cross, Thomas says he read the book so many times that the pages grew worn. He particularly admired the black activist's philosophy of self-reliance and, having also grown up in the segregated South, shared Malcolm X's distrust of government and white society. Yet, even as a young student with the words of Malcolm X in his ears, he developed and valued important friendships with whites.

Years later, in the early 1990s, when President George Bush was looking for a replacement for Thurgood Marshall, the Supreme Court's first African American justice, the Republican Party focused more on Clarence Thomas's conservative views. Had the White House vetted Thomas more thoroughly, let alone analyzed those views, it might well have been reluctant to nominate him. So convinced were they that here was a mere follower, they scarcely noticed that he'd given countless speeches while at the Equal Employment Opportunity Commission expressing a range of controversial opinions, not only about the law and the Constitution but also of his admiration of Louis Farrakhan and the black Muslim theory of self-reliance. However, both of these topics would come up at his confirmation hearing.

Clarence Thomas writes bitterly that at these hearings, the necessary public prelude to becoming a Supreme Court judge, he had to be "dehumanized and destroyed," precisely because he held views considered heretical for a black man and partly because, as he puts it, he was in a different ideological neighborhood and refused to buy in to the views that whites had "disseminated as the prevailing view for blacks."

He says his critics—the people who questioned whether he was smart or qualified enough to be on the court or those who suggested that he would meekly do whatever a white Supreme Court colleague told him—are in their own way as bigoted as the whites of his childhood in the deep South.

"People get bent out of shape about the fact that when I was a kid, you could not drink out of certain water fountains. Well, the water was the same. My grandfather always said that, 'The water's exactly the same.' But those same people are extremely comfortable saying I can't drink from this fountain of knowledge . . . They certainly don't see themselves as being like the bigots in the South. Well, I've lived both experiences. And I really don't see that they're any different from them."

At overwhelmingly all-white Holy Cross, he had been an outspoken activist who openly admired Malcolm X. This was the time when the American South was increasingly torn by urban race riots and political protests. For Thomas himself, the reality of "racism had become the answer to all my questions, the trump card that won every argument." He had become "an angry black man."

He argued then and still believes that white people have created a system where blacks have to stay in a certain place—only this time the boundaries concern ideas, not geography. As for the voices of white liberal reformers, he became, and still is, very skeptical, saying, "These people who claim to be progressive . . . have been far more vicious to me than any southerner and it is purely ideological."

Once again it was books that came to his rescue. While at Holy Cross College, he was able to enroll in an individual studies class and "felt the thrill of true intellectual growth." He read voraciously, including Ayn Rand's *Atlas Shrugged* and *The Fountainhead*, two works of quasi-philosophical style that I personally detest but seem to have inspired many individualist endeavors. Their main thrust is that there is virtue in the pursuit of individual achievements, coupled with a disdain for consideration of social values. Thomas says he took what he wanted from it and disagreed with the rest. "It went without saying that I was an individual: we are all individuals. The question was how much courage I could muster up to express my individuality."

And whether from Rand or just from first principles, the idea that government tends to "meddle with incompetence if not mendacity" in the lives of its citizens is central to Thomas's future politics.

JUDGE THOMAS'S FAVORITE READS

In his autobiography, Clarence Thomas says that his love of Churchill "kindled a love of reading for its own sake"—one that he had not acquired in college.

"Before long I was gobbling up such fat tomes as Paul Johnston's *Modern Times* and *A History of Christianity*, after which I branched out to Lincoln biographies." For "lighter fare" he read the Westerns of Louis L'Amour and Ayn Rand's political novels, "whose scathing criticisms of the dangers of centralized government impressed me even more after working in Washington."

"Reading Richard Wright's *Native Son* had made the strongest impression on me as a college student. What had happened to Bigger Thomas, I knew, could happen to any black man, including me."

In the darkest moments of his own real-life "inquisition" by the Senate panel supposedly reviewing his suitability to become a Supreme Court justice (but, he says, actually pursuing a more narrowly party political agenda), Thomas also recalls another famous story of injustice meted out to black men: *To Kill a Mockingbird*, in which Atticus Finch, a small-town southern lawyer, must defend Tom Robinson, a black man accused of raping a white woman. "He was lucky to have a trial at all—Atticus had already helped him to escape a lynch mob's rope."

Thomas says another of his favorite books is *Battle Cry of Freedom* by James McPherson, a history of the American Civil War, and at one point in his memoir, he urges one young man he meets to "keep on reading and dreaming."

But speaking of individuality, here, once again, books came to Thomas's aid. He took an independent study course on black novelists that included Richard Wright's *Native Son*. The novel describes the nightmare world of an innocent black man who finds himself caught up in a chain of events that eventually leads him to commit an act of violence that ultimately results in his death. Thomas also read Ralph Ellison's *Invisible Man*, which contains what seems to be Thomas's favorite quote, reproduced at length in his autobiography:

I was never more hated than when I tried to be honest. Or when, even as just now, I've tried to articulate exactly what I felt to be the truth . . . I was pulled this way and that for longer than I can remember. And my problem was that I always tried to go in everyone's way but my own. I have also been called one thing and then another while no one really wished to hear what I called myself. So after years of trying to adopt the opinion of others I finally rebelled. I am an *invisible* man.

Particularly striking is the line, "I have also been called one thing and then another while no one really wished to hear what I called myself." This seems to truly crystallize Clarence Thomas's own experience.

Anyway, to jump to the end, as it were, Thomas eventually studies for and passes the bar exam to become a lawyer. By now his perception of black justice has matured as he comes to terms with the fact he relays in the book that over 90 percent of black murder victims died at the hands of fellow blacks. He describes spending "a whole week trying to find a copy of *Race and Economics* and buying six copies when he finally did track it down knowing that I would want to have extra copies to lend or give away."

The reality was not as simple as blaming black people's woes on the "white devils" of Malcolm X's early days, he now realizes. As he puts it in his autobiography, "I also grew more wary of unsupported generalizations and conspiracy theories, both of which had become indispensable features of radical arguments."

The issue of the condition of blacks in the United States remained his central political cause. "As a young radical, I had found it easy to cloak my belief in the necessity of black self-reliance in the similar-sounding views of Malcolm X and the Back Muslims," he writes, in one of very few direct references to his radical days. Another time he says that he hated himself for "having succumbed in college to radical ideologies," and in a third reference he allows he had "been attracted to the Black Muslim philosophy of self-reliance ever since my radical days in college" and as a young man had praised Louis Farrakhan, aka "Louis X," one of the key figures in the Nation of Islam movement that Malcolm X became an evangelist for.

Ultimately for Thomas, it was the exquisitely crafted 1,458 words of the Declaration of Independence that encapsulated the core principles of natural law—specifically the promise that "all men are created equal" and have certain unalienable rights that come with that inheritance.

10

Follow Your Personal Legend

Malala Yousafzai and Oprah Winfrey

One of the most memorable phrases of the darkly brooding Brazilian author Paulo Coelho is "Life is the train, not the station," by which he means that life is about the journey, not the destination. Yet equally, we don't get trains to just any old place, nor is it enough just to live—we do need to have a sense of purpose.

That's a message Oprah Winfrey and Malala Yousafzai share. And if the two may seem an unlikely pair on the surface, they have some vital things in common: both come from very humble backgrounds, and both have become global icons for their dedication to an individual passion. Above all, both women are believers in the power of books and both are themselves inspired by certain bookish values.

Oprah was born into poverty in rural Mississippi to a single mother and raised in Milwaukee (a town with the dubious reputation of being the most segregated city in the United States). She has described being molested in her early teens, becoming pregnant at fourteen, and the child dying in early infancy. Yet today Winfrey is an American talk show host, actress, producer, and major philanthropist too. Of course, she is best known for *The Oprah Winfrey Show*, which was the highest-rated TV chat show in history. And if you're still not inclined to count her as a business entrepreneur, bear in mind that she was the first African American to become a multibillionaire!

While there are few people on the planet who haven't heard of Oprah, you'd be excused for not knowing about Malala Yousafzai, a Pakistani woman who, nonetheless, in 2014 became the youngest person to win the Nobel Peace Prize. She shares a passion for books with Oprah, and her Nobel win was in large part for her literacy campaigns. Other than that, their origins could not be more different. Yousafzai was born and brought up in the beautiful Swat valley region of Pakistan, an area of mountains, rivers, and shimmering sunsets. The serenity there was destroyed forever, however, when the Taliban seized the region in 2006, killing two thousand people. Schools became a particular target of the Taliban's torturous agenda, with the right to education one of many freedoms lost to the women of the Swat valley. As a young girl, Malala experienced these tragedies firsthand and decided to campaign fearlessly for basic education rights for herself and girls like her.

Malala tasted her first success at the tender age of eleven while writing blogs anonymously for the BBC Urdu-language site. She wrote about how life in the valley was changing under Taliban rule and about being prevented from attending school. In her January 3, 2009, BBC blog post, under the heading "I Am Afraid," she wrote, "I had a terrible dream yesterday with military helicopters and the Taliban. I have had such dreams since the launch of the military operation in Swat. My mother made me breakfast and I went off to school. I was afraid going to school because the Taliban had issued an edict banning all girls from attending schools. Only 11 out of 27 pupils attended the class because the number decreased because of the Taliban's edict. My three friends have shifted to Peshawar, Lahore and Rawalpindi with their families after this edict."

Inevitably, even though she never signed her name to these blog posts, over the course of the next three years, both Yousafzai and her father became known throughout Pakistan for their campaign to give Pakistani girls access to education. In 2011, she was nominated for the International Children's Peace Prize and awarded the Pakistan National Youth Peace Prize.

With this fame came enemies: death threats against her were published in newspapers and slipped under her door. On the morning of October 9, 2012, Yousafzai, whose first name means "grief-stricken," saw these threats become reality. Seated with her friends on a school bus heading home from school, she felt the bus stop and saw two Taliban soldiers come aboard. A young bearded man asked for Yousafzai by name and shot her three times in her head and shoulder, leaving her for dead.

That same day, she was given emergency treatment in a hospital in Saidu Sharif before being transferred via government helicopter to a Pakistani military hospital in Peshawar and four days later transferred again to an intensive care unit in Birmingham, England, for an emergency operation on her shattered skull.

The shooting and her incredible, indeed miraculous, recovery resulted in a global outpouring of support for Yousafzai and her family. On July 12, 2013, her sixteenth birthday, she visited New York and spoke in front of the United Nations. In October of that year, in acknowledgment of her work, the European Parliament awarded Yousafzai the prestigious Sakharov Prize for Freedom of Thought. Finally, in October 2014, Malala, along with Indian children's rights activist Kailash Satyarthi, was awarded the Nobel Peace Prize. Accepting the award, Yousafzai reaffirmed that "this award is not just for me. It is for those forgotten children who want education."

It's an incredible, indeed unique, story that may seem utterly different from the rise of Oprah Winfrey, but the two women share several characteristics, not least that (in their vastly different ways, of course) they both rose from obscurity to become worldwide sensations. They are also both deeply principled and both passionate advocates for books. However, behind the similarities are important psychological and political differences. As we'll see later in this chapter, for Winfrey, a book showed her a way of understanding herself, but for Yousafzai, books are tools for changing society. In 2013, only a matter of months after being shot by the Taliban, while inaugurating the large and impeccably modern library in Birmingham, England, she urged, "There is no greater weapon than knowledge and no greater source of knowledge than the written word."

Six months later, still not quite sixteen years old, she delivered another speech, this time at the United Nations, in which she was even more clear about her view of books as a revolutionary tool for social change (rather than dusty things kept in libraries or relaxing things to take to bed with a hot chocolate).

"Let us wage a glorious struggle against illiteracy, poverty and terrorism, let us pick up our books and our pens, they are the most powerful weapons. One child, one teacher, one book and one pen can change the world."

When Yousafzai met with President Barack Obama, she challenged him on the drone strikes in Pakistan that had killed thousands of people: "Innocent victims are killed in these acts, and they lead to resentment among the Pakistani people. If we refocus efforts on education it will make a big impact."

Certainly her own love of reading and education had already caused a dangerous ripple effect in her homeland. Her views offended and indeed continue to offend large sections of traditional Pakistani society, yet in following these views she was not as much enacting a political strategy as living out her earnest ethical convictions. These convictions were, Yousafzai has always been clear, to a large extent inherited from her father.

It seems her father had recognized and chose to nurture in Yousafzai something very special, even allowing her to stay up at night and talk about politics long after her two brothers had been sent to bed! In fact, her father's own story is a pretty remarkable one, if less colorful than Malala's, and also deserves to be remembered as it presents a needed contrast to stereotypes of Pakistani society that disempower the many educated and liberal voices in this diverse land.

Ziauddin Yousafzai was a teacher who had run a school in the village that admitted girls as well as boys. It was quite a large school, by Western standards, with over a thousand pupils, roughly half girls and half boys. In a 2013 interview with PBS, Yousafzai praised her father, saying he inspired her because he was a great social activist and he spoke out for women's rights even in what she calls "that hard situation." A determination to speak out and express your beliefs and convictions is one of the most important things that she learned from him. Her father's tale too is all about the importance of books. As he explained in an interview: "I thought, let me start a school of my own, I will have more freedom to practise the vision that I have. I started my school with 15,000 rupees— about £100. It was very meager capital. But the big capital and the big power that I had was my passion, my conviction, my connection to the community. I was so happy that the school I started, with just three kids, had 1,100 students—500 girls and 600 boys—by 2012."

But back to the daughter. The media feeding frenzy over "the little girl the Taliban shot," which started with *Time* magazine naming her (for three years running!) as one of the most influential people in the world, included numerous international prizes, such as being crowned the UN Messenger of Peace, and reached its peak with an asteroid being named after her!

A darker response, though, came from the All Pakistan Private Schools Federation, which claimed to represent 150,000 schools. Just a month after Yousafzai was awarded the Nobel Peace Prize, the federation announced an "I Am Not Malala" day, during which children at the schools were taught to condemn Malala Yousafzai and her ideas. Yet such bitterness and hostility was misdirected. After all, Malala wasn't just "Malala" either, as she herself put it later. On the contrary, she says, "I tell my story not because it is unique, but because it is not. It is the story of many girls."

That message is reflected in a book that the young Malala wrote, called *Malala's Magic Pencil*. This, despite obvious and forgivable shortcomings, became a huge best seller. The plot involves a girl, herself in symbolic form, longing for a magic pencil with which to "draw a better world." As none shows up, the girl instead dedicates herself to her schooling and realizes that she must instead use the ordinary tools around her to build a better world—a moral that is actually pretty similar to that in the novelist Paulo Coelho's tale of the alchemist, of which more in a moment. The solution was within her all along, we might say!

"Books and pens" are our most powerful weapons in the struggle for global justice, she says. But which books inspired her? One that she mentions often is *The Alchemist* by Paulo Coelho, a tale about a shepherd's search for treasure. Of course, the treasure the shepherd seeks is not where he imagines but rather lies much closer to home. As in Coelho's other works, the constant theme is that each of us are part of an unfolding cosmic story.

Yet even if Yousafzai particularly cites Coelho's book *The Alchemist* as an early inspiration, it is actually *Aleph* (2011) that most clearly provides a lesson for where she is today. In is in this, his fourteenth book, Coelho describes life as not merely a "train" but a journey needing a destination. The book recounts a middle-aged man's journey on the Trans-Siberian railway, replete with lurching carriages and nights spent listening to the clatter of the train wheels. The man is a successful but discontented writer. He's traveled extensively and earned worldwide acclaim for his books, but he finds himself lost and dissatisfied. At this point, a wise figure referred to simply as "J" inspires him through a story about the humble and ubiquitous bamboo plant. It seems, you see, that bamboo initially exists only as a tiny green shoot while its root system grows underground, invisible to the naked eye. Then, after years of apparent inactivity, it suddenly shoots up and can quickly reach the height of a house.

ALEPH
AUTHOR: PAULO COELHO
PUBLISHED: 2011

This is a novel, an autobiography, and a work of philosophy. The book tells the story of the author's "epiphany" (meaning spiritual awakening) while traveling on the Trans-Siberian railway. "Aleph" is the first letter of the Hebrew alphabet and is offered here as the receptacle of many deep and even mystical meanings.

In *Aleph*, Coelho writes, "Many things in life, personal and professional, are like the Chinese bamboo. You work, invest time, energy, do everything possible to nurture your growth and, sometimes, you don't see anything for weeks, months or even years. But if you have the patience to keep working, to keep persisting and nurturing, your fifth year will arrive and with it will come changes that you hadn't even dreamed of. Remember that one must be very daring to reach great heights, and at the same time, a lot of depth to stay grounded."

In real life, Coelho describes meeting people on the journey, including a twenty-one-year-old reader who insisted she had many things to talk to him about. "We met on the train and there was this connection between her, me and my books. I was old enough to be her grandfather but there is no age limit for people to act as a catalyst in your life," he told one interviewer, adding, "Of course, I don't take the Trans-Siberian every day but I try to give every day the opportunity for these experiences. If you're open to people on your way to work, it can happen. Or you can choose to be totally inwards and think only of yourself. You have to live in the moment."

The critical reception for what was, by then, Coelho's fourteenth book was cool. Julie Bosman introduced her *New York Times* interview with Coelho about the novel by calling him "a Twitter mystic."

A curious story told about the book, or rather the author, is that Coelho was always reluctant to allow others to modify his original tale, for example, in the process of translation. In an interview with the website Goodreads, he insisted that the book had "a life of itself," and this he felt had to be respected, thus giving a new sense to the term "book rights." An incident in 2003 reveals something about this and Coelho's commitment to these values. At this time, he allowed Warner Bros. to buy the film rights to his book, but it soon turned out that his idea of the book and the vision of the film producers were ultimately incompatible, the project stalled, and the movie never materialized. It seems that, among other inessential things, at one point the script envisioned a Hollywood-style battle sequence with ten thousand soldiers, something that, for the author, was definitely "not what the book is about." And, according to the *Guardian* newspaper, so strongly did Coelho feel the tug of authenticity that he offered $2 million to Warner Bros. to buy the film rights!

Pointing out Coelho's resolution to follow his personal legend and put art before dollars brings us back to the extraordinary story of Oprah Winfrey, whose success is all the more remarkable given that she started, on the face of it, with so many of life's cards stacked against her.

Given this, it's almost incredible to think that in 1998, at only forty-four years old, Winfrey would be named "One of the 100 Most Influential

People of the 20th Century" by *Time* magazine. But then, Winfrey is a very determined character. One story told about her is that just two days after the future media mogul started kindergarten, she complained to her teacher, saying, "I don't think I belong here 'cause I know a lot of big words." The teacher agreed and moved Winfrey to the first grade.

Winfrey's knack for seizing opportunities began to kick in when she moved to Tennessee to live with her father, Vernon Winfrey, a barber. While still in high school, she landed a job in radio as a reporter for a Nashville radio station, and at age nineteen she became the first African American to anchor a local evening news show. Her ability to deliver emotionally powerful questions and responses soon led to the opportunity to present a daytime talk show. This rapidly became the nation's favorite and won no fewer than thirty-four Emmy awards—seven of them awarded to Winfrey for best host. It's no wonder, then, that in due course she launched her own internationally syndicated production company. Throughout, the hallmark of her shows was a focus on self-healing and personal change.

It's quite a story, and many books have and will be written about Winfrey's achievements, but books also helped Winfrey along the way and inspired what would become for her a highly lucrative business strategy that, on the face of it, has nothing to do with business.

In an interview with Jeff Weiner, the CEO of the social networking site LinkedIn, Winfrey revealed that one book in particular came to her at a pivotal moment of doubt and helped shape all her future endeavors. In 1988, Winfrey had invited white supremacists to her talk show in an effort to gain insight into the source of their hatred. She immediately regretted this decision as it seemed to have given those people a recruiting platform to spread their hatred. (Twenty years later, two of those guests, now reformed, confirmed those suspicions to her.) Faced with doubt about how to recover from this misstep, Winfrey turned to a book called *The Seat of the Soul* by philosopher Gary Zukav. Published in 1989, the book was a sensation, a no. 1 *New York Times* best seller for thirty-one weeks.

Zukav, who was already famous for his new-age investigations of personal psychology and quantum physics (including one of my own favorite reads, *The Dancing Wu Li Masters*), offers a grand cosmological theory in *The Seat of the Soul*: "Each soul enters into a sacred agreement with the Universe to accomplish specific goals, or take on a particular task. All of your experiences of your life serve to awaken within you the memory of that contract, and to prepare you to fulfill it."

For individuals this means one thing. Every action, thought, and feeling is motivated by an intention, and that intention is a cause that exists as one with an effect. If we participate in the cause, it is not possible for us not to participate in the effect. In this most profound way, we are held responsible for everything we do, which is to say, for our every intention.

THE SEAT OF THE SOUL
AUTHOR: GARY ZUKAV
PUBLISHED: 1989

The central idea of this book is that humanity is evolving from a species that pursues power based on the perceptions of the five senses—external power—into a species that pursues a different kind of power that is based on spiritual values. This is what Zukav calls "authentic power." He contrasts the two kinds of activity, arguing that the pursuit of external power generates conflict—between individuals and lovers, within communities, and between nations—and has brought us to the edge of destruction.

Instead, authentic power "infuses" the activities of life with reverence, compassion, and trust and makes them come alive with meaning and purpose. Embracing the values of the soul transforms marriages into spiritual partnerships and reorients all aspects of our everyday lives.

"Reach for your soul. Reach even further, the impulse of creation and power authentic, the hourglass point between energy and matter, that is the seat of the soul. What does it mean to touch that place? It is exciting to come of age spiritually."

Huston Smith, professor of philosophy at MIT and himself the author of a book called *The Religions of Man*, called the book "remarkable" and complimented Zukav, saying that "one of our finest interpreters of frontier science" had shown himself to be equally able to explain and understand the human spirit. Many others, however, were unconvinced.

In an interview by the clinical psychologist and author Jeffrey Mishlove for the Public Television series *Thinking Allowed*, Zukav summarized the idea behind his book like this:

> My objective was not to make the soul legitimate in terms of science. The soul is legitimate, period. It doesn't need validation. At least that was my perception and so I wrote *The Seat of the Soul* to share the things that were most important to me. *The Dancing Wu Li Masters* was designed to open the mind, and *The Seat of the Soul* is a book designed to open the heart. And this is often the sequence that many people encounter as they move into an expanded awareness of who they are and why they are here.

This principle of intention became a guiding light for Winfrey. "The number one principle that rules my life is intention," Winfrey told Weiner. "And that is actually one of the reasons why I let the show go," she said, referring to giving up her talk show in 2011 to start her cable network called, significantly, OWN.

Zukav distinguishes between two kinds of do-gooders: those who are motivated by the positive effects of their actions on the recipients and the world and those who are really concerned with doing things that make them, well, feel good. Sooner or later the people on the end of actions that are really motivated by the second intention begin to resent being used like this.

From reading Zukav, Winfrey realized that for years the intention that had been driving her personal life and career had been the desire to be liked rather than a true strategy to do good in the world. And later, when invited to write the preface to the twenty-fifth anniversary edition of *The Seat of the Soul*, she explained in more detail how, after reading Zukav's book, she had called a big meeting with all the TV show's producers and announced a new strategy: "We are going to be a force for good, and that is going to be our intention."

Specifically, Winfrey had decided that there would be no more cooking segments with recipes for food she wouldn't dream of eating herself, and certainly no episodes during which, for example, audience members argued with white supremacists, as had happened on one show.

Winfrey also explained that there had been plenty of times where she'd heard ideas for the show that had plenty of details but *no positive intention*, and so from now on she would turn these down. Finally, she said, there were times when she felt that producers were manufacturing an intention that they themselves didn't believe in. She'd no longer accept this sort of inauthenticity.

Authenticity had become the key. In fact, Winfrey says, this philosophy still drives everything she does: "Do not bring me an idea that I cannot find my thread of truth in," as she told an audience at Skidmore College in 2017. She felt this so strongly that she even decided to end her hit TV show when she did because she felt that she had done all she could with it. She wouldn't allow herself to feign enthusiasm for her work just to continue a profitable venture.

On the other hand, her admiration of Zukav led to him being invited on her talk show thirty-six times, and she has said that *The Seat of the Soul* continues to inspire the work she does on her network OWN. Her newest show, *Belief*, is dedicated to exploring the power of spiritual experience as a force for good across the globe. The most recent edition of *The Seat of the Soul* includes a preface by Winfrey in which she says that "quite frankly, I don't believe I would ever have dreamed of creating such a network had I not read *The Seat of the Soul*."

That's quite an endorsement, but what sort of book is it, really? As to that, opinions are mixed. *Very* mixed. Zukav has been accused of ungrounded pseudoscience, and Winfrey has been called out for rushing uncritically into areas where wiser heads would have hesitated to go. Zukav's philosophy also seems derivative of other schools of thought. He offers nonattachment as the key to acceptance, but this is a position Buddhists have revered for centuries. He suggests that some truths must be accepted through commitment rather than understanding, but again this is a position others, such as the much-admired Danish philosopher Søren Kierkegaard, are famous for having proposed. Last but not least, there's a passage in Zukav's book about dolphins who decided to beach themselves in mass protest of life on earth. "This is their way of refusing to continue to live upon the Earth," explains Zukav earnestly. "They feel that they cannot fulfill the purpose for which they are born." This idea is certainly original to Zukav, but to recycle an old favorite barb of critics, if parts of his book are good and parts are original, it seems unfortunately that the original parts are not the good ones.

This is not to say that Zukav's writings cannot still serve a valuable purpose. Writers can be great communicators even if poor innovators. Zukav's book on physics, for example, *The Dancing Wu Li Masters*, deconstructs the Chinese name for physics, *Wu Li*, explaining that it has many subtle dimensions and can variously mean (depending on how it is pronounced) "patterns of organic energy," "my way," "nonsense," "I clutch my ideas," or "enlightenment." Zukav uses these shades of meaning to create the book's sections. The concept of "nonsense," for example, he uses to throw light on the otherwise baffling insights of Einstein's relativity theory and lead into discussions of some of the equally strange ideas of the ancient Eastern philosophical tradition.

But back to Winfrey and her own explorations of new-age philosophy. In 2007, Winfrey began to endorse a self-help program called *The Secret*, based on a book and film by an Australian television writer and producer called Rhonda Byrne. The central message of this (echoing Zukav but otherwise unrelated) was that people could change their lives through positive thoughts or vibrations that would, in turn, attract more positive vibrations and in due course bring many of the good things in life. It seems in one sense to fit Oprah's model of entrepreneurs with good intentions, but the initiative soon became mired in controversy. Peter Birkenhead of *Salon* magazine argued that this approach was psychologically damaging and accused it of trivializing important decisions and promoting a quick-fix mentality. Even Winfrey's stepfather, Vernon Winfrey, publicly condemned her new idea, saying, "That is not how I raised Oprah Gail" and that these days he found that he needed the show "like a hog needs a holiday."

THE SECRET
AUTHOR: RHONDA BYRNE
PUBLISHED: 2006

The Secret is Byrne's best-known book, promising to share with its readers nuggets of wisdom culled from world philosophies and religion that will help them to find success in every aspect of life, from relationships to health to wealth. The idea is that, well, "the secret" information that the book summarizes will enable readers to tap hitherto unsuspected "hidden powers" that lurk within them. It is a kind of revelation that is "life-transforming" for all who experience it.

The central idea of the book is that there is a kind of "law of attraction," which claims that thoughts can change a person's life directly. She says that all great men in history, such as Plato, Abraham Lincoln, Ludwig van Beethoven, Winston Churchill, and even Jesus, knew about and applied the law. She writes, "The Secret is the law of attraction! Everything that's coming into your life you are attracting into your life. And it's attracted to you by virtue of the images you're holding in your mind. It's what you're thinking. Whatever is going on in your mind you are attracting to you."

The book has sold thirty million copies worldwide and has been translated into fifty languages. However, some readers complained that it was not so much secret insights as "regurgitated trivialities," or even "absolute drivel," as one dissatisfied customer put it. The *New York Times* said caustically that the book might best be understood as "an advanced meme" (or intellectual virus) "whose structure has evolved throughout history to optimally exploit a suite of weaknesses in the design of the human mind."

The problem is, as Winfrey has found and Yousafzai doubtless will do too in time, that it is not enough to *start* along a particular path in life, whether inspired by a book or a person or something completely different, you have to be able to *navigate* along that route too, avoiding pitfalls. An inspirational book can only be a starting point—it can't substitute for having your own inner guidance system. Or—let's be generous—maybe what is needed is *a constant supply of new, inspirational books* to keep us all on track.

✛

Afterword

What Happened When Wittgenstein Met Tristram Shandy

Philosophers and philosophical works pop up as aspirational or influential texts more often than any others—and no wonder, philosophers are, after all, supposed to be the "big ideas" people. But where do philosophers get their ideas from? We usually imagine such thinkers starting from scratch, yet that's not quite right. In fact, philosophers, just like the rest of us, are often following up something they were told or read.

The writings of Plato are famously credited as the source for which all subsequent philosophy is merely footnotes–and with good reason–yet Plato too was influenced by his reading of texts by mystical figures such as Pythagoras. But to see how books influence books let's finish by taking perhaps the most famous, if by no means the smartest let alone the most productive, philosopher of the twentieth century, the Austrian eccentric Ludwig Wittgenstein. Wittgenstein only published one book in his lifetime, called obscurely the *Tractatus Logicus Philosophicus*, which is a mix of the views of his academic supervisor at Cambridge, Bertrand Russell, and a rather nasty tract by Otto Weininger called *Sex and Character*, which was also—wait for it!—much admired by one Adolf Hitler.

But that's politics. Sticking to Wittgenstein and philosophy, it is his second book, *Philosophical Investigations*, which is both rather better and more interesting to us. And without doubt, this was inspired in crucial ways by another text. And it is not the sort of book you would expect to be influencing an otherwise very earnest, even monomaniac philosopher like Wittgenstein. After all, the Irish clergyman Laurence Sterne's account of *The Life and Opinions of Tristram Shandy*, written in nine chunks with the first appearing as long ago as 1759, is not on the face of it a serious book at all, let alone a work of philosophy. Instead it is an extended parody of what is otherwise offered as the autobiographical, personal story of the life of a humble pastor living in the north of England.

The book is ostensibly Tristram's woeful narration of key episodes in his life, from the time as a toddler the sash window fell on his "manhood," accidentally circumcising him—"'Twas nothing, I did not lose two drops of blood by it—'twas not worth calling in a surgeon, had he lived next door to us—thousands suffer by choice, what I did by accident"—to his father's neglect of his education on account of his determination to first write a "Tristra-paedia," meaning a book to outline the system under which Tristram was to be educated. And all the time it is one of the central jokes of the novel that Tristram cannot explain anything simply, that he must make explanatory diversions to add context and color to his tale, to the extent that it is well into Volume III before he manages to even mention his own birth.

Wittgenstein liked the book so much that he constantly referred to it, and his contemporaries recall him claiming to have read and reread it a dozen times! Maurice O'Connor Drury, psychiatrist and loyal follower, for example, notes in his book, *Conversations with Wittgenstein*, that the celebrated philosopher once told him, "Now a book I like greatly is Sterne's *Tristram Shandy*. That is one of my favourite books."

The debt of Wittgenstein—and hence much modern philosophy—to Laurence Sterne's humorous novel is as remarkable as it is unexpected. The first influence is stylistic—but the style is also the content and provides new ways to see issues. Within the world of philosophy, Wittgenstein is celebrated for his "language games," yet the first round of the game was clearly played by Sterne.

Wittgenstein seems to have found inspiration in the permanent digressions that thwart the telling of Shandy's story as well as in the way that Sterne plays with words, often teasing the reader with the many ways that they can be used. Sometimes they are a straightforward record or a conversation, but other times they "point beyond the text" and force the reader to suddenly reevaluate all that has come before. In such changes of perspective, much of the humor lies.

Both Sterne and Wittgenstein demand "reader participation and response." Or as Wittgenstein says in the preface to *Philosophical Investigations*, "I should not like my writing to spare people the trouble of thinking. But, if possible, to stimulate someone to thoughts of his own."

The same playfulness that leads Sterne to use typographical tricks and techniques such as dots, dashes, blank pages, and even a "black page" reappear in Wittgenstein's book as intriguing graphics, including the famous doodle of a duck that might be a rabbit depending on what you are thinking as you look at it.

In a book called *Wittgenstein's Place in Twentieth-Century Analytic Philosophy* (1996), a British professor named Peter Hacker, who is counted in philosophy circles as one of the "principal commentators" on Wittgenstein's work, observes that "although the *Investigations* is written in brief and often apparently disconnected remarks, although it frequently jumps from topic to topic without indicating the reasons for such sudden transitions, and although it has seemed to many readers to be a philosophy that revels in lack of systematically, it is in fact . . . a highly systematic, integrated work, and anything but a haphazard collection or *apercus*."

Exactly the same could be said of Sterne's *Tristram Shandy*.

Similarly, in her book called *Wittgenstein's Art of Investigation*, Beth Savickey identifies key elements in Wittgenstein's work that are more literary than philosophical, let alone "logical," saying, "Wittgenstein's later writings are, perhaps, the only truly twentieth century philosophical writings we have. They are characterised by a participatory mystique, the fostering of a communal sense, the concentration of the present moment, and the repetition of grammatical techniques."

All of this is deeply "Shandyan," but oddly enough Savickey sees only a superficial link between the two writers—indeed she claims several German-language philosophers,[1] from Hegel and Schopenhauer and on to Marx and Nietzsche, are writers whose thinking was more directly affected by the Irish humorist. That seems a stretch, but it certainly makes two important points: first, that all kinds of books can have an influence well beyond their intended audience, and second, that that influence can sometimes be completely forgotten! Perhaps this book can be a small remedy for that.

---

1. Sterne being Irish, *Tristram Shandy* was, indeed, written originally in English, but it had been speedily translated into German in 1769. It is said that the celebrated German philosopher Schopenhauer liked the book so much that he wanted to provide the service himself—but the publisher declined his offer.

+

List of Books Featured in the Text

(Alphabetical, by author)
The Stranger, Albert Camus
Silent Spring, Rachel Carson
Aleph, Paulo Coelho
Be Here Now, Ram Dass
Origin of Species, Charles Darwin
The Story of Civilization, Will and Ariel Durant
The Deerslayer, or The First War-Path, James Fenimore Cooper
The Intelligent Investor, Benjamin Graham
The Autobiography of Malcom X, Alex Haley
The Wonderful Adventures of Nils, Selma Lagerlöf
Extracts from the Diary and Correspondence of the Late Amos Lawrence; With a Brief Account of Some Incidents of His Life, William R. Lawrence
The Story of Dr. Dolittle, Hugh Lofting
Moby-Dick, Herman Melville
Moral Man and Immoral Society, Karl Niebuhr
Down and Out in Paris and London, George Orwell
Common Sense, Thomas Paine
The Timaeus, Plato
Dice Man, Luke Rhinehart (aka George Powers Cockroft)
Where the Wild Things Are, Maurice Sendak
A Short View of Great Questions, Orlando J. Smith
The Life and Opinions of Tristram Shandy, Laurence Sterne
The Lord of the Rings, J. R. R. Tolkien
The Art of War, Sun Tzu
The Seat of the Soul, Gary Zukav

✛

Sources and Further Reading

INTRODUCTION

There are numerous versions of Sun Tzu's *The Art of War* available, including an audiobook, but the confusing thing is that the text described varies significantly depending on how it has been translated. I know from personal experience (of having my books translated into Chinese) that there really is a huge gap between cultures, and books like *The Art of War* use a lot of idioms and analogies that just don't work if translated too literally. Anyway, the book was translated into French and published in 1772 by the French Jesuit Jean Joseph Marie Amiot with the first annotated English translation published by Lionel Giles in 1910. In the introduction, Giles attacks a slightly earlier English translation in 1905 by Everard Ferguson Calthrop, a military man himself, under the title "The Book of War," saying, "It is not merely a question of downright blunders, from which none can hope to be wholly exempt. Omissions were frequent; hard passages were willfully distorted or slurred over. Such offenses are less pardonable. They would not be tolerated in any edition of a Latin or Greek classic, and a similar standard of honesty ought to be insisted upon in translations from Chinese."

Giles himself was a very learned chap who previously had made a detailed study of Confucius and worked at the British Museum. His text is online as part of the Project Gutenberg project that makes historically important texts available to everyone for free.

Did Buffett really say that about reading "500 pages a day"? Indeed, it is well substantiated. The quotation is based on the memory of Todd

Combs, who became an employee of Buffett's at his investment firm and who had enrolled at the Columbia Business School in 2000. He apparently heard Buffett say it circa 2002 as a student there. The quote has been repeated many times, including on October 26, 2010, in the *Wall Street Journal*, in the article "Buffett Flags a Successor—Fund Manager Named Leading Candidate as Next Investment Chief at Berkshire."

Larry Ellison's takeaway about "ignoring anger" is quoted by Reuters in an article titled "Salesforce Drama Steals Show at Oracle Conference," October 5, 2011, available online at www.reuters.com/article/salesforce com-oracle-idUKN1E7940ET20111005.

The foreword Marc Benioff wrote was for the edition *The Art of War—Spirituality for Conflict* by Thomas Huynh, published by Skylight Paths in 2008. This promises to offer detailed explanations and annotations of all the verses.

Mark Cuban's book *How to Win at the Sport of Business* was published by First Diversion Books in 2011, and Tom Corley's book *Rich Habits: The Daily Success Habits of Wealthy Individuals* was published by Langdon Street Press in 2011. Finally, Paul Martin's book *Making Happy People* was published by HarperCollins in 2005.

CHAPTER 1. MEET THE WILD THINGS

"Obama's reading list" mentioned here is discussed in an article titled "Obama's Secret to Surviving the White House Years," an interview with Michiko Kakutani, the book critic for the *New York Times*, on January 16, 2017, online at www.nytimes.com/2017/01/16/books/transcript-presi dent-obama-on-what-books-mean-to-him.html.

He expands on how he found the writings of two great reforming politicians, Gandhi and Mandela, particularly helpful. These books would be Mahatma Gandhi, *An Autobiography: The Story of My Experiments with Truth* (originally written in Gujarati but published in English in 1948 by the Public Affairs Press and reprinted in many new editions) and *Long Walk to Freedom: The Autobiography of Nelson Mandela* (published by Macdonald Purnell in 1994). Two other great political reads Obama evidently enjoyed are *Abraham Lincoln: His Speeches and Writings* edited by Roy Basler and Carl Sandburg in a book published by De Capo Press, 2001, and Martin Luther King Jr., *Stride toward Freedom: The Montgomery Story* originally published in 1958 by Harper & Brothers.

Two of Obama's own books that the chapter draws on are *The Audacity of Hope: Thoughts on Reclaiming the American Dream* (Crown/Three Rivers Press, 2006) and *Dreams from My Father: A Story of Race and Inheritance* (Times Books, 1995).

Hemingway's *For Whom the Bell Tolls* was first published by Charles Scribner's Sons in 1940. Hemingway's editor Maxwell Perkins's words, after reading the manuscript, that "if the function of a writer is to reveal reality, no one ever so completely performed it," are found in a letter of April 24, 1940, recorded in the book *The Sons of Maxwell Perkins: Letters of F. Scott Fitzgerald, Ernest Hemingway, Thomas Wolfe, and Their Editor* by Matthew Bruccoli and Judith Baughman (University of South Carolina Press, 2004).

Richard Gottlieb analyzed Maurice Sendak's picture book for *The Psychologist* in 2009. It is now also online at https://thepsychologist.bps.org.uk/volume-22/edition-10/eye-fiction-where-wild-things-are.

Jane Goodall's recommended reads are in an article called just that on April 26, 2018, for Radical Reads, online at https://radicalreads.com/jane-goodall-favorite-books.

Goodall's own classic text *In the Shadow of Man* was published in the United States by Houghton Mifflin in 1971 and reprinted in many editions. Goodall is the author of fourteen other books, including *The Chimpanzees of Gombe* (1986), *Visions of Caliban* (1991), and *Reason for Hope* (1999). That's not to mention numerous books specially for children, such as *My Life with the Chimpanzees* (Alladin, 1991), which starts by explaining how, as a child, Goodall was given a stuffed chimpanzee named Jubilee, and her fondness for this figure helped start her early love of animals.

Kathryn Reeds's May 7, 2010, interview for *The Harvard Crimson*, entitled "15 Questions with Jane Goodall," is online at www.thecrimson.com/article/2010/5/7/nbsp-fm-jg-people.

PBS offers videos and text about "Jane Goodall's Wild Chimpanzees," March 3, 1996, online at www.pbs.org/wnet/nature/jane-goodalls-wild-chimpanzees-jane-goodalls-story/1911.

Finally, the 2016 World Books Day interview published by the Jane Goodall Institute is online at https://news.janegoodall.org/2016/04/23/1013/ and has some great images of the books too.

CHAPTER 2. ROLL THE DICE

There are quite a few books about Google, such as Janet Lowe's *Google Speaks: Secrets of the World's Greatest Billionaire Entrepreneurs* (Wiley, 2009) and Ram Shriram's *Googled: The End of the World as We Know It* (Penguin, 2009), but then Google is a very big affair these days. However, Google's founders are a reclusive pair, and details of what they are really thinking and motivated by are hard to come by. Indeed, Michael Mace's account, *Map the Future*, is not really about Google but rather about the elusive ingredients of business success. So it is to articles like "Google Logic:

Why Google Does the Things It Does the Way It Does" published in the technology pages of *The Guardian* (www.theguardian.com/technol ogy/2013/jul/09/google-android-reader-why) and on the website of the Academy of Achievement (www.achievement.org/achiever/larry -page/#interview) that intriguing details must be sought.

Brin's comments on challenging Microsoft are preserved in a blog by Nicholas Carr called "Rough Type" (online at www.roughtype .com/?p=366) as well as noted in an article in the *New York Times*, April 13, 2003, by John Markoff and G. Pascal Zachary under the title "In Searching the Web, Google Finds Riches," and Asher Hakins's *Forbes* piece on penny-pinching billionaires, "The Frugal Billionaires," was published November 14, 2007. The interview with Barry Diller in *The New Yorker* was published online under the title "Inside the Googleplex" on October 2, 2009, and Ken Auletta tweaked the curtain on Google again on October 5 in an article called ominously "Searching for Trouble" in the same magazine.

Branson, on the other hand, seems to enjoy a bit of media attention, indeed a lot of media attention. His interview with Danny Baker in the *Radio Times*, the one where he says he was for a while "very much under the influence of the *Dice Man* books," is also recorded in an article by Sherna Noah in *The Independent*, May 21, 2013, entitled "Dice Man Books 'Influenced' Business Tycoon Sir Richard Branson." It is online at www .independent.co.uk/arts-entertainment/books/news/dice-man-books -influenced-business-tycoon-sir-richard-branson-8624831.html.

For the account of the man himself, his autobiography *The Virgin Way: Everything I Know about Leadership* was published by Portfolio in 2014 and (confusingly) also republished under the bolder title *Losing My Virginity: How I've Survived, Had Fun, and Made a Fortune Doing Business My Way* by Crown in 1999. Smart business move!

CHAPTER 3. SAVE THE PLANET—ONE PAGE AT A TIME!

Again, I am indebted to the high-quality journalism of *The New Yorker*, in this case Philip Hoare's article (November 3, 2011) "What *Moby Dick* Means to Me" (online at www.newyorker.com/magazine/2009/10/12 /searching-for-trouble#). Marie-Therese Miller's book, in the Conserva- tion Heroes series, simply titled *Rachel Carson* (Chelsea House, 2011), recalls Carson's early forays into writing. Carson's discovery later at college that biology gave her "something to write about" is recounted in Linda Lear's autobiography, also called *Rachel Carson* (1997) on page 80, referencing correspondence by Carson.

Indeed, Lear uses the phrase as the title for her fourth chapter in the autobiography. Carson's dismissal of pesticides as being as indiscriminate as a "caveman's club" was made in her book *Silent Spring*, first published in 1962, on page 297. Louis McLean's criticisms are recounted in *The Gentle Subversive: Rachel Carson, Silent Spring, and the Rise of the Environmental Movement* (New Narratives in American History) by Mark Hamilton Lytle, published by Oxford University Press in 2007. Bill Ruckelshaus's thoughts in the oral history interview with Chuck Elkins are online in a PDF entitled "Behind the Scenes at the Creation of EPA: An Interview with Chuck Elkins," part of the Environmental Protection Agency records at www.epaalumni.org/userdata/pdf/600A1DB1B9EF1E85.pdf.

Doug McLean's phrase, a "great herd of readers profess devotion to Herman Melville's classic *Moby Dick*, but novelists especially seem to love saying they love it," introduces the author David Gilbert's essay on Moby Dick for *The Atlantic* (August 2013), part of its By Heart series in which authors discuss their favorite books. It is also online at www.theatlantic.com/entertainment/archive/2013/08/the-endless-depths-of-i-moby-dick-i-symbolism/278861.

The influential *CBS Reports* program, with reporter Eric Sevareid, called "The Silent Spring of Rachel Carson" aired on April 3, 1963.

Frans Lanting's website is at www.Lanting.com. His 1997 book *Eye to Eye* was published by Taschen and consists mainly of 140 color photographs, prefaced by his personal introduction. "No one turns animals into art more completely than Frans Lanting," wrote *The New Yorker*—at least according to Lanting, see https://www.nationalgeographic.com/animals/article/frans-lanting-animals-gallery.

CHAPTER 4. SEARCH FOR LIFE'S PURPOSE

Steve Jobs's commencement speech for students was given at Stanford on June 12, 2005, and you can read it in full because it is archived online at https://news.stanford.edu/2005/06/14/jobs-061505/.

The PBS program entitled "One Last Thing" aired November 2, 2011. PBS.org has the show: https://www.pbs.org/show/steve-jobs-one-last-thing/. There's a nice annotated version of Jobs's *Playboy* interview with David Sheff on the Genius website: https://genius.com/David-sheff-playboy-interview-steve-jobs-annotated. Walter Isaacson's autobiography, all 656 pages of it, was published by Simon & Schuster in 2011, and David Price's *The Pixar Touch: The Making of a Company* was published by Penguin Random House in 2009.

If you want to know a bit more about the philosophy of existentialism, neither *Be Here Now* (published in 1971 by the Lama Foundation) nor Jean Paul Sartre's *Being and Nothingness*, first published in English by Routledge in 1956, far less his *Critique of Dialectical Reason* (published by Gallimard in France in 1960) will really help you, but then it seems that no one understands the term. Perhaps it doesn't have a fixed domain or meaning; such things happen in philosophy. However, to introduce some of my own books, I have given pointers as to what "existentialism is all about" in *Philosophical Tales* (Wiley-Blackwell, 2008)—Sartre is one of the strange tales—and *Cracking Philosophy* (Cassell Illustrated, 2016).

The Gardner Hendrie Oral Project interview with Evelyn Berezin for the Computer History Museum (March 10, 2014) is a rare and invaluable record of this innovator's life, influences, and experiences. An occasionally slightly inaccurate transcript is at https://archive.computerhistory .org/resources/access/text/2015/04/102746876-05-01-acc.pdf, and the actual three-hour interview is on YouTube at www.youtube.com/watch ?v=3wOWHkX4ilA.

The *New York Times* tribute to Berezin by Robert McFadden was published on December 10, 2018, under the rather clumpy title "Evelyn Berezin, 93, Dies; Built the First True Word Processor." It is online at www .nytimes.com/2018/12/10/obituaries/evelyn-berezin-dead.html.

Gwyn Headley's blog post on Berezin, "Why Is This Woman Not Famous?"(December 20, 2010), is online at http://fotolibrarian.fotolibra .com/?p=466.

As for *Astounding Science-Fiction*, it is also rather confusingly called *Amazing Science Fiction* and *Analog Science Fiction*, not to forget its original title of *Astounding Stories of Super-Science* (no wonder Evelyn got confused!). Under the *Analog* title, the magazine has a website that includes some of its wonderful early covers. See www.analogsf.com and www .analogsf.com/about-analog/vintage. However, Wikipedia has one of its better pages on the magazine, evidently lovingly put together by aficionados, which additionally points to the site archive.org, which has many of the early magazines in full! See https://archive.org/details/Astounding _Stories_of_Super_Science_1930, for example.

CHAPTER 5. SEE THE WORLD IN THE WIDER SOCIAL CONTEXT

Mike Duffy's website is https://thecitybase.com/about. "Today" is "in 2018." His comment for *Inc.* was part of a longer (but undated) piece called "32 Books Anyone Who Wants to Succeed Should Read" by Christina Des Marais. It is online at www.inc.com/christina-desmarais/32-books -highly-recommended-by-extremely-successful-people.html. Actually, Mike's choice is only number thirty!

Charles Dickens's *A Tale of Two Cities* was first published (as a book) in 1859 in London by Chapman and Hall. Project Gutenberg has the text at www.gutenberg.org/ebooks/98.

Mark Twain's essay "Fenimore Cooper's Literary Offenses" is online courtesy of the University of Virginia at http://twain.lib.virginia.edu /projects/rissetto/offense.html and includes harsh words coming from someone whose *real* name was Samuel Langhorne Clemens. James Russell Lowell's unkind little poem, actually a segment of a much longer poem satirizing several American authors, is preserved by the James Fenimore Cooper Society website at https://jfcoopersociety.org/articles /SUNY/1980SUNY-ASHLEY.HTML.

Marina Levitina recalls Russia's fascination with American adventure stories in her book *"Russian Americans" in Soviet Film: Cinematic Dialogues between the US and the USSR* (Bloomsbury, 2015). Further praise is unearthed in *A Study Guide for James Fenimore Cooper's "Pathfinder"* in the Gale, Cengage Learning series.

Robert Hughes's book is *American Visions: The Epic History of Art in America* (Knopf, 1997).

Riis's biographer Alexander Alland was writing in *Jacob A. Riis: Photographer & Citizen* published by Aperture in 1974. (Yes, the publisher did use the ampersand. Don't ask me why.)

There is a good selection of Riis's photographs (with annotations) in a page headed "Jacob Riis: Lighting Up the Slums with Flash Photography," curated by contemporary photographer Bill Dobbins online at https://blog.samys.com/jacob-riis-lighting-slums-flash-photography/.

George Orwell's book *Down and Out in Paris and London* was first published by Gollancz in 1933. *Animal Farm*, by comparison, was published in 1945, and *1984*—the dystopia featuring Big Brother—came in 1949.

CHAPTER 6. BE READY TO REINVENT YOURSELF

Henry Ford's homely advice about enthusiasm can be found all over the Internet, but it seems not to have a true source. Keith Sward gives a careful account of Ford's life in his book *The Legend of Henry Ford* and doesn't include it (Rinehart, 1948). The *Literary Digest* for January 7, 1928, included a special feature entitled "Henry Ford on His Plans and His Philosophy" in which he explains his philosophy that life is about gaining valuable experience and that this is "all we can get out of life." However, it is an earlier article, by Charles W. Wood, associate editor of *Forbes* magazine (January 1928) that provides the fullest account of Ford's philosophy of "experience." A book called *Going Below the Water's Edge* by

Ronald Fehribach (Author House, 2014) contains the full interview too, "master mind" and all.

A rather more practical approach is taken in a scholarly investigation of the production line called *The Machine that Changed the World* by James Womack, Daniel Jones, and Daniel Roos of Massachusetts Institute of Technology (Simon & Schuster, 1990). David Warsh compares Ford and Adam Smith in an article called "Adam Smith, Theorist" published June 7, 2015, on his site *Economic Principles* (formerly a newspaper column) online at www.economicprincipals.com/issues/2015.06.07/1753.html.

Richard Bak's book *Henry and Edsel: The Creation of the Ford Empire* was published by Wiley in 2003. Ford's concern that by underpaying workers "we are preparing a generation of underfed children who will be physically and morally undernourished" is discussed in Howard Means's book *Money and Power: The History of Business* (Wiley, 2002).

Tim Worstall published an article looking skeptically at Ford's pay rates called "On Henry Ford and His $5 a Day" for the free-market Adam Smith Institute. The article was published on June 13, 2010, online at www.adam smith.org/blog/tax-spending/on-henry-ford-and-his-5-a-day.

Aldous Huxley's 1932 classic *Brave New World* is one of the most inventive novels published in the twentieth century. It started out as a parody, and Ford apparently became a central figure by chance after Huxley happened upon a copy of Henry Ford's 1922 manifesto *My Life and Work* while on a boat traveling from Singapore to the Philippines. This fine document is preserved online by Wikisource at https://en.wikisource .org/wiki/My_Life_and_Work.

Ford's interview with German American journalist George Sylvester Viereck was in the August 5, 1928, *New York American*.

Jimmy Carter, American Moralist by Kenneth Morris was published by the University of Georgia Press (1997). You can actually hear President Carter's Georgia School of Law address if you go to www.americanrhetoric .com/speeches/jimmycarterlawday1974.htm. It also gives a transcription. *The Irony of American History*, the book by Reinhold Niebuhr said to influence Carter, was published by Charles Scribner's Sons (1952). Another Niebuhr text mentioned is *The Children of Light and the Children of Darkness* (University of Chicago Press, 1944).

Actually, there is a trove of the so-called Public Papers of the Presidents that includes all such things. Carter's records can be accessed online at https://quod.lib.umich.edu/p/ppotpus?key=title;page=browse;value=j. More conveniently for most, though, David Swartz "revisits" Jimmy Carter's truth-telling sermon to Americans in an article called just that for the academic experts' site The Conversation on July 13, 2018. The piece is online at https://theconversation.com/revisiting-jimmy-carters-truth -telling-sermon-to-americans-97241.

Whittaker Chambers's cover story for *Time* was in the March 8, 1948, issue. It was written just months before he testified "against Communism" before the House Un-American Activities Committee, testimony which would ultimately make him famous but also cost him his job at *Time*.

The University of Pennsylvania has Martin Luther King's "Letter from a Birmingham Jail" online at www.africa.upenn.edu / Articles_Gen / Letter _Birmingham.html.

CHAPTER 7. SET YOUR THINKING FREE

Where does Edison say "inventors must be poets so that they may have imagination"? Actually, I'm not quite sure, but it is quoted in Neil Baldwin's scholarly (542 pages!) account *Edison: Inventing the Century* (University of Chicago Press, 1995). Professor McCormick discusses this poetry issue for a National Public Radio show called "Thomas Edison: Inventor and Poet" (August 13, 2007), and the transcript is online at www.npr.org / transcripts / 12741251?storyId=12741251?storyId=12741251. McCormick adds, "He understood, I think, how poetry can fuel the creative process in ways that just, you know, the basic scientific process."

The text of Edison's essay "The Philosophy of Thomas Paine," written June 7, 1925, is online courtesy of the Thomas Paine National Historical Association at www.thomaspaine.org / aboutpaine / the-philosophy-of -thomas-paine-by-thomas-edison.html.

Thomas Paine's own great work, *The Rights of Man*, published in 1791, is available as an e-text at Gutenberg at www.gutenberg.org / files / 3742 / 3742-h / 3742-h.htm#link2H_4_0006, and the British Library has a nice facsimile of the first edition online at www.bl.uk / learning / timeline / item106644.html.

The National Park Service has a website called Where Modern America Was Invented, which looks at Edison's background, tells you where to actually visit today, and remembers him saying, "My mother was the making of me. She was so true, so sure of me. And I felt I had something to live for, someone I must not disappoint." It is at www.nps.gov / edis / index.htm.

Edison's writings on education teaching people how to think are mainly in his journals. The particular quote on "teaching people how to think" is reproduced in *Reconstruction and Reform: History of U.S., Book 7* by Joy Hakim (Oxford University Press, 1994).

The Library of Congress website has many Edison resources, including clips from early films: www.loc.gov / collections / edison-company-motion -pictures-and-sound-recordings / articles-and-essays / biography. When I say "films," these are rather modest in length. One features a man waving his hat, for example: www.loc.gov/item/00694118/. Another curiosity is the sound file of his "message to the American people" recorded during World War I: www.loc.gov/item/00694069/.

Bertrand Russell's saying that "the whole problem with the world is that fools and fanatics are always so certain of themselves, but wiser people so full of doubt" is actually a popular misquoting of Russell. In his book *Mortals and Others* (1931–1935), what Russell actually says is, "The fundamental cause of the trouble is that in the modern world the stupid are cocksure while the intelligent are full of doubt." He continues, "Even those of the intelligent who believe that they have a nostrum are too individualistic to combine with other intelligent men from whom they differ on minor points. This was not always the case." The book is a collection of essays by Bertrand Russell originally published in the *New York Journal-American*, and this essay was called "The Triumph of Stupidity" (May 10, 1933).

Walt Whitman's praise for the "scientific spirit" is preserved by the Walt Whitman Archive in its category of "Disciples"—that is, quotes preserved by his fans: https://whitmanarchive.org/criticism/disciples/traubel/WWWiC/1/med.00001.37.html. Does that make Kroto a disciple too?

The quote from Confucius, "I seek not the answer—but to understand the question," is loosely from *The Analects*, the collection of his sayings compiled by his disciples in the centuries following his death in 479 BCE. I say "loosely," as translations from Chinese are very subjective.

The passage from Plato imagining particles being transformed in cosmic fires is from *The Timaeus of Plato* (1888 Tr. R. D. Archer-Hind), specifically section 57a, pages 203–05.

Kroto recalls "the encouraging atmosphere" of Ottawa in his account of his life for the Nobel Prize Committee: www.nobelprize.org/prizes/chemistry/1996/kroto/biographical.

Finally, Ashutosh Jogalekar's blog post entitled "Ordering the Best Appetizer Platter; Harry Kroto's Many Passions" (July 1, 2009) is at http://scienceblogs.de/lindaunobel/2009/07/01/ordering-the-best-appetizer-platter-harold-krotos-many-passions.

CHAPTER 8. MAKE A HUGE PROFIT—AND THEN SHARE IT

The details for the "Non-fiction Favorites of CEOs" cited are *Winners Never Cheat Even in Difficult Times* by Jon M. Huntsman originally published in 2008 by Pearson FT Press.

Business Adventures: Twelve Classic Tales from the World of Wall Street by John Brook is available in reprint edition from Open Road Media, published in 2014; *Why Nations Fail: The Origins of Power, Prosperity, and Poverty* by Daron Acemoglu was published by Crown in 2012, and *One Thousand Ways to Make $1000*, a 1936 nonfiction book of personal finance by Frances Minaker, is today online at Gutenberg: www.gutenberg.org /ebooks/56006. But Buffett's key source, of course, is *The Intelligent Investor* by Benjamin Graham, first published in 1949 by Harper and Brothers, who are today part of HarperCollins.

Buffett's own book *The Essays of Warren Buffett: Lessons for Corporate America* (edited by Lawrence A. Cunningham) was published by Wiley in 2013. Buffett's address to Colombia University's centennial celebrations in 2015 is preserved by Colombia Business School and is online at www8.gsb.columbia.edu/articles/columbia-business/fast-forward -warren-buffett-51.

Buffett's comment on why his investment company had bought a large shareholding in the *Washington Post* newspaper company, which refers to what "we had learned from Ben Graham" and notably "that the key to successful investing was the purchase of shares in good businesses when market prices were at a large discount from underlying business values," is recorded by Glen Arnold in his book *The Great Investors: Lessons on Investing from Master Traders* (Pearson, 2011).

Buffett's annual letter for his company's investors written in 1987, which notes, "Whenever Charlie and I buy common stocks for Berkshire's insurance companies (leaving aside arbitrage purchases, discussed) we approach the transaction as if we were buying into a private business," is online at the finance website Alphavest at www.alphavest.com/an-essay -on-ben-grahams-mr-market-by-warren-buffett.

Buffett acknowledges ruefully that it took five years and more than $400 million in losses to "close up shop" on the complex web of 23,218 derivatives contracts with 884 counterparties that they ended up with after purchasing General Re (General Reinsurance Corporation) in the Berkshire Hathaway 2008 annual report. You can read more of this online at www.jameslau88.com/warren_buffett_on_derivatives.htm.

Buffett's 2008 op-ed for the *New York Times* entitled "Buy American. I Am," in which he says, "Let me be clear on one point: I can't predict the short-term movements of the stock market. I haven't the faintest idea as to whether stocks will be higher or lower a month—or a year—from now," is at www.nytimes.com/2008/10/17/opinion/17buffett.html. His comment that "we should neither try to predict these nor to profit from them. If we can identify businesses similar to those we have purchased in the past, external surprises will have little effect on our long-term results" is again in the Berkshire shareholder address cited above.

Buffett's comments made after surveying the wreckage of the subprime disaster are online at numerous media, including *Forbes* (www.forbes

.com/sites/bruceupbin/2010/09/02/a-plea-for-personal-responsibility
-in-the-corner-office/amp), where he is quoted saying, "It is the behavior
of these CEOs and directors that needs to be changed: If their institutions
and the country are harmed by their recklessness, they should pay a
heavy price—one not reimbursable by the companies."

Buffett can be found disagreeing that "analyzing stocks was useless" in
a book called *Buffett, Munger Marathon Investing: Passion Investing* by Jack
Burrow published by Friesen Press in 2017.

Adam Smith's pioneering work on early economic theory, *Wealth of
Nations*, was first published in 1776 and in many editions since. It is also
online as an e-book at Gutenberg: www.gutenberg.org/ebooks/3300.

Buffett's presentation to Georgetown University students in Washington, DC, at which he compared the US Federal Reserve to a hedge fund,
is online in an article headed "Buffett Calls Fed History's Greatest Hedge
Fund," by Noah Buhayar, published September 20, 2013. Buffett's views
on tax can be found in an article for the *New York Times* entitled "In Class
Warfare, Guess Which Class Is Winning" by Ben Steinnov, published November 26, 2006. Here he says, "There's class warfare, all right, but it's my
class, the rich class, that's making war, and we're winning."

Matthias Schwartz's article called "The Church of Warren Buffett: Faith
and Fundamentals in Omaha," was in *Harper's Magazine* in the January 2010
issue. It is online at https://harpers.org/archive/2010/01/the-church
-of-warren-buffett.

But on to Rockefeller. At his peak, at the start of the twentieth century,
Rockefeller's net worth was around 1.5 percent of the entire economic
output of the United States, records Karl Zinsmeister for the Philanthropy Roundtable in an article online at www.philanthropyroundtable
.org/almanac/people/hall-of-fame/detail/john-rockefeller-sr. This is
my source for facts such as that, in his lifetime, Rockefeller donated more
than $500 million (hundreds of billions of dollars in today's money) to
various philanthropic causes.

Rockefeller's 1909 memoirs are recalled in *The Philanthropy Reader* by
Michael Moody and Beth Breeze (Taylor and Francis, 2016). However, the
book that helped guide Rockefeller's thinking, *Extracts from the Diary and
Correspondence of the Late Amos Lawrence*, was published in 1856. It is now
an e-book at Gutenberg (www.gutenberg.org/ebooks/42522), and there
is a nice version at https://archive.org/details/extractsfromdiar00law
rence/page/n7.

John Thomas Flynn's biography of Rockefeller is *God's Gold: The Story
of Rockefeller and His Times* and was published by the Ludwig von Mises
Institute (2012).

Rockefeller's saying, "The secret to success is to do the common things
uncommonly well," although much repeated, may be apocryphal, a mis-

remembering of the words of another American businessman, Henry J. Heinz (1844–1919), who said "To do a common thing uncommonly well brings success." This is cited in John Woolf Jordan (1915), *Genealogical and Personal History of Western Pennsylvania*, p. 38.

"When a competitor did not want to be bought out, Rockefeller used ruthless means of persuasion." See, for example, an article by Sam Parr in *The Hustle* entitled "The Epic Rise of John D. Rockefeller," published March 9, 2016. It is online at https://thehustle.co/the-history-of-john-d-rockefeller-standard-oil.

The ledger of Rockefeller's gifts published by himself in 1897 is preserved by Colombia University Libraries Preservation Division and online at https://archive.org/stream/mrrockefellersle00rock/mrrocke fellersle00rock_djvu.txt.

The account, purporting to be of Rockefeller's first meeting with the Indian mystic, as "told by Madame Emma Calvé to Madame Drinette Verdier," is recalled in the book *The Complete Works of Swami Vivekananda*, Volume 9, published for example by Advaita Ashrama in 1947.

That one of Rockefeller's donations was to the University of Chicago is detailed on the beautifully illustrated blog Vivekananda Abroad: A Postcard Pilgrimage Illustrating the Travels of Swami Vivekananda. See http://vivekanandaabroad.blogspot.com.

CHAPTER 9. RECOGNIZE THE POWER OF SYMBOLS

The Autobiography of Malcolm X, "as told to Alex Haley," was originally published in 1965, the year of his assassination, by Grove Press. Will and Ariel Durant's *Story of Civilization* is a series of books written over decades, from 1935 to 1975, and was published by Simon & Schuster. Will Durant's *The Story of Philosophy* was first published in 1926 also by Simon & Schuster. It is likely that Malcolm X read Nietzsche only via Will Durant's account, but the phrase that caught his eye, "God is dead," first appeared in Nietzsche's 1882 collection *The Gay Science*. However, it is Nietzsche's *Thus Spoke Zarathustra* that is most responsible for making the phrase popular.

Clarence Thomas's autobiography *My Grandfather's Son* was published by Harper in 2007. Jan Crawford Greenburg's interview with Thomas for *ABC News* is online at https://abcnews.go.com/TheLaw/story ?id=3668863&page=1 under the heading "Justice Clarence Thomas Speaks Out: Jan Crawford Greenburg's In-depth Interview with Justice Clarence Thomas," dated October 3, 2007. And Ralph Ellison's *Invisible Man*, which contains Thomas's favorite quote, was published in 1952 by Random House.

Last but not least the "exquisitely crafted" 1,458 words of the Declaration of Independence can be read in their original form (via the wonders of the Internet) at www.ushistory.org/declaration/document/ under the heading "The Declaration of Independence: The Want, Will, and Hopes of the People."

CHAPTER 10. FOLLOW YOUR PERSONAL LEGEND

A selection of Malala Yousafzai's BBC blog posts has been collected online and can be read at www.bbc.com/news/world-asia-29565738 under the title "Moving Moments from Malala's BBC Diary." Yousafzai's page at the Nobel Prize Institute records her Nobel Lecture in Oslo, December 10, 2014, which includes her saying, "This award is not just for me. It is for those forgotten children who want education" as well as "I tell my story not because it is unique, but because it is not. It is the story of many girls." See www.nobelprize.org/prizes/peace/2014/yousafzai/26074-malala -yousafzai-nobel-lecture-2014.

The full text of her "glorious struggle" address to the United Nations has been preserved by the *Independent* newspaper under the heading "Malala Yousafzai Delivers Defiant Riposte to Taliban Militants with Speech to the UN General Assembly" (July 22, 2013) and is online at www.indepen dent.co.uk/news/world/asia/the-full-text-malala-yousafzai-delivers -defiant-riposte-to-taliban-militants-with-speech-to-the-un-8706606.html.

CBS News reported her meeting with President Obama in an article online October 11, 2013, under the heading "Obama Meets Malala at the White House," www.cbsnews.com/news/obama-meets-malala-at-the -white-house.

Her father, Ziauddin Yousafzai's, interview with PBS is part of his book *Let Her Fly* published by Ebury in 2018. Paulo Coelho's determination to protect his book's authenticity from Warner Bros. is recorded in a summary of milestones in the writer's life at www.theguardian.com /books/2008/jun/11/paulocoelho.

Time magazine's tribute to Winfrey comes in repeated inclusion in its annual lists of "The World's 100 Most Influential People." She is listed as an "artist" in the 2010 "Time 100" for example, which is online at http://content.time.com/time/specials/packages/completelist /0,29569,1984685,00.html.

The Oprah Winfrey Twitter feed has recorded Oprah's youthful boast "I don't think I belong here 'cause I know a lot of big words": https:// twitter.com/OWNTV/status/560890271194312704.

Jeff Weiner's interview with Winfrey on October 15, 2015, is on the Supersoul website, devoted to recording Winfrey's "supersoul conversations," at www.supersoul.tv/tag/jeff-weiner.

Gary Zukav's interview for the Thinking Allowed series is preserved in full and in text at www.intuitionnetwork.org/txt/zukav.htm.

Under the heading "The Book that Inspired Oprah Winfrey's Business Philosophy Has Nothing to Do with Business," the online magazine *Business Insider* has the story (November 5, 2015) about Winfrey discovering the principle of "intention," online at www.businessinsider.fr/us/oprah -winfrey-talks-about-her-favorite-book-2015-11.

The promise at Skidmore College, "Do not bring me an idea that I cannot find my thread of truth in," is recorded by Leah Ginsberg in an article called "The One Book that Changed Oprah Winfrey's Life and Business," published June 17, 2017, by CNBC, online at www.cnbc.com /2017/06/15/the-one-book-that-changed-oprah-winfreys-life-and-busi ness.html.

Peter Birkenhead's robust critique of *The Secret* was published in *Salon* under the heading "Oprah's Ugly Secret" on March 3, 2007, and is online at www.salon.com/2007/03/05/the_secret.

In a book review of April 11, 2010, entitled "The Queen of Talk Declined to Speak," the *New York Times* has the tale of Vernon Winfrey saying that he needs his daughter's show "like a hog needs a holiday," online at www.nytimes.com/2010/04/12/books/12book.html.

✛
Selected Bibliography

Acemoglu, Daron. *Why Nations Fail: The Origins of Power, Prosperity, and Poverty.* New York: Crown, 2012.

Alland, Alexander. *Jacob A. Riis: Photographer & Citizen.* New York: Aperture, 1974.

Arnold, Glen. *The Great Investors: Lessons on Investing from Master Traders.* Upper Saddle River, NJ: Pearson, 2011.

Bak, Richard. *Henry and Edsel: The Creation of the Ford Empire.* Boston: Wiley, 2003.

Baldwin, Neil. *Edison: Inventing the Century.* Chicago: University of Chicago Press, 1995.

Basler, Roy, and Carl Sandburg, eds. *Abraham Lincoln: His Speeches and Writings.* Boston: Da Capo Press, 2001.

Branson, Richard. *The Virgin Way: Everything I Know about Leadership.* New York: Portfolio, 2014.

Brook, John. *Business Adventures: Twelve Classic Tales from the World of Wall Street.* New York: Open Road Media, 2014.

Bruccoli, Matthew, and Judith Baughman. *The Sons of Maxwell Perkins: Letters of F. Scott Fitzgerald, Ernest Hemingway, Thomas Wolfe, and Their Editor.* Columbia: University of South Carolina Press, 2004.

Buffett, Warren. *The Essays of Warren Buffett: Lessons for Corporate America,* edited by Lawrence A. Cunningham. Boston: Wiley, 2013.

Burrow, Jack. *Buffett, Munger Marathon Investing: Passion Investing.* Victoria: Friesen Press, 2017.

Byrne, Rhonda. *The Secret.* New York: Atria (Simon & Schuster), 2006.

Camus, Albert. *The Stranger.* New York: Vintage, 1989.

Carson, Rachel. *Silent Spring.* Boston: Houghton Mifflin, 1962.

Coelho, Paulo. *Aleph.* New York: HarperCollins, 2010.

Cohen, Martin. *Cracking Philosophy.* London: Cassell Illustrated, 2016.

Cohen, Martin. *Philosophical Tales.* Oxford: Wiley-Blackwell, 2008.

Confucius. *The Analects (Penguin Classics).* New York: Penguin, 1979.

Corley, Tom. *Rich Habits: The Daily Success Habits of Wealthy Individuals.* Minneapolis: Langdon Street Press, 2011.

Cuban, Mark. *How to Win at the Sport of Business.* New York: First Diversion Books, 2011.

Darwin, Charles. *Origin of Species: 150th Anniversary Edition.* New York: Signet, 2003.

Dass, Ram. *Be Here Now.* San Cristobal, NM: Lama Foundation, 1971.

Dickens, Charles. *A Tale of Two Cities.* London: Chapman and Hall, 1859.

Durant, Will, and Ariel Durant. *The Story of Civilization.* New York: Simon & Schuster, 1935–1975.

Durant, Will. *The Story of Philosophy.* New York: Simon & Schuster, 1926.

Ellison, Ralph. *Invisible Man.* New York: Random House, 1952.

Fehribach, Ronald. *Going Below the Water's Edge.* Bloomington: Author House, 2014.

Fenimore-Cooper, James. *The Deerslayer, or The First War-Path.* New York: D. Appleton-Century Company, 1841.

Flynn, John Thomas. *God's Gold: The Story of Rockefeller and His Times.* Auburn, AL: Ludwig von Mises Institute, 2012.

Gandhi, Mahatma. *An Autobiography: The Story of My Experiments with Truth.* New York: Dover, 1983.

Goodall, Jane. *In the Shadow of Man.* Boston: Houghton Mifflin, 1971.

Goodall, Jane. *My Life with the Chimpanzees.* New York: Aladdin, 1991.

Graham, Benjamin. *The Intelligent Investor.* New York: Harper and Brothers, 1949.

Hacker, Peter. *Wittgenstein's Place in Twentieth-Century Analytic Philosophy.* Boston: Wiley, 1996.

Hakim, Joy. *Reconstruction and Reform: History of U.S., Book 7.* Oxford: Oxford University Press, 1994.

Haley, Alex. *The Autobiography of Malcolm X.* New York: Grove Press, 1965.

Hemingway, Ernest. *For Whom the Bell Tolls.* New York: Scribner, 1995.

Hughes, Robert. *American Visions: The Epic History of Art in America.* New York: Knopf, 1997.

Huntsman, Jon M. *Winners Never Cheat Even in Difficult Times.* Upper Saddle River, NJ: Pearson FT Press, 2008.

Huxley, Aldous. *Brave New World.* New York: Vintage, 2008.

Huynh, Thomas. *The Art of War — Spirituality for Conflict.* Nashville: Skylight Paths, 2008.

Isaacson, Walter. *Steve Jobs.* New York: Simon & Schuster, 2011.

King, Martin Luther Jr. *Stride toward Freedom: The Montgomery Story.* New York: Harper & Brothers, 1958.

Lagerlöf, Selma. *The Wonderful Adventures of Nils.* Wellington, NZ: SMK Books, 2009.

Lanting, Frans. *Eye to Eye.* Hollywood: Taschen, 1997.

Lawrence, William R., ed. *Extracts from the Diary and Correspondence of the Late Amos Lawrence; With a Brief Account of Some Incidents of His Life.* Salt Lake City: Project Gutenberg, 2013.

Lear, Linda. *Rachel Carson: Witness for Nature.* New York: Mariner, 2009.

Levitina, Marina. *"Russian Americans" in Soviet Film: Cinematic Dialogues between the US and the USSR*. London: Bloomsbury, 2015.

Lofting, Hugh. *The Story of Dr. Dolittle*. New York: Penguin, 1968.

Lowe, Janet. *Google Speaks: Secrets of the World's Greatest Billionaire Entrepreneurs*. Boston: Wiley, 2009.

Lytle, Mark Hamilton. *The Gentle Subversive: Rachel Carson, Silent Spring, and the Rise of the Environmental Movement* (New Narratives in American History). Oxford: Oxford University Press, 2007.

Mace, Michael. *Map the Future*. South Carolina: Amazon CreateSpace, 2013.

Mandela, Nelson. *Long Walk to Freedom: The Autobiography of Nelson Mandela*. London: Macdonald Purnell, 1994.

Martin, Paul. *Making Happy People*. New York: HarperCollins, 2005.

Means, Howard. *Money and Power: The History of Business*. Boston: Wiley, 2002.

Melville, Herman. *Moby-Dick*. New York: Random House (Modern Library), 2000.

Miller, Marie-Therese. *Rachel Carson*. New York: Chelsea House, 2011.

Moody, Michael, and Beth Breeze. *The Philanthropy Reader*. Abingdon, UK: Taylor and Francis, 2016.

Morris, Kenneth. *Jimmy Carter, American Moralist*. Athens: University of Georgia Press, 1997.

Niebuhr, Reinhold. *The Children of Light and the Children of Darkness*. Chicago: University of Chicago Press, 1944.

Niebuhr, Reinhold. *The Irony of American History*. New York: Charles Scribner's Sons, 1952.

Niebuhr, Reinhold. *Moral Man and Immoral Society. Study in Ethics and Politics (Library of Theological Ethics)*. Westminster: John Knox Press, 2002.

Nietzsche, Friedrich. *The Gay Science*, translated by Walter Kaufmann. New York: Penguin, 1974.

Nietzsche, Friedrich. *Thus Spoke Zarathustra*, translated by Walter Kaufmann. New York: Penguin, 1995.

Obama, Barack. *The Audacity of Hope: Thoughts on Reclaiming the American Dream*. New York: Crown/Three Rivers Press, 2006.

Obama, Barack. *Dreams from My Father: A Story of Race and Inheritance*. New York: Times Books, 1995.

Orwell, George. *Down and Out in Paris and London*. London: Gollancz, 1933.

Paine, Thomas. *Common Sense*. Cambridge: Cambridge University Press, 2011.

Paine, Thomas. *The Rights of Man*. Cambridge: Cambridge University Press, 2012.

Plato. *The Timaeus of Plato*, translated by R. D. Archer-Hind. London: Macmillan, 1888.

Price, David. *The Pixar Touch: The Making of a Company*. New York: Penguin Random House, 2009.

Rhinehart, Luke. *Dice Man*. New York: HarperCollins, 1999.

Russell, Bertrand. *Mortals and Others (1931–35)*. London: Routledge, 2009.

Sartre, Jean Paul. *Being and Nothingness*. London: Routledge, 1956.

Sartre, Jean Paul. *Critique of Dialectical Reason*. Paris: Gallimard, 1960.

Savickey, Beth. *Wittgenstein's Art of Investigation*. London: Routledge, 1999.

Sendak, Maurice. *Where the Wild Things Are*. New York: HarperCollins, 1984.

Shriram, Ram. *Googled: The End of the World as We Know It*. New York: Penguin, 2009.

Smith, Adam. *Wealth of Nations*. New York: Penguin, 1982.

Smith, Orlando J. *A Short View of Great Questions*. New York: Andesite Press, 2015.

Sterne, Laurence. *The Life and Opinions of Tristram Shandy*. New York: Penguin, 1991.

Sun Tzu. *The Art of War*, translated by Lionel Giles. El Paso, TX: Digital Pulse, 2009.

Sward, Keith. *The Legend of Henry Ford*. New York: Rinehart, 1948.

Thomas, Clarence. *My Grandfather's Son*. New York: Harper, 2007.

Tolkien, J. R. R. *The Lord of the Rings*. New York: Mariner, 2012.

Vivekananda, Swami. *The Complete Works of Swami Vivekananda, Volume 9*. Kolkata (Calcutta): Advaita Ashrama, 1947.

Weininger, Otto. *Sex and Character*. Bloomington: Indiana University Press, 2005.

Wittgenstein, Ludwig. *Philosophical Investigations*, 3rd ed. London: Pearson, 1973.

Wittgenstein, Ludwig. *Tractatus Logicus Philosophicus*. Salt Lake City: Project Gutenberg, 2010.

Womack, James, Daniel Jones, and Daniel Roos. *The Machine that Changed the World*. New York: Simon & Schuster, 1990.

Yousafzai, Ziauddin. *Let Her Fly*. London: Ebury, 2018.

Zukav, Gary. *The Seat of the Soul*. New York: Simon & Schuster, 2014.

Index

213

✚
About the Author

Martin Cohen is an author, editor, and philosopher who has written many popular books in philosophy and social science, including *101 Philosophy Problems, 101 Ethical Dilemmas,* an "anti-history" of great philosophers called *Philosophical Tales,* and *Wittgenstein's Beetle,* all widely translated. He has also written popular reference works, including two books in the For Dummies series on critical thinking skills and philosophy. He is currently living in the shadow of the Pyrenees in southwest France, writing full-time.